D1264820

*The Telephone and
Its Several Inventors*

To the many inventors who struggled
to perfect the telephone art, and received little
or no public recognition for their efforts

The Telephone and Its Several Inventors

A *History*

by
Lewis Coe

McFarland & Company, Inc., Publishers
Jefferson, North Carolina, and London

British Library Cataloguing-in-Publication data are available

Library of Congress Cataloguing-in-Publication Data

Coe, Lewis, 1911–
    The telephone and its several inventors : a history / by
Lewis Coe
        p.   cm.
    Includes bibliographical references and index.
    ISBN 0-7864-0138-9 (lib. bdg. : 50# alk. paper) ∞
    1. Telephone systems — History.   2. Electric engineers —
Biography.   I. Title.
TK6015.C64   1995
621.385′09 — dc20   95-13651
                                                          CIP

Manufactured in the United States of America

McFarland & Company, Inc., Publishers
  Box 611, Jefferson, North Carolina 28640

Contents

Acknowledgments   vii
Telephone Chronology   viii
Introduction   ix

1. The Patent   1
2. The Poor Schoolmaster   16
3. Yellow Breeches Creek   25
4. Under Pressure   31
5. Inventors Galore!   39
6. A Great Undertaking   47
7. Long Distance   58
8. A Man from Oberlin   67
9. Western Union   75
10. The Military Telephone   85
11. Down on the Farm   102
12. Collecting Telephones   116
13. Hackers and Phreaks   135
14. Over the Waves   144
15. The Singing Wires   156
16. How They Worked   173
17. The New Kids on the Block   180
18. Conclusion   186

Appendixes
1. Cities with Independent Telephone Companies   189
2. Cities That Once Had Independent Telephone Companies   190
3. Associations and Publications Related to Telephony   192

4. Insulator Manufacturers in the United States   194
5. Telephone Manufacturers   195
6. Some Communications Museums in the United States   197
7. Affidavits of Zenas Fisk Wilber   198
8. Affidavit of Alexander Graham Bell in Reply to That
        of Zenas Fisk Wilber   204
9. The Untold Story of the Telephone   206
10. Alexander Graham Bell's Original Patent Application, 1876 214
11. Alexander Graham Bell's Patent Application, 1877   220

Glossary   225
Bibliography   226
Index   227

Acknowledgments

SINCERE THANKS GO TO Roland Baumann of the Oberlin College Archives for his assistance in making their material on Elisha Gray available; to Cynthia Comer, head of reference, Oberlin College Library, for furnishing material on Elisha Gray; to Peg Chronister, curator of the Museum of Independent Telephony, for her assistance with information and photographs; to Dart Koedyker for assistance with photographs; to Col. John E. McCarty, U.S. Army (Ret.), for help in unraveling military red tape; to Stephen Prigozy for technical assistance; to George Swank of *Galvaland Magazine* for researching telephone history at Galva, Illinois; to Ruth Taylor Deery and Edmund Taylor, for gracious permission to quote the writings of their father, Dr. Lloyd W. Taylor, and for photographs of their father; and to L. E. Trump of Fairbanks, Alaska, who furnished information on the Alaskan telephone system.

Also, I would be completely remiss if I did not acknowledge my many friends at the Crown Point, Indiana, Community Library, and the Lake County, Indiana, Public Library. Their professional help and personal encouragement have made a sometimes difficult task seem a little easier.

Lewis Coe
January 1995

Telephone Chronology

1876   *February 14:* Bell files a patent application and Gray files a caveat.
1876   *March 7:* Bell telephone patent issued.
1876   *March 10:* Bell transmits first intelligible speech.
1876   *June 25:* Bell demonstrates telephone at Philadelphia Exposition.
1877   *January 30:* Second Bell patent issued.
1879   *November:* Bell–Western Union agreement.
1881   *January 10:* First demonstration of metallic circuit.
1882   Principles of "phantom" circuit discovered.
1885   Transposition of open wire lines: AT&T formed as parent company of Bell Telephone System.
1889   Signal Corps develops military field telephone.
1892   First Strowger dial phones installed in La Porte, Indiana.
1893–1894   Basic Bell patents expire.
1906   De Forest invents three-element vacuum tube.
1913   Kingsbury commitment compell Bell to accept long-distance calls from independent telephone companies.
1915   Opening of transcontinental telephone.
1925   Bell Telephone Laboratories founded.
1927   First transatlantic radio telephone.
1947   Invention of the transistor.
1948   First microwave radio relay system.
1951   Beginning of direct dialing long distance.
1956   First telephone cable across the Atlantic.
1960   First electronic switching system.
1962   *July:* First communications satellite launched.
1969   Carterphone decision compels Bell to allow connection of competing equipment.
1984   Divestiture of the Bell System.

Introduction

TODAY WE STROLL ALONG an "information superhighway" with sophisticated tools that are a far cry from the first telephones. Such communication devices as on-line computers, cellular phones, cordless phones, pagers, caller ID, call waiting, conferencing and 911 numbers are now taken for granted. Dick Tracy's "wrist radio," once a cartoon fantasy, is now almost a practical reality. The modern electronic switching exchange makes the old plug and jack switchboards look as ancient as Stone Age artifacts. We accept all these things and are quite willing to acknowledge Alexander Graham Bell as the inventor of the telephone.

The reader might ask, "what is the purpose of another book about the telephone?" It is true that there are dozens of books giving every phase of the telephone story. Unfortunately, almost all of them have been written with information supplied by the Bell Telephone Company. It is almost certain that any person seeking information about the telephone will end up reading the Bell version of history. This book will be seen by some as an attack on the Bell System. It will be critical of the Bell methods and self-serving attitude, yet the contributions of Bell himself and the company that bears his name will be freely acknowledged. The main purpose of this little volume will be to give due credit to the, for the most part, unknown inventors who contributed, each in his own way, to the modern telecommunication system.

Chapter 1

The Patent

THE BASIC PATENT LAW of the United States is governed by a 27-word clause drafted by the writers of the Constitution. None of the 55 men who wrote the words was an inventor himself. Section 8 of Article I grants to Congress the power "To promote the Progress of Science and useful Arts, by securing for limited Times to Authors and Inventors the exclusive Right to their respective Writings and Discoveries."

On March 7, 1876, the U.S. Patent Office issued to a young man named Alexander Graham Bell what has since been described as the most valuable patent ever issued. The patent was entitled "Improvement in Telegraphy," yet it was to secure for its inventor most of the basic principles involved in a telephone.

The Bell patent gave its holder a certain immortality as the inventor of the telephone. It also touched off a controversy that continues to this day. The immediate cause of the controversy was the fact that on the very same day that Bell filed his patent application, a caveat for a similar invention was filed by Elisha Gray. The caveat is no longer used, but at that time it was filed as a preliminary document describing an invention that in due time would be the subject of a formal patent application.

The year 1876 was historic in many respects. It was America's centennial year, to be celebrated by an exposition in Philadelphia. In Montana, Custer's command was wiped out at the Battle of Little Big Horn. Bell managed to complete a working model of his telephone and exhibited it to various dignitaries, including Emperor Dom Pedro of Brazil, at the Philadelphia exposition.

Bell's famous transmission, "Mr. Watson, come here, I want you!" took place on March 10, 1876. It is part of the myth and legend of the telephone, and by many it has been assumed that this was the first intelligible transmission of human speech. It may come as a surprise to some readers that speech had been transmitted by electricity before Bell. Also it is surprising to many to learn that the transmitter used by Bell on that historic occasion was not of his own invention.

1

It was, rather, a liquid contact transmitter described by Elisha Gray. In the liquid contact transmitter a needle dips into a small cup of water made conductive by the addition of a little acid. The needle is attached to a diaphragm which causes the needle to vibrate in accordance with the speech impinging on it. The vibrating needle varies the resistance of the battery circuit and thus the undulating current necessary for speech transmission is established.

The incident of March 10, 1876, proved to Bell that the telephone was a viable invention, but he also realized that the liquid contact transmitter would not be suitable for commercial use. The telephone that Bell demonstrated at Philadelphia used an electromagnetic transmitter that was merely a duplicate, in principle, of the receiving instrument—what we would call today a sound-powered telephone.

The first Bell telephone offered to the public consisted of a single magnetic unit which functioned both as a transmitter and receiver. This made it necessary to move the device from ear to mouth and vice versa when attempting to converse. This, of course, was very frustrating to the users. In an early ad, Bell attempted to instruct users in the proper method of operation: "After speaking, transfer the telephone from the mouth to the ear very promptly . . . much trouble is caused from both parties speaking at the same time. When you are not speaking, you should be listening."

The one feature of Bell's original patent that was unique was the electromagnetic receiver using a metallic diaphragm in a magnetic field. It was the forerunner of, and essentially the same, as the telephone receivers in use today. Even though he achieved his first results with the liquid type transmitter, Bell never used it again.

It seems incredible now that Elisha Gray failed to follow up his caveat with a patent application. He followed the course he did on the advice of his attorneys, who apparently shared his belief that the real money was in the telegraph field. At that time, the Morse telegraph was a booming business. Any device that promised to increase the message capacity of the existing wires was of great value to the inventor. Bell was in pursuit of the same goal—increased carrying capacity of telegraph circuits—yet he also seemed to realize, more than any of the others, the enormous potential of the telephone.

Gray's "harmonic telegraph," on which he alone held a patent, was the inspiration for the formation of the Postal Telegraph Company to challenge the Western Union monopoly. The harmonic telegraph was originally claimed to provide as many as 16 channels over a single wire. In actual practice only six channels were usable. Postal Telegraph started out with the Gray system and built some high-grade copper wire circuits suitable for carrying the multiple tone frequencies of the harmonic system. The company soon abandoned the Gray system and started using conventional Morse

Elisha Gray (1835–1901) (photo courtesy Smithsonian Institution).

equipment. Edison's invention of the quadruplex in 1875 had made it possible to send four messages simultaneously over a single wire.

Postal Telegraph, left with the high-grade copper wire circuits, eventually used them to good advantage in establishing its own limited long-distance telephone circuits. These circuits were only available along the major routes between large cities. Subscribers who had a need to make many telephone calls to other cities could have a Postal phone installed for this purpose. The instruments were magneto, local battery type instruments made by Kellogg Switchboard & Supply Company of Chicago.

Presumably the harmonic telegraph did not live up to expectations due to the state of technology at the time. For one thing, the effects of capaci-

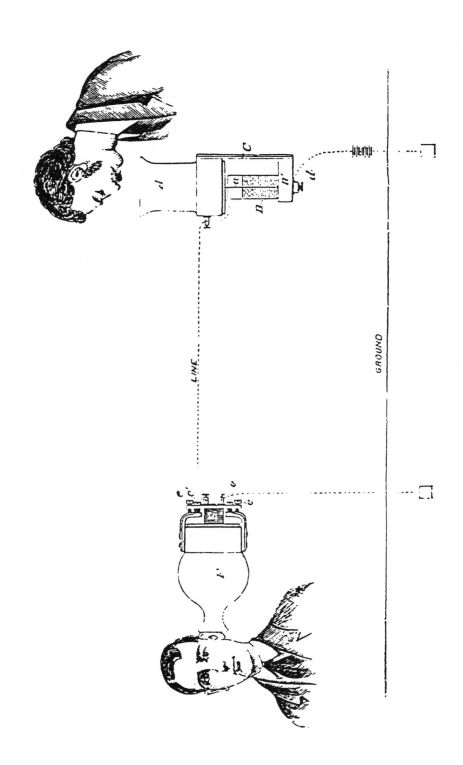

tance on long lines were not yet understood. Tests of the harmonic system using lumped values of resistance to simulate line circuits were not valid when the equipment was connected to an actual cross-country telegraph line. In later years, the invention of the vacuum tube, filter networks and line loading made the multifrequency system extremely important in communication technology. Western Union had a carrier system in operation which depended on the tone generating standard of a Hammond organ for the basic carrier frequencies.

In the Bell-Gray controversy, the most serious charge against Bell was the fact that he had apparently been allowed to see Gray's caveat and thereby was enabled to incorporate a claim to the variable resistance method of speech transmission. The variable resistance claim was written in on the margin of Bell's patent application. This added to the suspicion that he came upon the information after he had filed his original application and was allowed to modify it.

At that time, Bell did not know how to construct a variable resistance transmitter, but the principle was vital to all the transmitters that were subsequently developed. The evidence suggests, indeed the patent officer at the time admitted, that he had shown Gray's caveat to Bell, enabling the latter to modify his application. This was out and out fraud, yet the courts disregarded the apparent facts and sustained Bell's claims. Gray was to realize later that he had apparently shown Bell how to construct the transmitter with which the first results were obtained.

The last half of the 19th century was the golden age for inventors. It was a time when many of the great inventions were brought forth by individuals working alone. It was a time when patent law really protected the inventor against infringement. Inventions were zealously protected and the courts usually decided for the inventor. This was certainly true for Bell, as case after case was decided in his favor. The Bell patent, of course, was soon recognized as one of great value and attracted infringers by the dozen who wanted to get in on the telephone bonanza. The Bell Company were quite active in preserving the virtual monopoly they had on telephone communication. When any inventor appeared with a telephone device that appeared to have potential value, the Bell Company would try to buy him out. If this failed, they had an army of lawyers poised to file suits for infringement. It was said that anyone considering litigation against the Bell Company would soon find that all the competent lawyers in the field were already being retained by the telephone company. The Bell Company also encouraged its own employees to patent any idea, no matter how trivial, that had an application to the telephone business. In this way they built up

Opposite: **Illustration from Elisha Gray's caveat shows the liquid contact transmitter.**

neighborhood of another wire — an undulatory current of electricity is induced in the latter.

When a cylinder upon which are arranged bar-magnets — is made to rotate in front of the pole of an electro-magnet an undulatory current of electricity is induced in the ~~latter~~ coils of the electro-magnet

Undulations ~~may also be~~ are caused in a continuous voltaic current by the vibration or motion of bodies capable of inductive action; — or by the vibration of the conducting wire itself in the neighborhood of such bodies. ✗

In illustration of the method of creating electrical ~~currents~~ Undulations. I shall show and describe one form of apparatus for producing the effect. I prefer to employ for this purpose an electro-magnet A fig. 5. having a coil upon only one of its legs (b). a steel spring armature C is firmly clamped by one extremity to the uncovered leg d of the magnet, and its free end is allowed to project above the pole of the covered leg. The armature C can be set in vibration in a variety of ways — one of which is by wind — and in vibrating it produces a musical note of a certain definite pitch.

When the instrument A is placed in a voltaic circuit g b c f g the armature C becomes magnetic and the polarity of its free end is opposed to that of the magnet underneath. So long as the armature C remains at rest no effect is produced upon the voltaic current.

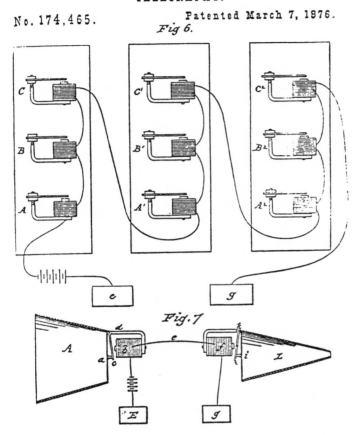

A. G. BELL.
TELEGRAPHY.

No. 174,465.

Patented March 7, 1876.

Fig 6.

Fig. 7

Illustration from Bell's first patent application. Figure 7 shows Bell's concept of a magneto type telephone.

a patent position that was almost invulnerable, yet they had some close calls.

Patent law, which worked so strongly to protect the inventor in Bell's day, is now considered to be much weaker. When a valuable idea is discovered now, it may be patented, yet the inventor is not assured of the full benefit of his discovery. Infringers, after assessing the profit potential of the invention, may decide to go ahead and manufacture it in open

Opposite: **The controversial marginal notation on Bell's patent application (courtesy of the Library of Congress).**

defiance of the patent. They figure to make enough money to defend against infringement suits and still show a profit.

This tends to defeat the system that was the keystone of the American economy for many years. Mark Twain once said, "A country without a patent office and good patent laws is just a crab and can't travel any way but sideways and backways." Contemporary writers, including Twain, professed to be alarmed by the coming of the telephone. They divined correctly that the telephone would soon constitute an invasion of individual privacy to a degree that had never existed before. Robert Louis Stevenson, upon seeing an American-made telephone in Honolulu in 1899, wrote to a local newspaper commenting on the problems of accepting the telephone. He characterized it as: "this interesting instrument . . . into our bed and board, into our business and bosoms . . . bleating like a deserted infant." Mark Twain, writing a Christmas piece for the *New York World* in 1890, said:

> It is my heart-warm and world-embracing Christmas hope and aspiration that all of us — the high, the low, the rich, the poor, the admired, the despised, the loved, the hated, the civilized, the savage — may eventually be gathered together in a heaven of everlasting rest and peace and bliss — except the inventor of the telephone.

Gardiner Hubbard sent Twain a good-humored response to the above and promptly got a reply addressed to "the father-in-law of the Telephone." Twain explained that his main irritation was with the Hartford telephone system, which he termed "the worst in the world." He further explained that since Professor Bell had invented the instrument in the first place he could not escape responsibility. "For your sake I wish we could think of some way to save him, but there doesn't appear to be any. Do you think he would like me to pray for him? I could do so under an assumed name, & it might have some influence." Twain went on to say that Bell was probably doomed, and so he had better come up and use the Hartford telephone, "that would probably reconcile him to Hell." Twain's running battle with the telephone started when the installers were putting the first one in his home. He told the men, "If Bell had invented a muffler or gag, he would have done a real service. Here we have been hollering 'Shut up' to our neighbors for centuries, and now you fellows come along and seek to complicate matters."

Like the Morse telegraph before it, the telephone went through a period when it was scarcely accepted by the public. Many thought it was a temporary fad. Others thought it was outright supernatural and maybe ungodly to convey the human voice by electricity over wires. In Chicopee, Massachusetts, a petition was presented to the village selectmen to have all the telephone poles taken down (it was rejected). In Philadelphia the telephone was coolly received by the businessmen of Walnut Street. They

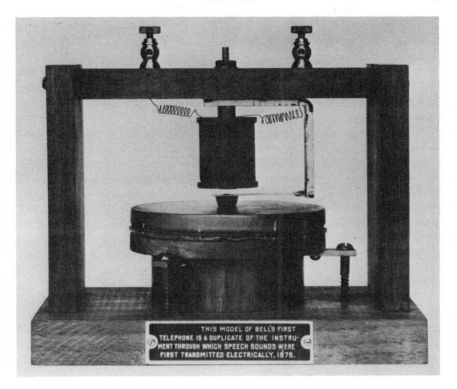

THIS MODEL OF BELL'S FIRST
TELEPHONE IS A DUPLICATE OF THE INSTRU-
MENT THROUGH WHICH SPEECH SOUNDS WERE
FIRST TRANSMITTED ELECTRICALLY, 1875.

The famous "gallows frame" transmitter used by Bell. It transmitted sounds but not articulate speech (courtesy of the Library of Congress).

were said to have exclaimed "Bless my soul! What's this, what's this? Telephone, do you say? We don't want it. Take it away!"

Japan, now one of our great competitors in industrial production, sent a representative to the United States in the 1890s with a view to finding out what had made the United States such a great nation. He concluded that it was our system of patents and protecting the inventors. His final conclusion was, "We will have patents."

Since the 1940s and 1950s, protection of inventors by patent law has been declining to the point where many individuals become discouraged with the prospect of inventing anything. It has been said that in today's patent climate, Alexander Graham Bell would have had only eight chances out of 100 to protect his telephone invention. The Lincoln-Edison medal awarded by the National Inventors Hall of Fame has an inscription attributed to Lincoln: "The patent system added the fuel of interest to the fire of genius." With all its faults, the patent system is taken seriously by large corporations. For example, IBM was listed in 1993 as receiving the most patents of any company in the world. One of the largest patent suits of modern times occurred when Polaroid sued Eastman Kodak for infringement of the Polaroid patents on instant cameras and films. On October 12, 1990, a settlement was reached which required that Eastman pay $925 million for their infringement of the Polaroid patents. In addition, Eastman had to pay rebates to owners of Eastman cameras, for which the Eastman instant film was no longer available.

After the issuance of Bell's patent in 1876, the Western Union Telegraph Company was considered to be the ideal entity to develop the telephone system envisioned by Bell. Western Union had a nationwide network of wires in place. The first telephone experiments between widely separated points had involved telegraph wires, and it was considered quite practical to use them for the telephone. It thus came about that Bell himself, looking for a quick source of cash, had offered his telephone patent rights to Western Union for $100,000. In retrospect, it can be seen that this represented one of the greatest bargains in communications history. Western Union, however, was riding the crest of success — the telegraph had made them one of the richest corporations in America and they had a virtual monopoly on the field. It is not too surprising then that they turned down Bell's offer.

In reading telephone history, even the version provided by the Bell Company, one can hardly escape the idea that a large part of the telephone invention was made by Thomas A. Watson. Bell had the vision to foresee the possibilities of electrical transmission of speech, but it was Watson who had the skill to transform Bell's vision into practical terms. Watson (1854–1934) was a skilled mechanic at Charles Williams' electrical shop in Boston at the time he became associated with Bell. In November 1876, Watson came upon the principle of the "magneto telephone," which used a coil of wire operating in the field of a permanent magnet. This was the prototype of the telephone receivers used to this day. It also functioned as a transmitter and made possible many of the early demonstrations of the telephone over ever longer circuits.

The improved receiver-transmitter was patented by Bell—Patent No. 186,787, issued January 30, 1877. This patent, together with the one issued in 1876, gave the Bell Company a virtual monopoly until 1893-1894. One of the early problems with the telephone was the need for a reliable device to signal subscribers and for the subscribers to call the central office. Once again, Watson's genius solved the problem. He developed the so-called "polarized" ringer for operation on low frequency alternating current.

The patent for the ringer, No. 210,886, was issued on December 17, 1878. The means for calling involved the development of a small hand-cranked magneto or generator. It was covered by Patent No. 202,495, issued to Watson on October 11, 1877. The ringer and generator were

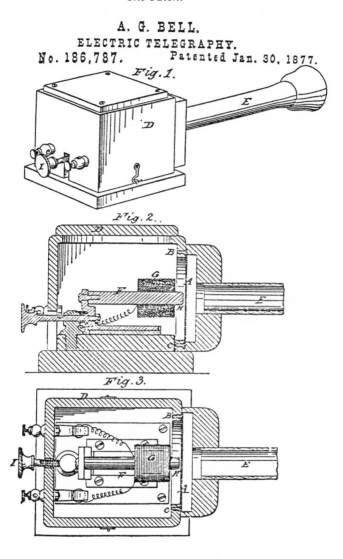

A. G. BELL.
ELECTRIC TELEGRAPHY.
No. 186,787.   Patented Jan. 30, 1877.

Fig.1.

Fig.2.

Fig.3.

A page from the second basic telephone patent.

such sound ideas that they continued in the telephone industry for many years.

In fact, the polarized ringer has long been a standard feature of all subscribers' telephones. Only in very recent years have electronic ringers using solid-state elements come into use. Although the magnetos went out of widespread use when the local battery system was superseded by the

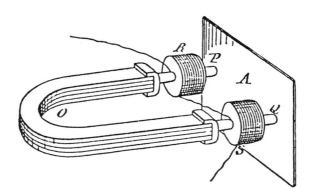

The electromagnetic receiver as invented by Thomas Watson. Forerunner of the telephone receivers still in use today.

common battery system, the ringing signal sent out by modern exchanges is the low frequency (17–20 cycles) alternating current first provided by Watson's generator of 1877.

The modern electronic ringers respond to the low frequency alternating current signals just as well as the older polarized ringers. Watson can claim some credit for originating the idea of the telephone booth. His landlady objected to the noise he was creating at all hours of the night with his telephone experiments. He created a makeshift sound deadening enclosure out of carpet.

Watson's contributions were recognized by the Bell investors in September 1876. He was persuaded to leave his job with Charles Williams and become a full-time employee of Bell's in return for a 10 percent interest in the telephone patent. If Watson's 10 percent share sounds niggardly considering the hardships and hard work he shared with Bell, it should be remembered that the decision on Watson's share would not have been Bell's decision alone. The financial backers, Hubbard and Sanders, probably had their voices in the matter. Even with his 10 percent share, Watson became a well-to-do man in later life, illustrating once again the tremendous profit potential of the telephone business. Watson stayed with the Bell Company until 1881 and by the time he left had accounted for some 60 patents in his own name. In fact, until his departure in 1881, Watson was the sole technical man of the new organization. He used his income from Bell to get into several other businesses, ending up with the Fore River Ship & Engine Company in 1901. Watson had been compelled to assume total responsibility for technical development because in July 1877 Bell had gone on a honeymoon trip to Europe. Bell, in fact, did little technical work on the telephone after the initial success. He was, however, active in demonstrations and testifying in the many lawsuits that were soon to follow.

In spite of the patent protection afforded by the early enforcement of the law, inventors of landmark devices had to fight a ceaseless battle against infringers. For example, Elias Howe, inventor of the sewing machine, had to engage in an ongoing legal battle to protect his rights. Once the sewing machine became known as an invention that would revolutionize the garment industry, a small army of infringers moved in. Howe was obliged to devote most of the income from his invention to protecting his patent rights in court.

Today's inventors face an increasingly discouraging prospect. A large corporation seeing an idea that looks promising may just go ahead and manufacture it, completely disregarding the inventor's rights. If the inventor decides to sue for infringement of his patent it may cost him at least $40,000 just to bring the case to court. Some companies callously disregard the inventor if they figure the potential profits will exceed the cost of legal action to defend the infringement. One large company told a lone inventor, "we have more people on our legal staff alone than you have in your entire company, go ahead and sue us!"

No where was the litigation more severe than in the early days of the electric communications industry. Alvin F. Harlow in his 1936 classic, *Old Wires and New Waves* says:

> Probably no other inventions in history have brought about as much legal embroilment, bitterness, venom, backbiting, slander, perjury and other chicanery and dissension as have those of communication—the telegraph, the telephone and, in but slightly milder degree—radio.

Morse, for example, once said plaintively that some people thought he had no right to claim his invention of the telegraph because he had not discovered electricity, nor the copper from which his wire was made, the brass of his instruments, nor the glass of his insulators. Morse, on the other hand, had tried to claim the property of electromagnetism as part of his telegraph invention. This claim was properly struck down in court because it was pointed out that the principle of electromagnetism was vital to all forms of telegraphy. To secure it to Morse exclusively would have made future improvements in the art impossible.

Bell's claim of the principle of "variable resistance" was allowed by the courts, however, even though there were strong indications that it had actually been discovered by Elisha Gray. The variable resistance principle was to form the basis for all successful telephone transmitting devices. It was just as fundamental as electromagnetism was to the telegraph, yet the courts decided against Morse and in favor of Bell. As the Bell Telephone Company prospered it was constantly working to make its patent position invulnerable. Soon able to acquire a staff of competent lawyers, it remained poised like a mother tiger, ready to defend its corporate position against all comers.

One of the early corporate decisions set forth a policy as follows:

> The business of manufacturing telephones and licensing parties to use the same for a royalty, shall be carried on and managed by a Trustee, under the name of the Bell Telephone Company, under and in accord with such general directions, rules and regulations as may be made for that purpose by the Board of Managers.

The following is from the catalog of C. E. Jones & Bro. of Cincinnati, Ohio, published during the 1880s and pretty well describes the telephone situation at that time:

> Since the introduction of the telephone, and its application to practical everyday use, we have devoted considerable time and labor to the development of apparatus — more especially Central Office Apparatus, such as switchboards, for the economical, reliable and speedy transaction of "Exchange" business, and call the attention of "Exchanges" and telephone managers to our illustrated circular, which we will send on application. We can furnish exchanges with all supplies, such as magneto bells, line wire, brackets, insulators, office wire and batteries of every description at bottom prices. We can furnish the magneto bells made by any of the licensed manufacturers of National Bell Telephone Co., at their regular rates.
>
> TO THE PUBLIC IN GENERAL
>
> And the users of private telephone lines in particular, we desire to say, emphatically, that we do not sell or rent telephones or microphones, or parts thereof. These instruments can only be RENTED of the National Bell Telephone Co., or their authorized agents, and it is impossible to get them in any other way.

Until the expiration of the basic patents in 1893-1894, the Bell rule of the telephone industry was almost absolute. The company maintained strict control of the sale and distribution of telephone instruments and would not permit non–Bell equipment to be connected to their lines. With the expiration of the Bell patents competition started to spring up in the form of independent telephone companies.

Bell, however, controlled the intercity lines, and for a long time would not permit connections by the independents. This severely limited the activities of the independents as they could only offer local service to their subscribers. Anyone wishing to use the "long distance" feature of telephone service was usually compelled to have two phones, the Bell and an independent.

Finally, as a result of constantly increasing pressure from government and the public alike, the so-called "Kingsbury Commitment" of 1913, in the form of a letter written by Nathan C. Kingsbury, ended the days of non-interconnection and also compelled AT&T (which became the parent company of the Bell System after the Bell Company moved from Boston to New York in 1885 and was reorganized) to get the approval of the Interstate Commerce Commission before buying out independent telephone companies. The new policy was hailed by President Wilson as an act of "business statesmanship." At the same time AT&T agreed to dispose of its holdings of Western Union stock, thus ending its dream of establishing a national telecommunications monopoly.

The first chink in the Bell armor apparently was the result of the "Carterphone" case in 1969. Carterphone Communications, Inc., a small manufacturer of telephone equipment, won an FCC ruling that allowed them to connect their equipment to Bell lines. The Carterphone equipment was a device to allow the connection of radio equipment to telephone lines for the purpose of relaying telephone calls to remote oil fields where no wire lines were available. It was a worthwhile service that filled a need but could not be used until the FCC ruling. The gates were down at last, and hundreds of companies entered the telephone field.

The final act of divestiture came on January 1, 1984, when the American Telephone and Telegraph Company, by then the world's largest company, was broken up into eight separate companies. Incidentally, the word "telegraph" in many telephone company names dates from the days when right-of-way franchises were originally granted for telegraph companies. With the name "telegraph" in a corporate title, the company was protected in its right to string wires for either telegraph or telephone use. These developments came as a shock to many Americans, who had become accustomed to the monolithic structure of the telephone company and the solid reliability of Western Electric equipment. Many feared that competitive telephone equipment would result in degraded service. It is true that low cost telephones have been the source of trouble, but those sold by reputable makers seem to work as well as the old reliable Western Electric equipment. In addition, many of the new electronic phones have features that were never offered in the old days before divestiture. There was a great deal of confusion when it was discovered that all service problems could not be handled by merely calling "the telephone company."

After the initial confusion, most people have come to feel that deregulation was something that had to happen. In general, telephone service is now equally as good as it ever was and in some respects much better. Meanwhile, AT&T has emerged as a slick and aggressive competitor in the complex field of telecommunications. Even after deregulation, AT&T is still the largest telecommunications company in the United States. Its annual revenues exceed $44 billion, and it has over 300,000 employees and over two million stockholders.

Chapter 2

The Poor Schoolmaster

MUCH OF THE CONTROVERSY that centered around the Bell patent was involved with the prior claims of Philipp Reis. It was held by many that Reis was the original inventor of the telephone and thus Bell could not rightfully claim the invention. Possibly the main reason that the Reis priority never stood up in court was that no one seemed to be able to demonstrate a Reis instrument in the transmission of articulate speech.

Once, when attorneys were attempting to demonstrate the Reis instrument in court they could not get the right adjustment on the apparatus, succeeding only in producing squeaks and squawks, but no speech. Finally, one of them in disgust exclaimed, "it can speak, but it won't." Such courtroom fiascos led one learned judge to issue a statement: "A century of Reis would never produce a working telephone." Just how the good judge could look 100 years in the future on a technical matter far beyond his ken was never explained.

Johann Philipp Reis was born on January 7, 1834, at Gelnhausen, in the principality of Cassel, Germany. His father was a master baker by trade, and also engaged in farming to augment the family income. Since his mother had died at an early age, the boy was raised by his grandmother. Both his father and grandmother contributed to the boy's preschool training and at the age of six he was sent to the common school of his town.

Reis's teachers soon recognized him as an exceptional student and recommended to his father that he be sent to a higher institution of learning. Unfortunately, his father died before Reis had completed his tenth year of common school.

Finally, Reis was entered in Garnier's Institute at Friedrichsdorf, and he finished his fourteenth year of schooling there. Then he went to Hassel's Institute at Frankfurt am Main. On finishing at Hassel's his instructors recommended that he be enrolled at the Polytechnic School at Carlsruhe. His guardian ruled otherwise and the lad was apprenticed to a mercantile establishment. Reis won the approval of his master during the apprenticeship, but devoted all of his leisure time to furthering his education.

Philipp Reis as pictured in Sylvanus P. Thompson's 1883 biography.

When his apprenticeship was over he entered the Institute of Dr. Poppe in Frankfurt. In 1851 Reis became a member of the Physical Society of Frankfurt. While a member of the society he had the benefit of association with the leading scientific men of Germany and from outside Germany, men like Faraday, Sturgeon, and Sir Charles Wheatstone. During 1854-1855 Reis was busy preparing himself to be a teacher. However, at that time all German youths had to serve a year in the military, and Reis had to defer his educational program to serve a year in the military at Cassel. After finishing his military service Reis continued his studies with the view of going to Heidelberg to complete his education. Then in 1858 he was offered a post as teacher at his old school, Garnier's Institute in Friedrichsdorf. The following year he was married and established his own home.

In 1860 Reis started the first research that was to lead to his telephone invention. In describing his apparatus he said: "I succeeded in inventing an apparatus, by which it is possible to make clear and evident the organs of hearing, but with which also one can reproduce tones of all kinds at any desired distance by means of the galvanic current. I named the instrument 'Telephon'."

Probably one of the world's first telephone lines was strung across the campus at Garnier's Institute, connecting two classrooms. A legend says that boys were afraid to make disturbances in the rooms for fear that Professor Reis would be listening on the telephone. In 1862 Reis attempted to publish a paper in Professor Poggendorff's well-known *Annalen der Physik*.

This paper was only the second to be rejected. This was a great disappointment for Reis, since he had been sponsored by two influential members of the scientific community, professors Bottger and Muller. Poggendorff was inclined to dismiss the transmission of speech by electricity as a myth. Reis, however, was convinced his work was rejected because he was, in his words, "only a poor schoolmaster."

During the years 1861–1864, Reis gave many public lectures concerning his telephone, including one before the Physical Society of Frankfurt. That august body soon ceased to take any notice of the telephone and as a result Reis resigned from the Society in 1867. Reis telephones had now been manufactured in considerable numbers and shipped all over the world, including one sent to the Smithsonian Institution in the United States.

After the lecture before the Physical Society, old Professor Poggendorff decided that the telephone was something worth noticing after all and invited Reis to submit a paper for publication in *Annalen der Physik*. Reis, however, had pretty well had it with Poggendorff by this time. His reply was a model of frosty Teutonic politeness, but it left no doubt as to his feelings on the matter. *"Ich danke Ihnen recht sehr, Herr Professor; es ist zu spat. Jetzt will ich nicht ihn schicken. Mein Apparat wird ohne Beschreibung in den Annalen bekannt werden."* A liberal translation of the foregoing would probably read: "I thank you very much, Professor, but you are a bit late. When publication would have meant a great deal to me you turned it down. Now, my apparatus has been shown and demonstrated all over the world. So thanks, but no thanks, I do not think publication in *Annalen der Physik* would serve any purpose."

Reis, who took his invention very seriously, could not understand why various scientific authorities dismissed his telephone as a philosophical toy. In 1872 he donated all his instruments and tools to Garnier's Institute. At the time he told Garnier that he had shown the world the way to a great invention which must now be left to others to develop. Suffering now from pulmonary consumption, he died in January 1874.

Reis telephones gave somewhat widely varying results. This was probably due, in part, to the employment of non-metallic membranes or diaphragms. Bell had the same problem with his transmitter using a non-metallic membrane in the transmitter. Variations in humidity caused the membranes to tighten or loosen with corresponding changes in sensitivity.

Another factor that limited the Reis instrument was the so-called "knitting needle" receiver. A steel rod about the size of a knitting needle was enclosed in a coil of wire and the assembly mounted on a wood box to act as a resonator. The undulatory current passing through the coil caused the needle to vibrate and generate sound waves. It is very likely that the Reis transmitters would have given much better results if used with a magnetic receiver of the type later used in all telephones.

Nevertheless, Professor Sylvanus Thompson, in his 1883 biography of Reis, published statements from many persons in the scientific field who had witnessed demonstrations of the Reis instrument. They were all unanimous in declaring that intelligible speech had been transmitted — not always perfectly, but well enough to convince the listeners that Reis had invented a means for transmitting speech by electrical current.

Reis had entrusted the manufacture of his telephones for public sale to the firm of J. W. Albert in Frankfurt. Mr. E. Albert of that firm commented on the membrane problem:

> The most important part was the membrane, because the delicacy of the apparatus depended principally upon that part. As it was not possible to make every membrane equally good, so it came about that instruments of different degrees of superiority came into use, and various decisions were arrived at as to the ability of the instrument to perform the functions for which it was designed. Those who happened to have a poor instrument were able to hear little; while those who possessed a good instrument were astonished as to its performance. A good instrument reproduced the words sung into it in such a manner that not only the pitch but also the words of the song were perfectly understood, even when the listener was unacquainted with the song and the words.

None of the early telephones were the perfect instruments we are accustomed to today. Bell himself, speaking before the American Academy of Arts and Sciences in May 1876, admitted the imperfections of his own instrument: "The effects were not sufficiently distinct to admit of sustained conversation through the wire. Indeed, as a general rule, the articulation was unintelligible, excepting when familiar sentences were employed."

Yet only two months previously Bell had been awarded a patent for one of the world's most valuable inventions. Professor Thompson sums up the Reis invention as follows:

1. Reis's telephone was expressly intended to transmit speech. (One of Reis's coworkers testified that the intention was to transmit speech. When music was used it was merely for convenience in testing and demonstrating. Bell did the same thing 15 years later.)
2. Reis's telephone, in the hands of Reis and his contemporaries, did transmit speech. (Any number of qualified persons testified to this fact.)

3. Reis's telephone will transmit speech. (Professor Thompson proved this by testing Reis instruments himself.)

Philipp Reis, the German orphan boy, deserved more remembrance than he ever got. He was plagued by ill health, and the last years of his life were tragic. Perhaps his invention of the telephone came too soon. Even in America, Bell's invention in 1876 was greeted with a good deal of skepticism. The Morse telegraph, introduced in 1844, also received grudging acceptance at first.

By 1876, the telegraph was firmly established, but the electrical transmission of the spoken word seemed like witchcraft. In the Germany of 1860, the public and the scientific community were much more reluctant to accept such advanced thinking. Also, Reis did not have wealthy financial backers, as Bell did.

Reis apparently was not greatly interested in the financial aspects of the telephone and pursued only the scientific side of his invention. Recognition by his peers was very important to him and he was bitterly disappointed when many of them dismissed it as a philosophical toy. Had Reis lived he would have undoubtedly improved his telephone and gotten a German patent.

The main reason that Reis's telephone was not recognized in the litigation over the Bell patent seemed to be that the attempts to demonstrate it in the United States were very inept at best. Bell was the ideal man to further his own interests. He had an imposing presence in public and was a fine orator. A forceful personality, Bell was what we would describe today as a "take charge sort of guy."

Bell was once asked the following question in a hearing held at the U.S. Patent Office:

If a Reis telephone, made in accordance with the descriptions published before the earliest dates of your invention, would in use transmit and receive articulate speech as perfectly as the instruments did which were used by you on June 25, 1876, at the Centennial, would it be proof to you that such Reis Telephones operated by the use of undulatory movements of electricity in substantially the same way as your instruments did upon the occasion referred to?

Answer by Bell:

The supposition contained in the question cannot be supposed. Were the question put that if I were to hear an instrument give forth articulate speech transmitted electrically as perfectly as my instruments did on the occasion referred to in the question, I would hold this as proof that the instrument had been operated by undulatory movements of electricity, I would unhesitatingly answer, Yes.

Surely, no better authority could be quoted to prove that Reis did indeed know how to adjust his instrument so that it would transmit the undulatory current necessary for speech transmission.

It is possible that Alexander Graham Bell, with his father, may have been in Scotland during the time that the Reis telephone was exhibited there. In a letter to the senior Bell, a certain Doctor Tait suggested that Bell might have gotten his idea for the telephone on that occasion.

This was vigorously denied by Bell, who piously responded: "Knowing all the stages of my son's laborious efforts before he finally achieved the telephone, I know that his work was not suggested, or directed, by anything Reis had done. At the time that the telephone first began to speak, the whole world was astounded. The very idea was entirely new."

This was a rather surprising statement in view of the known facts. It seems to be typical of the Bells that they believed their own views were sacred and too dignified to be challenged.

If Bell didn't see the Reis telephone in Scotland he certainly saw it at the Smithsonian Institution when he visited Joseph Henry. On this occasion Bell complained of his lack of electrical knowledge and Henry candidly advised him, "get it!"

All of the early telephone inventors were indebted to the prior work of Dr. Charles Grafton Page (1812–1868), a Salem, Massachusetts, physicist, who in 1837 discovered certain properties of electromagnets. Dr. Page found that when the current flowing through an electromagnet is interrupted a sound is given forth. This basic idea was to govern the whole future of telephony and was fundamental to all the telephones that were invented. It was not Reis or Bell who first conceived the idea of sending speech by electricity. The honor apparently belongs to a Frenchman, Charles Bourseul, who advanced the idea in 1854. He said: "Speak against one diaphragm and let each vibration 'make or break' the electric contact. The electric pulsations thereby produced will set the other diaphragm working, and the latter ought then to reproduce the transmitted sound."

Bourseul's ideas were published by a number of European scientific journals. Among the first was the *Didaskalia*, published at Frankfurt am Main. On September 28, 1854, it printed what is considered the earliest use of the term "Electrical Telephony." Unfortunately, Bourseul used the term "make or break" and it is thought that this led early workers, including Reis, astray.

Reis's first telephone was modeled on Bourseul's ideas; however, Reis had obviously discovered the principle of "microphonic" contacts, otherwise his instrument would never have transmitted articulate speech. Bourseul died without ever trying to put his idea to practical use, yet his contribution should not be minimized. He had an uncanny vision of the future at a time when the transmission of speech by wire was in the same category that we would label "science fiction" today. Much of the controversy that attended the work of Bourseul, and later Reis, has centered on the term "make or break" to describe the contact action of the transmitter. Yet Reis, according to many witnesses, did transmit intelligible speech. This seems to prove that he had discovered how to make the contact points of his transmitter microphonic. Reis himself used the term molecular action (*molekular Bewegung*) to describe the contact points of his transmitter, suggesting that he had indeed discovered how to adjust the points for speech transmission.

Oliver Heaviside joined the discussion about the Reis telephone and in reference to the transmitter commented:

> Variation of current with pressure. It seems established that Reis utilized the phenomenon in his transmitter, long erroneously supposed to work only by makes and breaks. Indeed, presuming that he was at the first unacquainted with, and to be adjusting his transmitter very finely, it would have been difficult for him *not* to have noticed that the current passed continuously with every light contact, and the wonderful change produced thereby, a harsh, disagreeable tone being replaced by a soft and smooth one, would be unmistakable. And, in fact, he did transmit speech in this way with unbroken current. If Reis had but employed carbon contacts instead of metallic, there can be little doubt that the practical introduction of telephony would have been much accelerated.

Perhaps motivated by Heaviside's comment, Francis Blake in 1877 invented a transmitter which used a carbon button for one contact instead of the metal to metal contacts of Reis's transmitter. After further development by Berliner, the Blake transmitter became the standard in the Bell System for many years. The whole subject was reexamined in 1932, as reported in the British *Post Office Engineers' Journal*. The post office experts tested the Reis instruments held in the Science Museum, London, and found that with the proper adjustment they would transmit speech. Of course, the test was conducted with modern telephone receivers and an induction coil to increase the volume. It was also pointed out that "talking transformers" were not uncommon in the British telephone system, suggesting that Reis's "knitting needle" receivers might have been more efficient than generally thought.

The Reis telephone was reviewed in great detail by V. Legat, Inspector of the Royal Prussian Telegraphs. His article, entitled "On the Reproduction of Musical Tones by Electromagnetism," was originally published in *Zeitschrift des deutsch österreichischen Telegraphen Vereine* during 1862. It was later published by the *Journal of the Telegraph* in America on December 1, 1877. Apparently recognizing the shortcomings of the original Reis "knitting needle" receiver, Legat designed a receiver using an electromagnet acting on a thin steel armature. The vibrations of the steel armature could be made more audible by a conical reflector that directed the sound to the listener's ear.

S. M. Yeates of Dublin, Ireland, purchased a Reis telephone in 1863 and started experimenting with it. Yeates also developed his own form of receiver. Yeates demonstrated his apparatus before the November 1865 meeting of the Dublin Philosophical Society, and reported that "both singing and the distinct articulation of several words were heard through it, and the difference between the speakers' voices clearly recognized." Dr. P. H. Van der Weyd became interested in the Reis telephone in 1869. He also constructed his own form of receiver, basically similar to the one used by Yeates. The good doctor did not believe the instrument would transmit articulate speech, but persons attending his demonstrations were positive that they could distinguish the words of songs being sung at the other end of the line.

Thomas Edison admitted that his work on the telephone, which culminated in the carbon transmitter, was greatly influenced by reading of Reis's earlier work. Edison, testing the Reis equipment, reported its performance as follows: "single words, uttered as in reading, speaking and the like, were perceptible indistinctly, notwithstanding, here also the inflections of the voice, the modulations of interrogation, wonder, command, etc., attained distinct expression." The earliest record of an electric telephone was contained in M. du Moncel's *Expose* published in Paris in 1854. This article described the work of Charles Bourseul, who undoubtedly inspired Reis to work on the telephone. Moncel published a book called *The Telephone* in which he paid tribute to Reis in the following words: "Nevertheless, it would not be just not to acknowledge that the Reis telephone formed the starting point of all the others. . . . It is probable that, in this manner, as in the greater number of modern inventions, the original inventor obtained only insignificant results, and that it was the man who first succeeded in arranging his apparatus so as to obtain really striking results, that received the honor of the discovery and rendered it popular."

Principal Dates in Reis's Life

1834   *January 7:* Philipp Reis born.
1850   *March 1:* Apprenticed to Beyerbach.
1855   Year of military service at Cassel.
1858   Settled in Friedrichsdorf.
1859   *September 14:* Married.
1860   Invented the telephone.
1861   *October 26:* Read paper "On Telephony by the Galvanic Current" before the Physical Society of Frankfurt am Main.
1861   *November 16:* Read paper to the Physical Society of Frankfurt am Main,

entitled "Explanation of a New Theory Concerning Perception of Chords and of Timbre as a Continuation and Supplement of the Report on the Telephone."

1861   *December:* Wrote out his paper "On Telephony," as printed in the *Jahresbericht.*

1862   *May 8:* Notice in *Didaskalia* of Reis's invention.

May 11: Lectured and showed the telephone to the Free German Institute in Frankfurt am Main. Article on the telephone, communicated by Inspector Von Legat to the Austro-German Telegraph Society, and subsequently printed in its *Zeitschrift.*

1863   *July 4:* Showed his improved telephone to the Physical Society of Frankfurt am Main.

September 6: Reis's telephone shown to the Emperor of Austria and the King of Bavaria, then visiting Frankfurt.

September 17: Meeting of the "Deutscher Naturforscher" at Stettin, Reis's telephone shown there by Professor Bottger.

1864   *February 13:* Meeting of the Oberhessische Gesellschaftfür Natur-und Heilkunde at Giessen; lecture by Professor Buff, and exhibition by Reis of his telephone.

September 21: Meeting of the Deutscher Naturforscher at Giessen. Reis gave an explanation of the telephone and the history of its invention, and exhibited it in action before the most distinguished scientific men of Germany.

1872   *September:* Meeting of the Deutscher Naturforscher at Wiesbaden: Reis announced to show his "Fall-maschine," but prevented by ill health.

1874   *January 14:* Philipp Reis died.

Chapter 3

Yellow Breeches Creek

BY THE 1880S, THE TELEPHONE was big news, and was obviously going to make a lot of money for Alexander Graham Bell. Such a bonanza could not avoid attracting other investors who were eager to cash in on one of the greatest inventions of the 19th century. Shrewd promoters began combing the bushes for any inventor who might have a claim that would challenge the Bell patent.

It was thus that the spotlight was directed towards one Daniel Drawbaugh. Drawbaugh, born in 1827, was an amiable rustic who hailed from the hamlet of Eberly's Mills, hard by the banks of Yellow Breeches Creek, in the hills just west of Harrisburg, Pennsylvania. Drawbaugh operated a blacksmith shop and was generally considered to be slightly eccentric. His wife once became so disgusted with his mindless tinkering that she smashed all of his equipment. Nevertheless, he was a prolific inventor, and held 60 patents which he had sold for small sums.

With this kind of background he would seem to have been an unlikely inventor of anything as complex as the telephone. In 1863 he started experimenting with telephones. Where he got the idea was never disclosed. In 1867, he made a telephone with a teacup for a transmitter that he later claimed had worked fairly well. By 1870, he was supposed to have produced an electrical instrument that would transmit speech from one room of his house to another. When he boasted that some day he would talk across the Atlantic, a neighbor, William Darr, the village undertaker, replied, "Try it first across Yellow Breeches Creek." Daniel never forgave him for that remark! An example of Drawbaugh's casual approach to "invention" was shown in the telegraph instrument he devised. To test it out, he traveled in the dead of night to the nearest railroad where there was an overhead telegraph line. He threw a wire up over the line to demonstrate the operation of his instrument. This was not the act of a responsible person. He might have gotten enough voltage from the line to activate his instrument, but in so doing he grounded out the line, making it unworkable and possibly interfering with vital train order messages.

It happened in 1880 that a group of investors heard of Drawbaugh and decided that his claims might challenge the Bell patent. They applied for a patent on his behalf and organized the People's Telephone Company. The event was reported by *The New York Journal of Commerce* on August 23, 1880:

> A company has recently been formed in this city with a capital of $5,000,000 for the purpose of manufacturing telephones. The company is to be known as the People's Telephone Company, and a number of leading capitalists in this city and Cincinnati are interested in it. The telephones are to be manufactured under the patents of Frank A. Klemm and Abner G. Tisdel, and the application for patents of Daniel Drawbaugh of Eberly's Mills, Cumberland County, Pennsylvania, filed July 21, 1880. It is claimed by those interested in the new enterprise that Drawbaugh is really the inventor of the telephone, and had completed one years before Professor Bell or any one else had manufactured one. He was, however, in very humble circumstances, and his neighbors who knew of his experiments looked upon him as a harmless lunatic. He continued improving his original telephone, and it is claimed that the one which the new company proposes to furnish is superior to any now in use. The company has fitted up a factory in Brooklyn, and in three months will be prepared to supply 1,000 of the new telephones.

When they started producing telephones they were immediately sued for infringement by the Bell Telephone Company in the Southern District Court of New York. Thus began one of the hardest fought legal battles in telephone history and one that nearly defeated the mighty Bell Company. The People's Company had retained an able lawyer, Lysander Hill, who called hundreds of witnesses. Of these, at least 49 testified that they had talked or heard speech on Drawbaugh's telephone before the Bell patent was issued.

Drawbaugh, unfortunately, was not a very good witness in his own behalf. He was not able to give any coherent account of how he invented his telephone. He said, "I don't remember how I came to it, I had been experimenting in that direction. I don't remember getting it by accident either. I don't remember of anyone talking to me of it." The main issue was to establish the date when Drawbaugh had demonstrated his telephone to the various witnesses. Many of the witnesses were very vague about the dates and could not identify the particular instrument that had been demonstrated for them.

When Bell lawyers asked him why he had not patented his invention he gave the excuse that he was too poor to pay for a patent application. This was not a very plausible explanation in view of his previous patents, but it earned a lot of sympathy from the public, who tended to side with a poor man from a backwoods community fighting the wealthy Bell Company. The testimony in this case ran to 6,000 pages, and it was finally heard by the

U.S. Supreme Court. At one point in the trial in August 1883, it appeared that Drawbaugh might actually win, and Bell stock dropped fifty points.

The Bell faction tried every trick in the book to discredit Drawbaugh, labeling him a "clown," an impostor, and other derogatory terms. In spite of these attacks, Drawbaugh stands forth as an individual of some substance. He was a skilled mechanic and had earned a living entirely through his own skill and ingenuity. He was devoted to his family, and over the years had occupied a number of substantial dwelling houses in the community of Eberly's Mills. The models he exhibited were definitely based on electrical principles, not "string telephones" as was sometimes alleged. The main problem was that neither he nor his witnesses could convince the court that he had invented these things before the date of Bell's patent.

There was a strong suspicion that Drawbaugh merely copied the ideas of others and claimed them as his own. For example, his so-called "wireless system" was merely the reinvention of earth current communication, which had been known since 1837. Obviously, when he demonstrated such things to his unlearned neighbors they were perfectly willing to believe that he was the original inventor. It seems rather significant that of the 19 telephone patents actually held by Drawbaugh, all were dated after Bell's original patent. The earliest was 1882.

It was a day when powerful monopolies were riding roughshod over the little people. Attacks on Drawbaugh's character only served to arouse public opinion in his behalf. When the case finally reached the Supreme Court in 1887, there were seven judges sitting, and the vote was four to three in favor of Bell. The Bell Company, with characteristic braggadocio, called it a "unanimous decision." It was far from unanimous—it was a close squeak for the Bell Company. Bell followers have often cited the case as showing how narrowly the valuable telephone patent was preserved for responsible management. This implied that the management of the People's Telephone Company would have in some way been less in the public interest than that of Bell, demonstrably one of the most powerful and ruthless monopolies in the country.

Whatever the merits of the case, Drawbaugh did not do so badly. He got the spotlight of public attention for three years before retiring to the obscurity of Eberly's Mills, and he was paid $20,000 for his patent rights. The Bell attorneys earned $70,000 for their fee on the case and had no cause for complaint. One by one the Bell Company had disposed of all who had the temerity to challenge their patent, but Drawbaugh came the closest to unseating the mighty corporation that for many years had a stranglehold on telephonic communication.

The Supreme Court decision in the Drawbaugh case was a close call for the Bell Company, one of the closest in their long history of litigation. The dissenting opinion read:

We think that the evidence on this point is so overwhelming, with regard to both the number and the character of the witnesses, that it cannot be overcome. . . . We are satisfied, from a very great preponderance of evidence, that Drawbaugh produced and exhibited in his shop, as early as 1869, an electrical instrument by which he transmitted speech . . . by means of a wire and the employment of a variable resistance to the electrical current. . . . We are also satisfied that as early as 1871 he reproduced articulate speech at a distance by means of a current of electricity, subjected by electrical induction to undulations corresponding to the voice in speaking — a process substantially the same as that claimed in Mr. Bell's patent. Perhaps without the aid of Mr. Bell, the speaking telephone would not have been brought into public use to this day; but that Drawbaugh produced it, there can hardly be a reasonable doubt. . . . It is perfectly natural for the world to take the part of the man who has already achieved eminence. It is regarded as incredible that so great a discovery should have been made by a plain mechanic, and not by the eminent scientist and inventor.

The court documents also stated:

The defendants contend that long before Bell had perfected his invention, and long before its mental conception by him, Drawbaugh had not only made the same invention, but had perfected improvements in its organization and detail which Bell never reached, and which were only reached years afterwards by the work of many other inventors in the same field of improvement. Their theory of the facts is stated with substantial accuracy in the answer to the bill of complaint. The answer, among other things, avers that Drawbaugh "was and is the original and first inventor and discoverer of the art of communicating articulate speech between distant places by voltaic and magneto electricity, and of the construction and operation of machines and instruments for carrying such art into practice." . . .

The proofs on both sides lead to the general conclusion that Drawbaugh was not an original inventor of the speaking telephone, but had been an experimenter, without obtaining practical results until the introduction of the instruments into Harrisburg. It is very probable that after reading in the *Scientific American*, loaned to him by Mr. Shapley in October 1876, the article purporting to describe Bell's telephone, but which really describes better the Reis apparatus, he undertook to improve his old devices. At that time, or after he had examined the telephone instruments at Harrisburg and carried one of them home to study, he may have altered the organization of his instrument and made the intermediate exhibits between F and D. If he exhibited them at his shop and was able to transmit speech through them, this fact will account for the testimony of the witnesses who identify these exhibits, and may be mistaken as to the time they saw them. The real history of his talking machine is known only to himself, and it will not be profitable to conjecture when he made the advanced instruments which he claims to have made in February 1875, and the later instruments. It may be that in discrediting his narrative, and rejecting the theory of the facts which rests upon it, the value of the corroborative testimony has been underestimated. However this may be, no doubt is entertained as to the conclusion which should be reached upon the proofs. Succinctly stated most favorably for the defendants the case is this: One hundred witnesses, more or less, testify that on one or more occasions, which took place from five to ten years before, they think they saw this or that device used as a talking machine. They are ignorant of the principle and of the mechanical construction of the instruments, but they heard speech through them perfectly well, and through one set of instruments as well as the other. This case is met on the part of the complainants by proof that the instruments which most of the witnesses think they saw and heard through were incapable of being heard through in the manner described by them; and further, that the man who knew all about the capacity of his instruments never attempted to use them in a manner which would demonstrate their efficiency and commercial value, but, on the contrary, for ten years after he could have patented them and for five years after they were mechanically perfect, knowing all the time that a fortune awaited the patentee, and with no obstacles in his way, did not move, but calmly saw another obtain a patent, and reap the fame and profit of the invention. Without regard to other features of the case it is sufficient to say that the defense is not established so as to remove a fair doubt of its truth; and such doubt is fatal.

A decree is ordered for complainant.

If Daniel Drawbaugh was truly a clown, as he was labeled by the Bell Telephone lawyers, then Antonio Meucci could easily have earned the title of "super clown." Meucci who was a resident of Havana, Cuba, around 1849-1850, claimed that during that period he had discovered how to transmit words over a wire using several batteries to produce electricity. He called his device the "Speaking Telegraph." Meucci came to America in 1850 and established his residence at Clifton, on Staten Island. He had several occupations, including candle making and the manufacture of paper from vegetable fiber. He even operated a brewery at one time.

He resumed his experiments with telephony and claimed that before 1860 he had "good working instruments." By 1865, he claimed, his instruments were the equal of any that came later. Meucci claimed that his instruments were in use at his home and were known to his friends. Unfortunately, the original models disappeared, and Meucci was always very vague in describing just how they were constructed. Finally, in 1871, he induced three of his friends to invest money in his telephone and they were taking steps to procure a patent. The patent attorneys they consulted were quite candid in telling the group that they were not in condition to secure a patent—more work was needed.

One device claimed by Meucci was apparently nothing more than an acoustic telephone, the so-called "lover's telegraph" or "tin can" telephone. Although Meucci managed to get his name in the history books, his proposals were not considered worthy of attention by the Bell Telephone Company, who had a policy of buying out or suing any potential telephone inventor. Possibly they were convinced that Meucci posed no threat to the Bell patent when they heard of his proposal that two persons could converse by sitting in insulated chairs and letting the electric current pass through their bodies!

The final denunciation of Meucci came from a Bell attorney who said, "Meucci is the silliest and weakest imposter who has ever turned up against the patent." Giovanni E. Schiavo, a historian, in 1958 examined the Meucci claims again in some detail. Reading these claims only reinforces the opinion that Meucci did not understand the basic principles of the telephone, either before or for several years after Bell invented it.

Chapter 4

Under Pressure

ONE NAME THAT SURFACES repeatedly in accounts of early telephone history is that of Emile Berliner (1851–1929). Born in Hanover, Germany, he was the fourth in a family of 11. His formal schooling ended at the age of 14. When he was 19 he decided to seek fame and fortune in the United States. Leaving family and friends behind, he boarded the *Harmonia* for the two-week voyage to New York. It was 1870, before the Statue of Liberty welcomed newly arrived immigrants, and there were no immigration quotas. With the help of family friends Berliner found his first employment in Washington, D.C.

He returned to New York in 1873 and then started work as a traveling salesman of men's furnishings for a Milwaukee, Wisconsin, firm. In 1875 the young man was back in New York, where he found employment in the laboratory of Dr. Constantine Fahlberg, the discoverer of saccharine. In 1876, Berliner returned to Washington and resumed his former employment as a store clerk. Without formal education after age 14, the young clerk, now 26, took every advantage of opportunities to improve his education.

The Bell telephone invention was the sensation of the day after its exhibition at the Philadelphia Centennial. Bell's original telephones were sound-powered devices and thus had a very limited range of transmission.

Berliner became interested and started to pursue his own experiments in telephony. He soon formed the opinion that a successful telephone transmitter would have to employ a battery to enable the voice to carry to long distances. Bell's sound-powered concept simply would not do. At this point the young inventor was undoubtedly influenced by the original telephones of Philipp Reis, but he did not at first grasp the function of Reis's metal to metal contacts.

Berliner's first models employing metal to metal contacts did not work. Discouraged, he confessed his problem to a friend who was a telegrapher in a fire alarm office. Berliner told his friend that he was interested in becoming a telegraph operator. In demonstrating the operation of a telegraph key, his friend interrupted and said "you are not pressing the key firmly enough." Berliner then asked, "you mean the strength of the current depends on the pressure on the key knob?" Then his friend told him that for this reason women telegraphers were not used on long distance circuits because their touch was too light. This, of course, was a fiction, because women operators employed the same pressure on the key as the men. Even a small woman had easily enough strength to depress a telegraph key correctly. However, this little fairy tale was enough to give Berliner the idea he needed. He realized that contact resistance varies with pressure, especially when the pressure is quite light.

What followed was essentially Berliner's reinvention of the Reis telephone of 1860. Berliner developed the principle of variable resistance between metal contacts to a high degree. All of his experimental models would transmit articulate speech. If any vindication of Reis was needed this certainly was it.

One of Berliner's most successful models was the so-called "soap box transmitter," which was completed in April 1877. The box was an ordinary wooden box about seven by twelve inches in size. The bottom was knocked out, and over the opening was placed a thin metal sheet to act as a diaphragm. Supported on the other side was a screw tipped with a polished steel button that could be adjusted to bear on the diaphragm. This device easily transmitted speech. The actual box is preserved in the United States National Museum. Inside it is tacked a card reading:

> Introduced in evidence in Circuit Court of United States District of Massachusetts. In equity 3106; U.S.A. vs. American Bell Telephone Company and Emile Berliner, Defendant's exhibit. Berliner's soap-box Transmitter. M.S.C. Special Examiner.

Berliner once proved to government attorneys that his principle of variable resistance contacts would even work with an ordinary telegraph key. He hooked one up with a battery and telephone receiver and had the government lawyers conversing by talking into the telegraph key acting as a microphone. Somewhat chagrined, the Federal attorney turned to the telephone company lawyer and exclaimed: "It does seem incredible."

Reis invented a telephone in 1860 and had plunged into obscurity even before his death in 1874. Berliner invented a telephone transmitter in 1877 and was immediately plunged into years of notoriety amidst a vast legal tangle surrounding his invention. Of course, Berliner worked in the late 1800s when public acceptance of new inventions was probably a little higher than it was in the Germany of 1860.

Berliner might have plunged into obscurity as well, except that he came to the attention of the Bell Telephone Company. Bell at that time was desperately searching for a better transmitting element for its phones. The

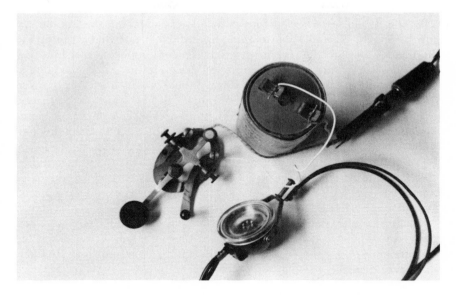

Replication of Berliner's telegraph key microphone — it works! (Photo by Lewis Coe.)

sound-powered instruments they were using just did not lend themselves to the wide expansion of the telephone system that was vital to Bell's prosperity.

Bell realized that the principles embodied in Berliner's device were vital to any successful transmitter that would be developed in the future. The Berliner transmitter, employing metal to metal contacts, would transmit speech but it was of limited usefulness for commercial service. Nevertheless, Bell hired Berliner and had his patent rights assigned to the company. About the same time, Bell also acquired rights to a transmitter invented by Francis Blake.

Blake's transmitter was almost the same as Berliner's except that Blake had hit upon the happy idea of using a carbon button for one of the contact points. The resistance characteristics of the carbon made it easy to get the widely varying value of current required for good speech transmission.

The Blake transmitter showed a lot of promise, but it was not long before its weakness was discovered. The instruments as manufactured and tested would not stay in adjustment—a fatal defect for public telephone use. Bell, having both Berliner and Blake on their payroll, put the two to work to solve the problem. Finally, Berliner discovered how to correct the defect in the Blake transmitter, and soon they were being mass produced and widely used. In fact, the Berliner-Blake transmitter was standard with Bell for many years.

This would seem like a happy ending to the story, but the trouble was just beginning. The trouble stemmed from the fact that Bell acquired the Berliner patent in 1878 (Berliner's original patent application of 1877 had never been acted on) and then, either by design or incredible bungling in the patent office, the actual patent was not issued until November 18, 1891. There were two schools of thought to explain this 14-year delay in issuing the Berliner patent. One school held that a series of "interference" claims were filed by rival inventors, some hoping to be paid off by the Bell Company to drop their claims. The other school of thought, and one that got a lot of public support, was that the Bell Company managed to manipulate the delay for the express purpose of prolonging their virtual monopoly for another 17 years after their basic patents expired. This would have placed Bell in a very strong position until 1908.

Given the predatory business practices of the Bell Telephone Company, it was hard to convince anyone that there was not dirty work at the patent office. Some people felt that the Berliner patent had more commercial value than the original Bell patent.

This kind of thinking was fueled by such figures as were published in a Washington dispatch dated November 18, 1891, in the *Chicago Inter-Ocean*:

> A curious computation was made by experts about the Patent Office today as to the value of the Berliner patent to the Bell Company. The capital stock of that company being $15,000,000 and the maximum rise in the stock 30 points, it follows that the value of the Berliner microphone patent as determined by stock quotations, is $5,000,000. On this basis, by computation, the patent added one third to the value of the Bell Telephone Company's capital stock.

Another typical editorial of the time was this one published in the *Rochester Herald* (N.Y.) of December 4, 1891. This was two weeks after the issue of the Berliner patent in Washington.

> For a long time prior to November 17th the stock of the Bell Telephone Company stood at or near $180. For about a week preceding that date, it advanced some three or four dollars. On the Friday before, there were sales at $193; Monday it had gone up to $198, and on the day the Berliner patent was issued, the stock reached $210. These quotations show that people inside the Bell combination knew what was going on at the Patent Office, confirming opinion long held by many that the Bell Company had altogether too confidential relations with that office. The *Boston Journal* says: "It is claimed that the patent covers every known form of battery transmitter." It will be seen from these statements by the papers of Boston, which is the home of the Bell Company, that the monopoly expects to retain its grip upon this country for seventeen years longer. It has sought to accomplish this result by the dishonorable trick of keeping up a sham contest in the Patent Office over the Berliner application through the past fourteen years. That such proceedings are possible in a bureau of the national

government is a fact discreditable to the officials of that bureau during the period named and an outrage on the people of the United States. The time has come for a complete revolution in that office and a change in the laws bearing upon this question.

Public agitation, fanned by such editorial comments, soon reached the level where the government felt that some action had to be taken. A bill in equity was filed in the Circuit Court of the United States in and for the District of Massachusetts on February 1, 1893. The case finally reached the Supreme Court, and on May 10, 1897, Mr. Justice Brewer handed down a verdict in favor of Berliner and the Bell Company. It was held that the government had failed to prove any fraudulent intent on the part of the Bell Company. The vote was six to one, with Mr. Justice Harlan dissenting.

Once again, the superb legal talent marshalled by the Bell Company had managed to leave the company unscathed. The public, however, was hardly convinced. Most people thought it was all just too neat to be honest. Yet it was all legal, it was on the record books, and the only folks who really had no complaint were the Bell stockholders. Perhaps the best comment on the situation was given by writer Paul Bocock in *Munsey's Magazine* (November 1900). His story, titled "The Romance of the Telephone," said in part:

> Interwoven in the story of the golden growth of the telephone, are such marvelous oaths, such charges of corruption and treachery, such tales of ruin and oppression, such accusations against men high in the public esteem, such sacrifices of truth and honor, such disappointments and defeats of the many who have sought to share the reward of the one, that the bare relation of them all, were that possible, would surpass any romance ever written.

American Bell could now claim a new transmitter patent broad enough to cover almost all forms of telephone transmitters and running until 1908, yet even their own people apparently recognized the unfairness of the court decision. In the latter part of 1891, James Storrow, an American Bell lawyer, wrote to Bell President Hudson and said: "The Bell Company has had a monopoly more profitable and more controlling — and more generally hated than any ever given by any patent. The attempt to prolong it by the Berliner patent will bring a great strain on that patent and a great pressure on the courts." Hudson ignored this advice, and the result was the suit that finally ended in the Supreme Court decision in favor of Bell.

Eventually a suit brought by Bell against the National Telephone Manufacturing Company resulted in the Berliner patent being construed in a very narrow category. This effectively ended the Bell monopoly and enabled independent telephone companies to spring up all across the country after the turn of the century. Bell's strategy against the independents had been to fight them in the courts instead of trying to provide better service at lower rates. The public was becoming tired of the arrogant attitude of Bell. By 1897 Bell was beginning to lose some court cases. One Bell historian said: "Where the Bell company enjoyed monopoly privileges, officials of the company were discourteous and dictatorial and the service was not satisfactory."

Almost coincident with Berliner's work was that of David E. Hughes. Born in England, Hughes at the time of his experiments was professor of natural philosophy at the College of Bairdstown, Kentucky. Hughes discovered that loose metallic contacts carrying battery current can generate the undulating current necessary for sound transmission. His discovery was disclosed in a paper which he wrote and sent to Professor Huxley in England. It was read by Huxley before the Royal Society in London on May 8, 1878. Hughes called his device a "microphone," a term coined by Wheatstone in 1827 to describe an acoustic listening instrument. The term is still used today in reference to any instrument designed to pick up sound. Telephones all use one, only in telephone practice it has always been called a "transmitter." The first Hughes microphone was a group of three ordinary iron nails in loose contact. Later, the principle was used with carbon rods, or pencils. The carbon gave greatly improved sensitivity. It was said that a fly's footsteps could be heard—and remember, this was before electronic amplification was available.

The Hughes carbon-pencil microphone was the subject of further development in France by a man named Ader and his associates. They developed models using six to 12 carbon pencils in series-multiple circuits. This enabled higher battery current to be used with correspondingly higher output. In 1884 at the Paris Electrical Exposition, Ader anticipated modern stereo sound reproduction. He placed microphones at each end of the stage of the Grand Opera, each wired on a separate circuit to earphones in the Exposition Hall, enabling listeners to use a receiver at each ear and experience the binaural transmission of sound. Like the liquid contact transmitter of Gray and Bell, and the metallic contact transmitter of Berliner, the Hughes microphone was not practical for commercial telephone use. It was, however, an important step along the way towards the microphones and transmitters that we now take for granted.

During the years when the Bell System had no other transmitter except the Berliner-Blake, they found that while this instrument delivered good speech quality, it was low on output. This made it a problem on the long distance circuits that were coming into increasing use. Thus it was that they were quite interested in the transmitter invented by a British clergyman, Henry Hunnings, of Bothwell in Yorkshire. Hunnings received a patent on September 16, 1878, for a new type of telephone transmitter. It involved multiple contacts between a diaphragm and a cavity filled with carbon granules. Because of the multiple contacts, the Hunnings transmitter could handle greater current and provide a relatively higher output. The main weakness was that the carbon granules tended to "pack," rendering the instrument insensitive. Because it seemed promising, the Hunnings U.S. patents were purchased by Bell. The transmitter was redesigned in 1885 to use a horizontal diaphragm and hard carbon granules. Also, the electrodes were gold-plated to reduce contamination of the surfaces. The resulting transmitter gave higher output than anything previously used. Over 10,000 of the Hunnings transmitters were manufactured and widely used by the Bell Company on their long-distance lines.

The final development of carbon button transmitters was largely the result of the research conducted by Thomas Edison while he was employed at Western Union. The 1879 accord between the Bell Company and Western Union gave Bell full use of the patents held by Western Union. The final development of the Edison transmitter was credited to A. C. White, a Bell engineer, who, in 1890, invented what came to be known as the White "solid back" transmitter. The name solid back came from a heavy metal strap across the back of the unit that supported the rear end of the carbon chamber. Careful design produced a unit that was even higher in output than the Hunnings "long-distance" transmitter. Packing of the carbon granules was minimized, although it was always a problem with carbon button transmitters.

The White transmitter, or variations thereof, was practically a standard until the handset type of transmitter button was invented in the 1920s. Carbon buttons continued to be used in all telephones until the appearance of the comparatively new telephone that used the electret type of transmitter. Improved techniques of manufacture enabled the production of small, carbon button type transmitters for operators' headsets that were about the diameter of a quarter coin and very light. Pity the poor operator who worked in the days when the Blake transmitter was standard—it weighed about six pounds! In the 1990s we have tiny microphones for operators' headsets that are less than the diameter of a lead pencil and able to deliver high quality speech with good sensitivity.

Although Berliner's metal contact microphone was practically worthless for commercial use, it gave the Bell System for the first time a variable resistance transmitter. Combining the work of Berliner and Blake, they managed to survive the years until the agreement with Western Union in 1879 gave them access to Edison's carbon button transmitter patents. Berliner contributed a more useful invention to telephony when he patented the induction coil in 1878. The importance of the induction coil was that it matched the transmitter, a low resistance device, with the line resistance, which might be 500 ohms or more. The induction coil was what is called in electrical terminology a "step up transformer." By its use, the efficiency of the telephone was improved enormously over the earlier, primitive circuits that might involve only a transmitter and receiver in series with the local battery and the line. Edison also shared in the induction coil idea and patented it in 1878.

Telephone induction coils actually trace their ancestry back to the early experiments of Michael Faraday and Joseph Henry. Before the general use of alternating current electricity, an induction coil was the only means of generating high voltage electricity at will. The largest such coil ever built was the creation of William Spottiswoode of London in 1876. Spottiswoode's coil was 44 inches long and was capable of generating a spark 42 inches long. In America, many of the early experiments were conducted by Charles Grafton Page in 1838. Page, a physician of Salem, Massachusetts, graduated from Harvard College in 1832. He soon became an electrical experimenter and continued in this work until his death in 1868.

Berliner was also an active inventor in other fields, inventing a talking machine and a method for duplicating disk records in 1887. In 1908 he invented a lightweight, rotating cylinder aircraft engine. In 1925 he invented acoustic tiles and other materials for deadening sound. Yet the fact remains that his real contribution was the indirect service he rendered to Bell, enabling them to prolong their monopoly another 17 years. This may not have been his intention, but he was a Bell employee and it is pretty safe to say that he did exactly what he was told.

Chapter 5

Inventors Galore!

BY THE LAST HALF of the 19th century, the telephone was an idea whose time had come. Following the success of the Morse telegraph, which established the idea of transmitting intelligence electrically, it was only a short time before the obvious possibility of transmitting the human voice electrically had occurred to many people in widely separated parts of the world. The telephone was fated to follow the telegraph, just as the discovery of radio soon opened the doors to television.

George B. Prescott, in his book *The Electric Telegraph*, published in 1866, speculates on the possibilities of transmitting music by telegraph. Prescott relates how skilled telegraphers could tap out the rhythm of popular songs of the day so skillfully that the tunes could be recognized at the other end of the wire. Carrying his speculation a step further, he predicted the transmission of musical tones of several thousand hertz per second. No one had figured out exactly how to do it yet, but Prescott's work shows what was on a lot of minds at the time.

While the time of the telephone had arrived technically, it didn't mean that the general public was ready to accept it. Even many scientific authorities dismissed it as a "philosophical toy," causing many early workers to slacken their efforts or quit entirely. Philipp Reis, plagued by ill health and little recognition for his telephone, just gave up and said it would be up to others to carry on the work he had started.

In America, Edward Ferrar was experimenting with a telephone in 1851. His equipment was said to be the equal of anything later claimed in the Bell patent. Ferrar received some advice (which in hindsight must have been bad) from Professor Silliman of Yale University. As a result he gave up his experiments, thereby losing his chance for a place in history. The good professor was probably echoing what was unfortunately a prevailing opinion of the time, "don't waste your time on an impractical device like the telephone."

Another 1851 inventor was S. D. Cushman of Racine, Wisconsin. Cushman was a telegraph construction man and was working on a new idea for lightning arresters, then an important need for the fledgling telegraph industry. While working near one of his arresters one day he was startled to hear the faint sound of frogs croaking in a nearby swamp. The details are not known, but apparently something in the lightning arresters, possibly an inductance coil or capacitor plate, was acting as a microphone and a reproduction device as well. A series of experiments followed in which his brother, W. P. Cushman, B. F. Blodgett and a Mr. White, took part. They were able to talk back and forth over distances of two or three miles. In 1854 the Cushman device was used for communication between the ends of a rope walk. For some reason, Cushman did not attempt to patent his idea, either in 1854 or thirty years later when it was discovered by the Bell Company, who signed Cushman to a three-year contract in May 1882.

James W. McDonough of Chicago claimed the invention of a telephone receiver before December 31, 1867. In August 1871, McDonough drew a diagram showing a telephone transmitter and receiver intended for transmission of speech over wires. He filed a patent application in April 1876, calling it a "teleloge" meaning "far speech." This patent was not granted until 1881. By that time Bell was seeking out all possible claimants to the telephone invention. McDonough was quietly bought out and disappeared into the limbo of other telephone inventors.

This illustrated the thorough intelligence gathering of Bell, who searched out every inventor who had any presumptive claim to the telephone, no matter how unlikely. Then they either hired the person, bought his patent rights, or sued him for infringement in court. The legal climate of that day seemed to be overwhelmingly in favor of the Bell Company. The telephone company finally involved poor Cushman in a court case, and the judge ruled against him, saying that what he had done was only an "abandoned experiment." This was typical of the highhanded legal procedures of the day, when jurists with only a sketchy knowledge of the matter at hand attempted to rule on technical matters that were far beyond their ken.

An argument much used, which affects the consideration of inventions made by others — put forward when it was urged that Bell had never gotten his apparatus to talk when his invention was patented — was "that the subject matter of a patent was protected for all it would or could perform, whether the inventor knew it or not, and whether claimed or unclaimed." Seemingly this was the principle applied to Bell's invention, but by some curious twist of the legal mind the principle was forgotten when it came to considering the work of other inventors.

The earliest efforts to reproduce speech at a distance concentrated on mechanical means. Large, megaphone-type devices were able to send speech sounds to distances beyond that reached by the unaided human voice. The peculiar whistled language used by the Canary Islanders on the island of Gomera to communicate across the valleys is said to cover as much as five miles under ideal conditions.

Eventually it was discovered that voice vibrations could be carried through solid wires or rods of metal or wood. Perhaps the first recorded experiments were those of Charles Wheatstone in 1821–1823, when he demonstrated his "magic lyre." In this experiment, wooden rods ran between a piano in one room to a sound box in another room and the sounds of the piano were reproduced in the remote sound box. Even Wheatstone's experiments may not have been the first to discover the mechanical transmission of speech. Writing in 1664, one Robert Hooke said: "I can assure the reader that I have, by the help of a distended wire, propagated the sound to a very considerable distance in an instant, or with as seemingly quick a motion as that of light, at least, incomparably swifter than that, which at the same time was propagated through the air; and this not only in a straight line, or direct, but in one bended in many angles."

Credited to Amos E. Dolbear in 1854, the "string telephone," or "lover's telegraph," was undoubtedly inspired by Wheatstone's experiments. In this device, a string or wire is stretched between the closed ends of two cylindrical containers. Speaking into the open end of one container sends the voice vibrations over the string or wire to the distant container. In later years, children often made these telephones from discarded tin cans, hence the name "tin can telephone." By making the connecting link a taut metallic wire, carefully supported, ranges up to a quarter mile could be achieved. As made by children, the tin can telephones always seemed to work. Possibly this was because over the short distances usually involved, the shrill voices of the users could normally be heard with or without the telephone.

When Bell demonstrated his invention in England for the first time, it stimulated an intense popular interest in the subject. Capitalizing on this interest, the novelty shops made up inexpensive versions of the "tin can telephone" and sold them by the thousands to an eager public. A commercial version of the tin can telephone was listed in the Montgomery Ward catalog of 1895, "complete with 200 feet of connecting wire."

Dolbear, the inventor of the "tin can telephone," was not a simple backwoods rustic to be easily intimidated by the mighty Bell telephone company. Dolbear was born in Norwich, Connecticut, in 1837. He started his schooling at Ohio Wesleyan University and then entered the University of Michigan. His major was mining engineering and he received the degrees of A.M. and M.E. in 1867 and the Ph.D. in 1873. After receiving his doctorate he was appointed professor of physics and astronomy at Tufts College in Massachusetts in 1874. One of his first inventions was what he called an "electric writing telegraph" in 1864. This was an anticipation of Elisha Gray's "telautograph." Western Union turned down the idea, assuring

Anyone can make a "tin can telephone." All that is needed are two cans and a length of fine wire or string. (Photo by Lewis Coe.)

Dolbear that "there was no future in it." This was the same Western Union that once turned down the chance to buy Bell's telephone patent outright for $100,000. Also in 1864, Dolbear invented what he called a "talking machine." Unfortunately, he did not pursue work on this device which actually was identical with Bell's original type of electromagnetic receiver and transmitter—a sound-powered telephone. If Dolbear had patented his device, Alexander Graham Bell would never have been heard of—but he didn't, and by the time he realized what he had it was too late.

In 1879, Dolbear invented what he called a "static telephone." This device employed closely spaced metallic plates to form a capacitor whose characteristics were varied at voice frequencies. This created the undulating current necessary for voice transmission. Modern condenser microphones and loudspeakers work on exactly the same principle. It should be explained that the terms "capacitor" and "condenser" mean the same thing in electrical terminology. The word capacitor is used almost exclusively now, since the earlier term caused confusion between two entirely different things, electrical condensers and steam condensers. When Dolbear attempted to patent the condenser idea, he was promptly sued by the Bell Company. When this case finally reached the Supreme Court, the decision was in favor of Bell. In this rather remarkable decision, the court maintained that Bell had patented the very idea of conveying speech by electricity. New means of doing this were not considered patentable.

Next, Dolbear discovered the principle of induction, and found that his static transmitters and receivers could communicate at a 50-foot distance without connecting wires. When he applied for a patent on this idea in 1882, the patent office turned it down with an astounding explanation, saying that the device was "contrary to science and would not work." This must have caused Dolbear to scratch his head and mutter, "what do you have to do to patent a new idea?" Actually, Dolbear had demonstrated his idea before several scientific groups prior to applying for a patent. The principle is still used today in inductive sound distribution systems, such as churches, where the listeners can wear headphones not connected by wires, and hear the services. It has also found use in public museums where visitors can rent headsets and hear taped descriptions of the exhibits.

Dolbear finally did receive a patent on his system of wireless communication in 1882, but this was for wireless telegraphy employing a spark coil as the transmitting device. The telephone had been on his mind all the while, and in September 1876 he started work on a model of what was later the identical type of electromagnetic transmitter and receiver used by Bell. It was suggested at the time that Bell had heard of Dolbear's work and was guided towards his own version accordingly. Bell, of course, denied this. Dolbear seemed to accept the situation philosophically and once wrote to Bell, remarking how common it was for two persons working independently to hit on the same idea without any knowledge of the other's work. Nevertheless, Dolbear felt that he had in some way been deprived of credit for the telephone invention. One of the Tufts alumni remembered the way in which Dolbear displayed a box to a freshman physics class in 1895 and declared, "This is the first telephone that was ever invented, I invented it." Years later, some of the alumni had a bronze plaque affixed to a wall of Ballou Hall at Tufts in commemoration of Dolbear's claim.

Dolbear was an important witness in the famous Dowd case of 1878 in which Bell sued Western Union for infringement of the basic telephone patents. In this case, Dolbear was a witness for Western Union, along with Elisha Gray and Thomas A. Edison. In September of 1877 he had negotiated an agreement with the Gold and Stock Company, a division of Western Union, to apply for patents on all his telephone inventions and assign them to Gold and Stock. By the terms of this agreement, he was to be compensated for the patent and legal expenses involved, plus one-third of the net profits from the patents and an allowance of twenty-five dollars a week to support further research. He made a patent application in October and was thus involved in both patent interferences and the Dowd case.

When Dolbear discovered after selling his telephone rights for $10,000 that Western Union would have paid $100,000, he considered himself to

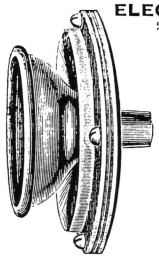

ELECTRICAL GOODS.

24170 The Elgin Accoustic Telephone, made wholly of metal, nickel plated, self-supporting, not even a screw to hold it in place. The telephone will work on a line ½ mile long, and is the neatest, most durable and best working mechanical telephone on the market. Telephones, per pair (2), with 200 feet wire, wire for hangers and directions for putting the phone in working order complete.

Weight, 3½ lbs......$5.00
24171 Copper Wire, No. 18, for Elgin Phone, per pound (125 feet).........   ...$0.31

Acoustic, or "tin can" telephone could be purchased from the Montgomery Ward catalog of 1895.

have been "outrageously swindled." He confessed at the same time that he would have accepted an offer of only $5,000! His telephone of 1879 used a static or condenser type of transmitter and was thought not to infringe on the Bell patent. However, in 1881, after the Dolbear Electric Telephone Company had been organized, it was sued by the Bell Company on the grounds that Bell patents covered all forms of speech communication, no matter how obtained. This action went all the way to the Supreme Court and was decided for Bell in 1886.

After the telephone had been invented, and no satisfactory answer had been given as to who actually invented it, the inventors went right on inventing. The telephone, it seems, stirred inventors to get involved with it somehow. In 1912, Lincoln C. Stockton was awarded a patent for a "Portable Face Mask for Telephone Use." This bag-like device clamped over the mouthpiece of a candlestick telephone and supposedly prevented nearby persons from overhearing the conversation.

Perhaps the goofiest telephone invention appeared in 1916. Paul P. Banholzer of Philadelphia received a patent for a gadget for which the claim was made "that this instrument will further introduce the dot and dash system of telegraphy, which can be understood by any wire operator. Furthermore, the sound it produces is unmistakable and carries much farther than the voice." This device was merely a telegraph key clamped to the upright stem of a candlestick phone. By mechanical action the dots and dashes could be heard over the phone. No possible application of the thing sounds reasonable, except that it might be used by student operators to practice with each other over the phone.

In 1929, Edward O. Hunter invented what he called a "finger thimble for telephone dials." This gadget, looking like an oversized sewing thimble, was supposed to protect the finger of a person making many rotary dial calls.

The Hush-a-Phone was a device that had been in use since 1921. It was a small enclosure that clamped over a telephone mouthpiece and tended to prevent persons nearby from overhearing the conversation. It required no electrical connection to the telephone and could not possibly degrade the service. In the 1940s, AT&T discovered this device and decided that it violated the dictum that only Western Electric–manufactured equipment could be connected to AT&T lines. This was a ridiculous assumption on the part of AT&T, yet they were upheld by the FCC. The Hush-a-Phone Corporation took their case to the U.S. Court of Appeals and were vindicated when the Court ordered the FCC to reverse its decision. The Hush-a-Phone case became important in subsequent litigation involving the use of non–Western Electric equipment on telephone lines.

Lee De Forest, in the process of acquiring over 300 patents in his lifetime, was involved in almost constant litigation to defend his rights. His invention of the three-element vacuum tube, or audion, was one of the great landmark inventions of the electronic world, yet it immediately came under fire of infringers. The most audacious of these were H. D. Arnold of the Western Electric Company and Irving Langmuir of General Electric. Both of them had discovered that the audion could be greatly improved by a higher vacuum to rid the tube of gasses. Langmuir was actually issued a patent on his process, and with this patent the General Electric Company would have been in a position to dominate the entire field of electronics. De Forest's company filed suit against General Electric, and a long, drawn-out court case finally reached the Supreme Court. In a decision handed down in May 1931, the court said:

> That the production of the high vacuum tube was no more than the application of the skill of the art to the problem in hand is apparent when it is realized that the invention involved only the application of this knowledge to the common forms of low-vacuum discharge devices such as the Fleming and De Forest tubes.
>
> Once known that gas ionization in the tube caused an irregularity of current which did not occur in a high vacuum, it did not need the genius of the inventor to recognize and act upon the truth that a better tube for amplifying could be made by taking out the gas.
>
> Arnold, who was skilled in the art and who had made studies of electrical discharges in high vacua, when shown a De Forest audion for the first time on November 14, 1912, immediately recognized and said that by increasing the vacuum the discharge would be sufficiently stable and have adequate power

levels to enable the tube to be employed as a relay device in transcontinental telephony.

The very fact that all of significance in the Langmuir improvement was obvious to one skilled in the art as soon as he saw the unimproved tube, lies athwart of a finding of invention.

This court decision was hailed by the press as "another smashing victory over the radio trust."

One of the bright spots in Bell System history was the founding of the Bell Laboratories in 1925. Previously, research involving the telephone had been carried on by company engineers who were interested primarily in projects of direct benefit to the telephone company. Now, a highly talented group of scientists was working in diverse fields. Some of these projects, of course, were of direct benefit to the telephone company. Others tended to be the kind of thing that benefited all mankind instead of just the Bell stockholders. One of these was the invention of the transistor in 1947. The transistor marked the beginning of the present age of electronics. The inventors, William Shockley, Walter H. Brattain, and John Bardeen, were awarded the Nobel Prize in Physics in 1956.

Transistors now are a vital part of almost any electronic device, but in the beginning the first commercial application was in the hearing aid. Electronic hearing aids had been developed in the pre-transistor days. Using miniature vacuum tubes and exceedingly clever design in physical construction, the makers had come up with hearing aids that were much better than anything previously used. The vacuum tube hearing aids worked well and were welcomed by the people that depended on them. However, there were some disadvantages. The units, even after maximum reduction of size, still required a small case to contain the batteries and amplifier. The batteries were relatively expensive and required frequent replacement. Transistors changed all this and the devices became smaller and smaller until now — when they are small enough to fit in the wearer's ear.

Inventors, as a class, are not usually discouraged by the negative experiences of others — they just keep on inventing. Otherwise, they might just as well follow the advice of Charles Duell, director of the U.S. Patent Office, who declared in 1899 that "Everything that can be invented has been invented."

Chapter 6

A Great Undertaking

DURING THE LATTER HALF of the 19th century it seemed that great discoveries were often made by individuals not specifically qualified in a particular field. For example, Morse was a portrait painter, Bell a teacher of the deaf, and Marconi an Italian youth who might well have ended up as a gentleman farmer.

Surely, though, no background could be more unusual than that of Almon B. Strowger, inventor of the automatic switching system for telephone exchanges. Strowger (1839–1902) was an undertaker in Kansas City, Missouri. He is credited with inventing the first successful automatic switching system for telephone calls. According to legend, Strowger became convinced that the telephone operators were interfering with his calls for the benefit of his competitors. He thought that if the human operator could be eliminated, such annoying practices would end.

Persons familiar with switchboard operations in a town the size of Kansas City would question the ability of operators to interfere with Strowger's calls. He thought otherwise, and started work on a device to solve the problem. Kansas City at that time had two telephone systems in competition with each other, the Bell and the Home. Strowger's problem may have been merely that he did not have both phones. One can only admire the persistence of this diminutive, 110-pound man, who with little previous knowledge of the subject, and using makeshift materials, proceeded to make a crude working model of the device that eventually revolutionized the telephone industry. Strowger's first model was called the "collar box" because it was fashioned from an ordinary paper collar box, a common item at the time.

Strowger continued to perfect his switch and was issued a patent, No. 447,918, on March 10, 1891. Meanwhile, a chance encounter with a Chicago salesman, Joe Harris, led to a business partnership that was organized as the "Strowger Automatic Telephone Exchange" in 1891. This was the beginning of the firm that would later be known as the Automatic Electric Company. The company grew rapidly, and by 1921 it had 10 acres of plant space and

3,000 employees. Strowger's patent is generally conceded to be the lineal forebear of the original dial telephone switchboard. The patent was so strong that even the mighty Bell System could not circumvent it, and was compelled to pay license fees until 1905.

To fully appreciate Strowger's contribution, one must consider the problems inherent in the manual switching systems that had been in use since the first Bell exchange. In the manual system, an operator gets a signal from the subscriber, either by a magnetic drop annunciator as originally used, or a signal lamp in later systems. The operator inserts one plug of a cord set into the calling line jack. After getting the number wanted, the other side of the cord set is plugged into the called party's jack and a ringing signal sent out.

This simple and direct system worked well enough when the telephone was new and switchboards were small in size. The expanding use of the telephone, however, caused switchboards to become larger and larger. The sheer physical size of switchboards with hundreds of lines started to be a problem. The switchboards eventually grew so large that supervisors often wore roller skates to get from one end of the board to the other in a hurry. By 1929, supervisors with their short skirts, Clara Bow haircuts and graceful skating style presented an entrancing picture, but they were clearly not the answer to the rapidly expanding needs of the telephone service.

The first commercial installation by the new Strowger company was in the city of La Porte, Indiana. With much fanfare, the first automatic switching system was placed in service on November 3, 1892. Public interest in the project generated so many new subscribers that the Strowger company fell behind in their construction work and had to ask the La Porte city council for a time extension on their contract. Similar systems were installed in Noblesville and Crawfordsville, Indiana, soon after.

These early Strowger switching exchanges worked well enough if properly operated by the subscriber. However, all were eventually abandoned as the original type of push-button selector led to many wrong numbers. These first automatic phones had four push buttons labeled "hundreds," "tens," "units," and a "release" button to reset the mechanism. It was necessary for the caller to count the pulses, pushing a button eight times for an "8," etc. It was not until 1896 that a dial selector resembling the modern rotary dial was developed and ended the need for callers to count the pulses. The first Strowger dial selectors had eleven finger holes, ten for the digits and the eleventh for signaling the long-distance operator.

By 1900, automatic switching was well developed, yet many years passed before manual exchanges were eliminated completely. A clever device was designed to solve the problem of interchanging calls between dial and manual exchanges. A dialed call coming into a manual exchange

Push buttons of the Strowger automatic telephone installed in La Porte, Indiana, in 1892. (Photo by Lewis Coe.)

area keyed up a synthetic voice which told the human operator on the manual switchboard what number to ring. These so-called "call announcer" machines utilized strips of sound movie film to create the synthetic voice. This technique, borrowed from the movies, was used because at that time (the late 1920s) magnetic recording of the type used today was not yet available. Operators in manual exchanges had dials handy to call into automatic areas.

In general, smaller communities were the first to get dial service, as the problems of changeover were simpler. The conservative Bell System, with large investments in comparatively new manual exchanges, did not change over until the equipment was fully depreciated. As late as the mid–1950s there were still a few manual exchanges in Chicago and other large cities.

The Automatic Electric Company was purchased by GTE in 1956. In 1972, to commemorate the 80th anniversary of Strowger's first exchange, GTE presented the city of La Porte with a replica of one of the first automatic phones. Arrangements were made to have the historic phone placed on permanent display in the museum operated by the La Porte County Historical Society.

After Strowger made the original invention he was fortunate in acquiring the services of skilled designers who took his basic idea and improved

Replica of 1892 phone presented to the city of La Porte, Indiana, in 1972 and on display at the La Porte County Historical Society museum. (Photo by Lewis Coe.)

it. Men like A. E. Keith and John and Charles Ericson were instrumental in the early development of the Strowger switching system. The mechanism was compared to the proverbial Dutchman's wife, "not much for looks, but is hell for work."

An exchange sold to the Citizens Telephone Company of Grand Rapids, Michigan, in 1904 was still going strong after 15 years. The maker had guaranteed to replace any worn or defective parts for the first seven years of service. It was said that the total cost of the guarantee to the maker had been about 15 cents per connected telephone. The Strowger switch as developed by Automatic Electric Company became very successful and was installed worldwide. The Bell System had adopted the step-by-step system as early as 1919; Western Electric did not start manufacturing such equipment until 1926. Prior to 1926, the Western Electric Company did the installation work of automatic exchanges, but the equipment itself was manufactured by Automatic Electric.

As good as the Strowger system was it had certain limitations in operating speed, and it also had a space problem as exchanges grew larger and larger. The crossbar switch was developed by AT&T to solve some of these problems. Eventually even the crossbar method began to exhibit the same problems as the earlier systems. With the invention of the transistor in 1947, possibilities for electronic switching began to emerge. Since 1965 many electronic switching exchanges have been installed, and electronic switching is now the accepted method. Electronic switching exchanges are much faster in operation than the best electro-mechanical system and they are very compact in physical size.

Development of electronic switching required several years prior to 1965. During this period, the exchange at Morris, Illinois, was selected to act as a guinea pig for the first unit. First, a laboratory mock-up of the Morris exchange was tested, followed by actual commercial use at Morris. One of the unique features of electronic switching was the "flash cutover" to the new system, replacing the hours of tedious labor required in the past to cut over from an existing system to a new one.

Before Strowger died in 1902 he was said to be greatly discouraged by the general lack of recognition that he had received for his contribution to the telephone industry. His name is not even mentioned in many standard biographical reference books. His contribution might be considered minimal, since the automatic system was really developed by the skilled engineers who joined Automatic Electric. Yet he had the basic idea and did something about it. Many years might have elapsed before someone else came along to do the job. Strowger's grave is in the Greenwood Cemetery, St. Petersburg, Florida. Along with Elisha Gray and the many others, he is one of the forgotten men of the telephone industry.

Strowger might have been better known if he had had more of the self-promoting characteristics of Alexander Graham Bell. Bell was his own best press agent and never lost an opportunity to cash in on the advantage he had gained from his patent. For example, Bell showed up at the bedside of President Garfield after the assassination attempt on July 2, 1881. Bell was working on a machine called an "induction balance." He persuaded the president's medical men to let him try a haywire and untested machine in the hope of locating the bullet that was lodged in Garfield's body. In those days, before X-rays, there was no way of locating a bullet except by probing. Needless to say, Bell could not locate the bullet, but he got a lot of publicity in his attempt to do so. The president died, of course, on September 19, not from the effects of the bullet, which had not touched any vital organ, but from infection caused by clumsy attempts to probe for the bullet without provisions for surgical cleanliness.

The telephone system has gone full circle from Strowger's original push buttons to the rotary dial and now back to push buttons. Judging by the "wrong numbers" most people still receive, it is apparent that subscribers still have trouble with those buttons.

Automatic Electric was to the independent telephone industry what Western Electric was to Bell. It ultimately became the supplier of equipment to the largest independent of them all, GTE. The company was formerly known as General Telephone & Electronics and was engaged in

a variety of enterprises not directly related to its prime business of supplying public telephone service. Since deregulation, GTE has had to change its image as a regulated public utility to that of an international telecommunications competitor. The company has gone after the cellular telephone market in a big way and it is now considered the second biggest provider of that service. Cellular service is attractive to the telephone companies because new customers are added at insignificant cost compared to conventional service. About 16.1 million U.S. telephone subscribers, more than any of the regional Bell companies, are now served by GTE.

The ten largest independent telephone companies include GTE, by far the largest, and the following nine:

United Telephone System
Continental Telecom, Inc. (CONTEL)
Centel Corporation
ALLTEL Corporation
Puerto Rico Telephone Company
Rochester Telephone Corporation
Century Telephone Enterprises, Inc.
Lincoln (Nebraska) Telephone & Telegraph Company
Telephone and Data Systems, Inc.

Even though the principles of automatic dialing were understood by the turn of the century, there was no great rush on the part of the telephone companies to put it into actual use. For one thing, many telephone engineers felt that the manual system was superior. It did not require the subscriber to do anything more than lift his receiver off the hook and ask for the number he wanted. Another advantage was that the circuits were continually subject to monitoring by the operators, who could quickly tell if something was wrong. In the dial system, the subscriber hears an impersonal dial tone, and that is the only indication that the line is working. The manual switchboards in use had been steadily improved over the years and were very efficient in operation. Also, the manual boards represented a large investment which had to be written off almost completely when an automatic system was installed.

The Bell System's cautious approach to automatic switching was interpreted by some to mean that they were opposed to any form of automation. This was probably not the case, and most Bell engineers were honestly concerned with maintaining the standards of service to which they were committed. It was also thought by the Bell people that the savings in labor from eliminating the operators would be offset by the increased number of

Opposite: **Bell attempting to locate the bullet in the body of President Garfield. (Photo courtesy of the Library of Congress.)**

maintenance people needed to keep an automatic system working. The first Bell approach to automation came in the 1913–1917 period, when a "semi-automatic" system was the subject of intensive research. In this system, a subscriber first reached an "A" operator and gave her the number he wanted. The "A" operator then dialed the number requested. Probably the first push button dialers were those used by the "A" operators. The first trials, involving about 10,000 lines, were conducted in two offices in Newark, New Jersey, in 1913. Other large-scale tests of the semi-mechanical system were conducted in Newark, New Jersey, and Wilmington, Delaware, in 1917.

World War I prevented any further work on automatic switching. By 1919, the Bell System had decided to go ahead with automatic switching and made the following statement in the Annual Report:

> During the past year the Engineering Department has been engaged in planning and directing the introduction of machine switching or automatic switchboards into the Bell System. . . . Such studies show that in the large cities machine switching equipment should be employed for extensions necessary to provide for growth, and for reconstruction to replace worn out equipment. Our experience has shown that by this procedure we are enabled constantly to change to new types of apparatus as they are developed, with the least amount of disturbance to the service, in the minimum time and without disturbing effects upon the employees or on the financial situation.

The fact that operator wages started to rise sharply around the time of World War I was probably a significant factor in the decision to go fully automatic. The cutover to automatic exchanges did not occur immediately. The first one was in Omaha, Nebraska, in 1921, and the first metropolitan use was the cutover of the Pennsylvania exchange in New York City in 1922.

While the Bell System was going through its period of indecision regarding automatic switching, the Strowger system, as manufactured by Automatic Electric, was enjoying rapid growth. Due to the Strowger patents, Bell was sharply limited as to what they could do in automatic switching until 1905. In fact, Bell's main supplier, Western Electric, did not begin manufacturing automatic switching equipment until around 1926. Even then, Automatic Electric continued to furnish equipment to the Bell System until 1936. Although the equipment was manufactured by Automatic Electric to Bell specifications, it was usually installed by Bell technicians.

By 1914 the Strowger system had been greatly improved from its original form and was finding widespread acceptance by the independent telephone companies. Furthermore, the dial system was more or less readily accepted by the subscribers. It had been thought that subscribers would

Automatic Electric dial phone, 1906. (Photo courtesy Museum of Independent Telephony.)

object to the dialing process. Formerly, they had only to lift the receiver and give a number to the operator. Now, they were involved in a mechanical operation and were responsible for their own errors. The subscriber, being occupied with the dialing process, tended to ignore the time required to complete a connection. Most liked the dial because they thought it was faster and that it afforded complete privacy. Also, subscribers felt that they were using the most "modern" equipment. This latter factor, that of modernity, was now a cause of concern to telephone officials. They feared that subscribers who might have to use the older manual system for some time to come would become antagonistic towards the "obsolete" type of equipment they were forced to use. Dialing of long-distance calls had to wait until the development of high capacity cable and radio systems gave the large number of circuits required. Limited dialing of toll calls over certain high traffic routes occurred earlier. Nationwide direct dialing of toll calls was commenced in 1951.

Starting in mid–1955, negotiations were in progress that might have changed the future of General Telephone, the largest independent of them all. Donald Power, president of General, was approached by Sothenes Behn, chairman of International Telephone and Telegraph Company, with the idea of a merger between ITT and General. The ITT Company was the corporation built by Behn and his brother Hernand, starting with a small Puerto Rican telephone company. The corporation had manufacturing facilities in the United States and Europe, and it was extensively involved in worldwide communications systems. The proposed merger was seen as offering numerous advantages to both companies. The merger never took place, largely because of power struggles within ITT. Colonel Behn was gradually losing his control of ITT, which he had ruled as his own personal fiefdom since the death of his brother in 1933. A new man, W. H. Harrison, was gradually assuming power, and the old days when Behn gave sumptuous luncheons in his swank penthouse atop the building at 67 Broad Street had come to an end.

The main problem confronting the proposed merger was who was going to head the combined companies. Donald Power of GTE was a very capable man and the logical choice for the job. Behn envisioned that he and Power might run the new company. This was not agreeable to Harrison, who was not about to play second fiddle to anyone. He had enough influence with the ITT board to terminate the negotiations, which were broken off in 1956.

That same year, W. H. Harrison died of a sudden heart attack. A month later, Sothenes Behn officially resigned as chairman of ITT. His health deteriorated rapidly, and he died in June 1957 and was buried in Arlington National Cemetery with full military honors. During World War I, Behn had served as a lieutenant colonel with the Signal Corps and was awarded the Distinguished Service Medal.

In the early years, the independent telephone companies were severely handicapped in their efforts to secure a share of the telephone market. The Bell System held the all-important patents on loading of open wire lines and cables. This meant, for example, that the independent companies had to use heavier gauge copper wire on their long-distance circuits to make up for the lack of loading. Also, they could not make use of underground cables much over ten miles in length, again because of the lack of loading equipment to reduce the transmission losses. In the case of the open wire lines, it was estimated that the Bell System was saving around 40 percent on copper costs alone which gave it quite a competitive advantage. Around 1915 there was much animosity between the Bell System and the independent companies. One outburst in the trade press summed it up:

> The Bell, despite the many severe lessons taught it by the Independents, is the same greedy, domineering, arrogant corporation it was in the palmy days of its monopoly wherever it had undisputed control . . . the people are determined to have justice in telephone service and rates and realize that they must depend on Independent companies to secure it.

Chapter 7

Long Distance

STARTING IN 1876, THE ENGLISH physicist Oliver Heaviside (1850–1925) had put his mastery of Maxwell's electromagnetic theory to use in analyzing the problems of telephone transmission over wire lines. Heaviside's approach to the problem involved adding lumped values of inductance to transmission lines. He was able to prove mathematically that adding inductance to the line, since inductance had the opposite electrical sign of the capacitance which was one of the main sources of loss, would have the practical effect of reducing attenuation. Resistance, which was the other source of loss, could be managed to some extent by increasing the size of the line conductors.

Most electricians of the time could not follow Heaviside's line of reasoning, which involved higher mathematics. One of them argued that it would be like "putting bumps in the road to make the carriages run faster." It should be explained that the term "electrician" as used in those days would apply to a person we would call an engineer today. At that time most telephone transmission problems were solved by application of the "KR law."

The KR law was an empirical formula based on the capacitance of the line and the resistance in ohms. Heaviside's views soon put him in head to head confrontation with William Henry Preece. Preece was the acknowledged expert on these matters and headed the British Post Office communications system from 1877 to 1899. It was Preece, later to be knighted, who had given the first encouragement to Marconi in the development of wireless. Progressive enough to see the possibilities of Marconi's work, he nevertheless was hopelessly wedded to the KR law when it came to telephone transmission. Due to the eminence of Preece's position, the KR law remained the standard design method in England and to some extent in America. Changes were on the horizon, though, as Heaviside's theory became better understood and his work was taken up by George Campbell and Michael Pupin in America.

Heaviside was not given to being diplomatic in expressing differences of opinion. Some of his papers directed to Preece were refused publication in English journals. The following quotation is typical:

> In the meantime I may remark that if the reader wished to master these things, he must give up any ancient prejudices he may be enamored of about a "KR" law and the consequent impossibility of telephoning when "KR" is over 10,000. When pointing out, in 1877, the true nature of the telephonic problem and the absurdity of the "KR" law applied thereto generally, I predicted the possibility of telephoning with "KR" several times as great. It has since been done, in America, of course. A short time since, in noticing the KR = 32,000 reached by the New York–Chicago circuit, I further predicted that it would go up a lot more. It did very shortly after. The record is now about 50,000 (Boston–Chicago) for practical work, I believe. But there is no need to stop at 50,000. That can be largely exceeded in an enterprising country.

In another instance Heaviside wrote this highly satirical comment concerning a formal paper that had been published by Preece:

> A very remarkable paper on the "Coefficient of Self-Induction of Iron and Copper Telegraph Wires" was read at the recent meeting of the B.A. by William Henry Preece, F.R.S., the eminent electrician. The fact that it emanates from one who is—as the *Daily News* happily expressed it in its preliminary announcement of Mr. Preece's papers—one of the acknowledged masters of his subject, would alone be sufficient to recommend this paper to the attention of all electricians. But there is an additional reason of even greater weight. The results and reasoning are of so surprising character that one of two things must follow. Either, firstly, the accepted theory of electromagnetism must be most profoundly modified; or, secondly, the views expressed by Mr. Preece in his paper are profoundly erroneous. Which of these alternatives to adopt has been to me a matter of the most serious and even anxious consideration. I have been forced finally, to the conclusion that electromagnetic theory is right, and consequently, that Mr. Preece is wrong, not merely in some points of detail, but radically wrong, generally speaking, in methods, reasoning, results and conclusions.

One almost feels a certain sympathy for William Preece in the face of these caustic attacks. Heaviside was undoubtedly correct as far as theory goes, but he could have been a little more tactful in putting his point across. Preece, after all, was a man who had assumed the tremendous responsibility of the British communications system. He had made it work, and he stayed with the methods that had worked for him before. Heaviside saw no need for tactfulness. To him, truth as proved by mathematics was the only thing that mattered. Heaviside continued to lament on the inability of others to understand his theories. In his book *Electromagnetic Theory* he said: "But to convince other people is quite another matter. They may not be competent to understand the evidence. Or they may be fully competent, but not have sufficient acquaintance with the subject; or not to have the time to examine it; or not have the energy; or have no interest in it. Then, as Elijah said to the priests of Baal, you must 'Cry Aloud'."

Heaviside continued to "cry aloud," and he was finally successful in having his theories accepted. He was, however, practically an outcast in the British scientific community. Only through the efforts of William Thompson and Oliver Lodge was he finally admitted to membership in the Royal Society. Coming from a family of artists and wood engravers, Heaviside had not followed the family tradition. Apparently self-educated to a large extent, he received his early education from his mother.

Instead of pursuing a formal education, he became absorbed by mathematics at an early age. It was his habit to lock himself in the airless confines of his attic bedroom and work late at night on mathematical problems. He did not even use a slide rule, working out complex equations by longhand arithmetic. His mother left his meals outside the locked door and hoped that he would eventually eat. He never married. Heaviside had an offer in 1881, which he did not accept, to go to America and work for Western Union in installing the new Wheatstone telegraph equipment that had been imported from England. He did some consulting work for the British communications industry, but this young man could not work long in a routine job. His mind was completely occupied with proving complex theories by means of mathematics. He never had a large income, and most of it came from the sale of his books and papers.

Heaviside in his final years complained that his contributions to the telegraph and telephone industry had never been adequately recognized. This was largely his own fault, as his abrasive manner with others tended to repel those who would have otherwise sung his praises. The last years of his life were spent in poverty and isolation in the house known as "Homefield" in Torquay (it is now known as "Highwold"). By 1921, he had become increasingly reclusive, depending on a friendly local constable to bring him his food and other necessities. Heaviside's papers had been refused by several scientific English journals because the editors considered them too difficult for their readers. One editor wrote:

> Both our referees, while reporting favorably upon what they could understand, complain of the exceeding stiffness of your paper. One says it is the most difficult he ever tried to read. Do you think you could do anything, viz., illustrations or further explanations to meet this? As it is, I should fear that no one would take advantage of your work.

When another scientist complained that his papers were difficult to read, Heaviside replied: "That may well be, but they were much more difficult to write."

Heaviside had discovered the idea of inductive loading, but he had not made any great attempt to reduce it to practical terms. Still, he was the first to suggest it and to prove that if it were properly applied it could increase the range of long-distance telephony. For this reason, he must be remembered as one of the great contributors to the science of the telephone.

The idea of placing inductance in a telephone line to balance out the capacitance seemed simple enough. To reduce it to practical terms was an incredibly complex task. The problem was to construct inductance coils that had very low ohmic resistance as compared to their value of inductance. Since the coils were inserted in series with the line, the resistance component acted to attenuate the voice currents. If the resistance was too high it would offset the gain that was to be achieved by inductive loading. Another fixed property of loading, no matter how efficiently it was accomplished, was that it contributed no amplification of the signal as was later done by repeaters. All loading could do was reduce the attenuation of the signal. The men in America who reduced Heaviside's theory to practical terms were George Campbell of AT&T and Michael Pupin.

Pupin, a Serbian immigrant, had arrived in the United States in 1874. It is said that he had neither a penny to his name nor a word of English on his tongue. In the space of 25 years Pupin had acquired a Ph.D. and was a professor of mathematics at Columbia University. He was the kind of man who could understand Heaviside's reasoning and reduce the ideas to practical form. He applied for a patent on the loading coil in December 1899 and received his patent in June 1900. Pupin's patent was promptly purchased by the Bell Telephone Company, who were acutely aware of the need for loading to increase the range of their long-distance lines.

Campbell of AT&T had been working on the problem of loading concurrently with Pupin. Along with Pupin, he was one of the few engineers who could appreciate Heaviside's work and reduce it to practical terms. Loading was at first applied to the open wire lines which formed the long-distance network of the day. The practical limits were reached in 1911 with the Chicago to Denver line. Here very heavy line conductors were used to minimize losses due to the resistive component, and loading coils were spaced every eight miles. As early as 1905, loading had been applied to the cable running between New York and Philadelphia. Even the relatively short field wire circuits of the U.S. army have benefited from the principle of loading. The Signal Corps has portable loading coils, consisting of a small carrying case with four binding posts to connect the incoming and outgoing field wire.

With the practical limits of loading reached, the only other way to increase distance of transmission was to use some form of repeater. The first was a mechanical device, invented by a Bell engineer named Shreeve. It consisted of a receiver element with the diaphragm mechanically coupled to a carbon transmitter button. The voice signals coming on the input side activated the carbon button, and the signal was retransmitted with new power to the destination. The Shreeve repeater was used to some extent, but it was not a perfect repeater in any sense. True repeaters had to await the invention of the audion tube by Dr. Lee De Forest in 1906. Until then, long-distance service, especially at the maximum ranges, was a source of constant complaint by the public. The circuits were often noisy, the voices weak and indistinct and most folks resorted to the old reliable Morse telegraph when communication was required to a distant point.

The title, "The Father of Radio," that Lee De Forest (1873–1961) bestowed on himself in his 1950 autobiography could certainly be justified by his many contributions to the art. By the same token, he would have been justified in calling himself "The Father of Long-Distance Telephony." This remarkably gifted inventor, who amassed a total of well over 300 patents in his lifetime, was born in Council Bluffs, Iowa, in 1873. His father was pastor of the First Congregational Church there. The family moved to Waterloo, Iowa, where De Forest's earliest childhood memories were established at age five. The next move was to Muscatine, Iowa, on the banks of the Mississippi. De Forest started school there, but the family was soon on the move again. His father had accepted the presidency of Talladega College in 1879.

The move to Alabama was not easy for the De Forest family, confronting as they did an abrupt change from the Midwestern life-style to which they were accustomed, to the entirely different environment of the Deep South during those days of Reconstruction. De Forest's father wanted his son to enter the ministry, but the boy had different ideas. He was early drawn to science and mechanics and this was to be his main preoccupation throughout life. One of his early inventions, at age 11, was a "perpetual motion machine." Unlike many of the early inventors, De Forest obtained a good classical education before embarking on his life's work. He graduated from the prestigious Sheffield Scientific School at Yale, and ended up with a Ph.D. His doctoral thesis was "Reflection of Hertzian Waves from the Ends of Parallel Wires."

Shortly after graduating from Yale, De Forest applied to Marconi for a job with his company. Marconi had just arrived in New York to superintend the reporting of the America's Cup Race by wireless, a novel feat for the time. Unfortunately, the great inventor of wireless was preoccupied with many other matters and took no action on De Forest's application. He had no way of knowing what a talented young man he was losing, one who could have been a great asset to the budding Marconi organization. The Spanish-American war broke out during De Forest's graduate years at Yale, and in a rash spirit of patriotism the Yale men tried to enlist as an elite unit, the "Yale Light Artillery Battery." They ended up as a mere platoon in the Connecticut Volunteer Militia Battery. They got as far as a training camp at Niantic, Connecticut. Then the war was over before they had a chance to participate.

Dating from his work in graduate school, De Forest had been in search of a better detector of Hertzian waves. This is what led him to experiments with the Fleming valve that had been invented in England in 1904. The Fleming valve (in the United States called a tube) consisted of an evacuated glass bulb in which was embedded a filament and a plate electrode. The device functioned as a one-way conductor of electrical current — a rectifier. As such, it was finding some use as a wireless signal detector. It was stable and predictable in operation, but contributed no gain to the circuit and was not much better than the mineral detectors commonly used. In 1883, Thomas Edison was experimenting with one of his incandescent lamps. He discovered that by inserting a metal plate in the tube he caused a one-way flow of current from filament to plate. He also discovered that a reversal of filament heating voltage produced a change in the flow of current through the lamp.

The so-called "Edison effect" was an important portent of things to come, but it was disregarded generally by Edison and others. De Forest got to thinking about it and decided the Edison effect was trying to tell him something. On an impulse he placed a third element within the envelope of a Fleming tube. Immediately it was discovered that a small change in voltage on the third element, or grid, as it came to be known, would produce a proportionately large change in the plate current. This was the principle of electronic amplification that was to make possible better telephony, radio, and a host of other useful devices.

The next discovery was the principle of oscillation, or regeneration. This characteristic was obtained by coupling a small amount of the plate current energy back into the grid circuit. This discovery increased the sensitivity of radio receivers enormously and made possible the first practical transmitters for radio telephony.

De Forest called the new tube the "audion." The name had been coined by his lab assistant Clifford D. Babcock. Some historians claim that he did not realize the potential of his invention. This hardly seems likely — he knew exactly what he had and what it was capable of doing. His first customer, of course, was good old AT&T, desperate for a means of extending its telephone circuit from coast to coast. De Forest always claimed he was defrauded in the sale of the telephone rights to the audion. He was asking $450,000 for the audion rights. The telephone company, taking advantage of the inventor's financial straits at the time, managed to get the price down to a mere $50,000. This apparently was done by employing a go-between, a lawyer by the name of Sidney Meyers. Meyers concealed the fact that he was a representative of AT&T. The telephone company was actually prepared to pay as much as $500,000 for the rights. The services of

Meyers saved AT&T $450,000 and defrauded De Forest and his stock-holders of a like amount.

Even at that time, the rights were estimated to represent a value of six million dollars to the telephone company. De Forest had done the basic research on the audion tube while working for the Federal Telegraph Company in Palo Alto, California. Even though he had sold the telephone rights to AT&T, De Forest and Federal retained what were called the "shop rights" to the audion invention. This enabled Federal eventually to go into the radio communication business in competition with RCA. During World War I, all electronic patents were taken over by the government. When the war ended, AT&T's patents were returned to the telephone company, but AT&T had made a deal with RCA, and all the patents ended up in what was called the "RCA Patent Pool."

This suited the goals of David Sarnoff, president of RCA, who sought to control all radio enterprises by simply owning all the vital patents needed to construct any kind of radio apparatus. He would have reached his goal, except for one thing: those "shop rights" still owned by Federal. The California company was able to launch a worldwide radio communication service in open competition with RCA. The operating company using Federal equipment was the Mackay Radio and Telegraph Company.

In 1928, Federal and Mackay became part of the International Telephone and Telegraph Company. Patents were still held by RCA which Federal could not circumvent. Federal's designers had to use a lot of ingenuity to meet the current needs. For example, when Federal started to manufacture their own high-power transmitting tubes, they discovered that all the basic patents covering the vital grid structure of a tube were held by the RCA patent pool. Looking around, Federal found an obscure patent for building reinforcing rod structures in concrete building columns.

It was exactly what was needed for the grid structure, and the somewhat surprised inventor was glad to find a buyer for his patent. Thus, in one way or another, Federal managed to field a line of radio equipment that was used worldwide, not only at fixed radio stations, but in the thousands of seagoing ships that were required to carry radio equipment. There were certain items that just couldn't be improvised. Then the ideas were just stolen and used on the quiet. For this reason, casual visitors to Mackay Radio stations were prohibited.

One of the real struggles of De Forest's career came when his claim to be the inventor of the principle of regeneration brought him into conflict with E. H. Armstrong. The court battles lasted for several years. Armstrong had been active in developing the use of regeneration in improving the performance of radio receivers. Many people considered him to be the true inventor of this valuable feature. De Forest, however, countered with his laboratory notes from his days with Federal Telegraph. He claimed that he had discovered the effect of feedback while experimenting with audio frequency amplifiers. The long court battles had traumatic effects on both men. The final legal decision went to De Forest. This was a crushing defeat for Armstrong and his supporters. It was probably a case of simultaneous invention. Such cases are often decided on legal grounds that have no relation to the actual merits of the inventions involved.

In his lifetime, De Forest had acquired over 300 patents covering almost every phase of electrical communication. One of his unusual inventions was the "Theremin." Actually, the Theremin is usually credited to Leon Theremin, a Russian inventor. Theremin was born in 1896 in St. Petersburg, Russia. He had started work on his musical instruments as early as 1920 and eventually came to New York, where he had a laboratory in the 1930s. During World War II, Theremin returned to Russia where he worked in the intelligence field. After the war he worked as a scientist for the KGB. He had licensed his musical instrument patents to RCA, and these were the patents that were later successfully challenged by De Forest. Theremin died in Moscow in November 1993 at age 97. In his autobiography De Forest does not acknowledge this; he gives the impression that he had the idea long before anyone else. At any rate, De Forest claimed the device as his own and patented it in 1925. The Theremin was a musical instrument that produced violin-like sounds by the interaction of two radio frequency oscillators. The device was housed in a freestanding wooden cabinet. Two metal rods protruded from the sides of the cabinet. It was played purely by hand motions in relation to the two metal rods — one hand raised or lowered the tone while the other governed the volume. In the hands of a skilled player, the Theremin could deliver pleasing music, but it never achieved any real popularity. Theremins were used to produce some of the eerie sound effects of early horror and science fiction movies. The 1925 patent for the Theremin was licensed to the Wurlitzer company. The resulting instrument was known as the Hammond "Novachord." The De Forest company sued RCA in 1931, charging infringement of 13 patents covering the use of electronics in musical instruments and won the case.

De Forest's invention of the audion tube is considered by many to be his greatest accomplishment. It opened the door to the modern age of electronics and should rank De Forest with Morse, Bell and Marconi. The telephone, in particular, owes a special debt to De Forest. His invention of the audion was timely, enabling the telephone company to offer transcontinental service in 1915. Western Union had done it with the Morse telegraph 54 years earlier.

On January 25, 1915, AT&T held the formal ceremony opening the transcontinental line for commercial service. It is sad to report that Lee De Forest, the man who had done as much as anyone to make it possible, was not invited to attend. It so happened that De Forest's own company had an exhibit at the Panama-Pacific International Exposition in San Francisco in 1915. The American Telephone & Telegraph Company also had an exhibit to call attention to their new transcontinental line. A booklet entitled "The Story of a Great Achievement" was handed out to visitors. De Forest was quick to note that the booklet did not even mention his contribution. Reacting quickly, the feisty inventor rushed a printing job overnight, and by the next day his people at the De Forest booth were handing out booklets that looked exactly like the telephone company version. Of course, the De Forest booklets gave the full story of his contribution to the great achievement of transcontinental telephony in the following words:

> That amplifier was at last discovered—not by telephone engineers, whose minds had for years spun in the old rut of receiver-microphone "Siamesed" together. [De Forest refers to the Shreeve repeater, which consisted of a magnetic receiver mechanically coupled to a carbon transmitter button.] In 1912 Lee De Forest found that when a strange device called the Audion was properly connected in the line between a transmitter and receiver, it actually amplified the voice currents, giving a reproduction of perfect fidelity without a trace of lag or distortion, yet with a great increase in volume, or intensity. It is this device—patented by De Forest in 1906 and licensed by him to the telephone company in 1913—which at last and alone enables you today to talk from the Panama-Pacific Exposition to New York or Maine.

The transcontinental telephone line, which De Forest's audion had made possible, was completed in 1914-1915 and opened for commercial service in 1915. It was built using four No. 8 copper wires with Pupin loading coils every eight miles. Electronic repeaters were located at Pittsburgh, Chicago, Omaha, Denver, Salt Lake City, and Winnemucca, Nevada. The four-wire group could handle three telephone conversations and four Morse telegraph circuits. The total length of the circuit was about 3,400 miles. The 398-mile stretch of line from Wendover, near the Utah line, to Wadsworth, near Reno, Nevada, traversed some of the most rugged desert country in North America. It passed near Indian villages and through country that had changed little since covered wagon days. The line poles were spaced about 35 to the mile, making a total of around 13,900 poles for the stretch across Nevada. The poles came from northern California and were transported by sea, rail, horse and mule drawn wagons, motor trucks and tractors. Digging of the thousands of holes for the line poles was done by a Beltz power posthole digger which had been adapted to digging the holes for the line poles. This was probably the first use of a power digging machine to replace the back-breaking labor of digging the holes by hand.

Chapter 8

A Man from Oberlin

OBERLIN IS A CHARMING little Ohio town 35 miles southwest of Cleveland. It is, of course, the location of Oberlin College. The college was founded in Oberlin in 1833 and the town has just grown around it. The campus is a pleasant mix of old and modern architecture. The wide areas of grass and trees make it a relaxing environment for students. A prominent feature of the campus is the memorial for the 18 Oberlin missionaries who were murdered at the Shansi mission in China during the Boxer Rebellion of 1900. (A new book by author Nat Brandt, *Massacre in Shansi*, Syracuse University Press, Syracuse, New York, 1994, tells this tragic story in detail. Another Brandt book, titled *The Town That Started the Civil War*, tells of the abolitionist activity in Oberlin.)

Oberlin is noteworthy for some firsts in education. It was the first college to champion women's rights and become coeducational. Also, in 1835, it was one of the first to admit black students. The town of Oberlin was a center of abolitionist sentiment in pre–Civil War days. It was an important junction point on the Underground Railroad that spirited fugitive slaves on their way to Canada. When the fugitives reached the shores of Lake Erie they could board a boat for Canada and were then safely beyond reach of their pursuers. One of Oberlin's famous graduates was Charles Martin Hall, the discoverer of a practical process for producing aluminum. Hall's invention made him independently wealthy and he shared generously of his wealth in endowments to his alma mater.

To this pleasant campus in 1857 came a young man named Elisha Gray. Born in Barnesville, Ohio, in 1835, Gray was a farm lad who was trying to earn his living by manual trades such as blacksmithing and carpentry. He was not physically able to continue in these trades and was persuaded by friends to get some education. Gray only studied in Oberlin for two years at preparatory school. Accounts of Gray's stay at Oberlin vary. Some say he spent two years at preparatory school and two years at the college. At any rate he did not graduate from Oberlin. His contacts with Oberlin professor Charles Churchill were apparently the beginning of his lifelong interest in electricity and telegraphy. This was a time when great discoveries were being made by individuals working alone. In the new field of electricity and communication there was an almost unlimited opportunity for inventors to patent new ideas that would contribute to the rapidly growing technology of communications.

Displaying an exceptional talent for electrical science, Gray moved to Cleveland and was soon inventing a variety of devices used in telegraphy and other electrical fields. General Anson Stager, who headed the Military Telegraph Corps during the Civil War, took an interest in Gray and introduced him to a man named E. M. Barton. This led to the organizing of the firm of Gray & Barton. Barton was a former Western Union employee whose duties had included examining and testing new products to see what value they might have to Western Union. Gray's purchase of an interest in the Barton shop had been financed by Stager. It was at his suggestion the new company moved to Chicago in December 1869. The company finally became the Western Electric Company, first a supplier of equipment to the Western Union Telegraph Company. The present Graybar Electric Company takes its name from the original partnership of Gray & Barton. E. M. Barton once quipped, "Of all the men who *didn't* invent the telephone, Gray was the nearest." Around 1874, Gray left the Western Electric Company to begin independent research. Ironically, the Western Electric Company was to become the main supplier of equipment for the Bell Telephone Company.

Gray's main interest in research lay in the field of telegraphy. His harmonic system used tones of a different frequency to transmit multiple messages over a single telegraph wire. The basic idea of tone telegraphy apparently originated with the famous "bathtub experiment" of 1874. Gray discovered his nephew playing with some electrical apparatus in the bathroom. The boy had hooked up an ordinary induction coil, connecting one lead to the zinc lining of the bathtub. Holding the other wire in his hand, he could hear the tone from the induction coil when he touched the zinc surface of the tub. The induction coil would have been similar to the "medical batteries" of the period. In Gray's time, these coils were called "rheotomes," a term no longer used. These medical batteries operated by subjecting the body to a mild electrical shock. Since the machines came with electrodes to fit all the orifices of the human body, the treatments were mildly stimulating, to say the least. Gray, taking over the experiment from the boy, discovered that by changing the frequency or tone of the vibrator he got a corresponding tone when he touched the bathtub lining. This is said to be the beginning of his experiments with tone telegraphy. Tone telegraphy never became practical during Gray's lifetime, but eventually became a very important principle in multichannel telegraphy.

This was an idea that was exceedingly attractive to the telegraph company at that time. The Morse telegraph was commencing to develop an enormous volume of traffic between major cities, and any means of providing more message handling capacity was welcomed with open arms. Alexander Graham Bell was in pursuit of the same goal. His patent application was for a method of multiple tone telegraphy, and the word "telephone" was not even mentioned. Gray was actually ahead of Bell with the multiple tone telegraph and in 1881 succeeded in selling the idea to the newly formed Postal Telegraph Company for $300,000. Gray had worked with water rheostats during his Gray & Barton days, and it is thought that this gave him the idea for the liquid contact telephone transmitter. The water rheostat was a device for varying electrical current. A barrel of water was used with two round plates immersed. One of the plates could be adjusted to vary the spacing to the other plate and thus the conductivity.

The liquid contact telephone transmitter worked on the same principle. Instead of large plates in a barrel of water, the telephone transmitter employed a needle dipping into a small cup of water. The water was slightly acidulated to make it conductive to electricity. The needle was attached to a diaphragm that vibrated with the speech sounds. Bell used this device for his first successful transmission of speech. Gray used it for the same purpose, but both inventors realized that the liquid contact transmitter was not practical for commercial use.

Even though Gray was not a graduate of Oberlin, his life was linked closely to the college. In Oberlin Gray met his wife, the former Delia M. Shepard. They were married in 1862. Oberlin College awarded Gray an honorary degree in 1878, and he served as a visiting professor teaching courses in electricity and science. Gray once explained the flow of electric current by the following analogy:

> When you were a boy did you never set up a row of bricks on their ends, just far enough apart so that if you pushed one over they all fell, one after another? Now, imagine rows of molecules or atoms, and in your imagination they may be arranged like the bricks, so that they are affected one by the other successively with a rapidity that is akin to that of light waves, and you can conceive how a motion may be communicated from end to end of a wire hundreds of miles in length in a small fraction of a second, and no material substance has been carried through the wire — only energy. We do not mean to say that the row of bricks illustrates the exact mode of molecular or atomic motion that takes place in a conductor. What we mean is, that in some way motion is passed along from atom to atom.

Losing the telephone patent was a great disappointment for Gray. He once wrote to his attorney: "I have read Bell's claims, and it seems to me he could not have described my invention better if he had copied it. How in the name of patent law could Wilber issue that patent without declaring an interference?" Gray's feelings, which varied from being philosophical over loss of the telephone patent to bitter resentment over unfair treatment at the patent office, were stirred again by a remarkable series of affidavits issued in 1885-1886 by Zenas Wilber, the patent office examiner who issued the Bell patent (see Appendix 7).

Wilber was known in Washington as an alcoholic. A Washington police lieutenant said that complaints had reached the police of Wilber's being drunk and disorderly at least 20 times in a one-year period. Also, Wilber was known to be in the habit of borrowing money from anyone he could. His first affidavit, issued October 21, 1885, categorically denied that there was the slightest irregularity in the issuance of the Bell patent. Everything was strictly according to patent office procedure, he said under oath. Then Wilber did a complete flip-flop. In his last affidavit, issued April 8, 1886, he made a complete "confession," admitting that he had taken a $100 bill from Bell, and also that he had borrowed money from Bell's attorney. He also admitted that he had given Bell the complete details of Gray's caveat. The final affidavit in this remarkable exposure of dirty linen came in an affidavit by Bell himself (see Appendix 8). He, of course, denied all of Wilber's allegations. Despite these serious charges and denials, which certainly could have supported a libel suit, the whole matter was quietly dropped—nobody sued anybody. Yet, the damage was done, the seed of suspicion against Bell was planted and lingers to this day.

Persons who knew Gray thought it was partly his lackadaisical attitude in legal matters that caused him to abandon his caveat. If he had followed the caveat with a patent application, Bell's patent would have been held up indefinitely until the conflicting claims were resolved. Nevertheless, Gray's attorneys advised him to follow the course he did, and it has been characterized as the greatest mistake of his career. Gray had received the necessary financial backing to pursue his research in multiple tone telegraphy from Samuel S. White, a wealthy manufacturer of dental equipment in Philadelphia. When Gray filed his caveat at the patent office, his attorney promptly wrote to White advising him of the interference between Gray's caveat and Bell's patent application. The letter to White stated, "the Commissioner holds that he (Gray) is not entitled to an interference and Bell's application has been ordered to issue. . . . We could still have an interference by Gray's coming tomorrow and promptly filing an application for a patent. If you want this done, telegraph me in the morning, on receipt of this, and I will have the papers ready in time to stop the issue of Bell's patent." This letter reached White at a time when Elisha Gray was visiting him in Philadelphia. White was obsessed with the money-making possibilities of the multiplex telegraph and advised Gray to concentrate on that field.

Gray himself, and most other experts in the telegraph field, felt that the telephone was not worth pursuing. Bell, with his professional background in speech, saw the possibilities of the telephone more clearly than anyone else. In his patent application he was just plain lucky, as any serious opposition by Gray would have challenged the Bell patent. Even with his limited knowledge of electricity, Bell had managed to elucidate the basic principles of telephony very clearly, yet determined action by Gray, who was far more knowledgeable in the field of electricity, would have affected the history of telephony in a very profound way. In May 1874, Gray had given demonstrations of his equipment before telegraph experts in Washington, New York and Boston. One Western Union official was quoted in *The New York Times* as saying that Gray had taken "the first step toward doing away with manipulating instruments [that is, telegraph keys] altogether. In time," the official continued, "the operators will transmit the sound of their own voices over the wire, and talk with one another instead of telegraphing."

However easygoing he might have been in legal matters, Gray was certainly an industrious inventor. The disappointment over the telephone patent did not deter him from pursuing a busy career in inventing other devices. After the death of Joseph Henry in 1878, Gray was considered by many to be the most knowledgeable man in the United States on electrical matters. After the Dowd case settlement in 1879, Gray received a letter from William F. Channing, an electrical inventor. The letter, as quoted in *The New York Times* of April 30, 1888, said in part "you can not avoid this issue of originality, even by the most perfect business settlement. The question is one of scientific history which you and Professor Bell must meet. There is no covering it up. Unless you and Professor Bell can agree upon a statement as to joint invention or otherwise, the verdict will probably be that one or the other of you was dishonest, with some stains or suspicions on the name of both . . . ."

One of the most important of Gray's inventions was the telautograph, invented in 1887. Inventions of the past often seemed to emerge at precisely the point in history when they were timely and sensational. Others, appearing almost after the fact, have received relatively little notice from the public. Such was the case with the telautograph, "the machine for writing by electricity" that was invented well after the Morse telegraph and the telephone were in widespread use. All of the early telegraph inventors, including Morse, thought in terms of a visual reading device. Morse's first receiver traced the dots and dashes on a moving paper tape, which then had to be decoded by the operators. After the tape system had been in use for about six years, operators began to discover that the clicking of the recorder mechanism created a sound pattern that could be read by ear. The discovery of sound reading, purely accidental, made the Morse system so simple and practical that it remained the principal means of telegraphic communication for over 90 years.

It was not until 1886 that inventors became interested in the idea of transmitting handwriting by wire. That it should be handwriting was normal, as the typewriter had not yet come into widespread use and most written communications were handwritten. The first machine, called the "writing telegraph," actually saw some limited commercial use. The writing was received on a moving paper tape and since there was no pen-lifting mechanism for the receiver, all of the characters were joined by a continuous line on the tape.

Telegraphic writing soon attracted the attention of Gray. His machine was a vast improvement over the earlier versions. It had a pen-lifting mechanism and the message was written in conventional format on a standard sheet of paper. A company called the Gray National Telautograph Company was chartered in 1888. Gray was reportedly paid six million dollars for the patent rights to the machine. Telegraphic writing was a sensation at the 1893 World's Fair in Chicago. An improved machine in 1896 staged an impressive demonstration in transmitting handwriting 431 miles from Cleveland to Chicago. Since the machines were used principally in the larger metropolitan areas they were not too well known by the general public. A typical application was in the old Dearborn Street railway station in Chicago. Here, a telautograph in the main concourse gave baggage and mail handlers information on trains arriving and departing the station.

Perhaps the ultimate triumph of the telautograph was its selection for fire control communication at the coastal defense batteries on the Atlantic and Pacific coasts. In those days before aircraft, the only defense systems needed were strong fortified points around major seaports to repel naval attack. The coastal defense batteries were the 19th-century equivalent of Star Wars and were shrouded in extreme secrecy. In 1895, the *Scientific American* lamented that the press had not been permitted to inspect the installations for several years. The huge, slow-moving projectiles fired by the guns were extremely accurate. Their weight and slow velocity made them immune to the normal variables in the rules of ballistics, and they could be depended on to hit a specified point in the target area. Contrary to the usual rule of artillery, the muzzles of the guns were elevated to shorten the range and lowered to increase it. The guns could be depended on to hit any coordinate in the target area. Their effectiveness depended on the accuracy of the observers in calling out the target location. Speedy and accurate communication was needed between the observers and the guns. Telephone and telegraph did not prove practical due to the deafening noise in the gun pits when the battery was firing. Special models of the telautograph were designed and mounted in weatherproof cases with glass front panels. The telautograph instruments were redesigned in the period between 1940 and 1960 to incorporate the latest developments in electronics. The present versions will operate over any standard telecommunications link and are not limited in range. Many telautographs have remained in use 100 years after their invention, but they are now largely replaced by fax machines.

Alexander Graham Bell was growing weary of the constant haggling over the telephone. After the death of Elisha Gray in 1901, Bell wrote in a letter:

> Ever since the commencement of litigation in telephone matters, I have been obliged to keep silence—my counsel always advising me that the Courts would look after my reputation and sustain my rights—which they have always done. This was pretty hard to do at first, and I can remember how I used to writhe—in silence—under the unscrupulous attacks which were made upon me. But as years went by I became callous and indifferent as to what people thought or said about me or the telephone. For some time past I have felt that the articles which have appeared in the public press demanded some reply, but I did not care to undertake it myself, and my old defenders have all passed away. I had almost reached the conclusion that the time had come for me to speak out in my own behalf, when the sudden death of Elisha Gray caused me to change my mind. I had a very high respect for Elisha Gray, and have always had the feeling that he and I would have become warm friends had it not been for the intermeddling of lawyers and the exigencies of law suits. Whatever Mr. Gray may have thought of me, I have always had the kindest feelings towards him, and it therefore seemed inopportune that I should say anything in conflict with his claims at a time when we are all mourning his loss.

Herbert N. Casson's book *The History of the Telephone*, published in 1910, was probably not written in the executive offices of the Bell Telephone Company, but it might as well have been. In this book Casson quotes a man named George C. Maynard, who was apparently a Bell licensee in the city of Washington, D.C.:

> Mr. Gray was an intimate and valued friend of mine, but it is no disrespect to his memory to say that on some points involved in the telephone matter, he was mistaken. No subject was ever so thoroughly investigated as the invention of the speaking telephone. No patent has ever been submitted to such determined assault from every direction as Bell's; and no inventor has ever been more completely vindicated. Bell was the first inventor, and Gray was not.

One of Gray's staunchest supporters came forth in 1937 in the person of Dr. Lloyd W. Taylor, head of the physics department of Oberlin College. Dr. Taylor was convinced that Gray was the real inventor of the telephone, even though Bell held the legal claim. Taylor published a paper in the *American Physics Teacher* in December 1937 setting forth a mass of evidence supporting his views (see Appendix 9). Dr. Taylor was planning to publish a full length book on the Bell-Gray controversy. Due to his unfortunate death in a mountain climbing accident on Mt. Saint Helens, Washington, in July 1948, the book was never finished. The manuscript is held in the College Archives at Oberlin College. Dr. Taylor was a meticu-

Dr. Lloyd W. Taylor, head of the physics department of Oberlin College, defended Gray's claim to the telephone invention. (Courtesy of Ruth Taylor Deery.)

lous researcher and had access to many original Gray documents. Among these was a scrap of paper he found in the attic of the old Gray residence in Highland Park, Illinois. On the paper Gray had written, "The history of the telephone will never be fully written. It is partly hidden away in 20 or 30 thousand pages of testimony and partly lying on the hearts and consciences of a few whose lips are Sealed, — Some in death and others by a golden clasp whose grip is even tighter."

Unlike many other 19th-century inventors, Gray earned large sums of money for his patents. Typical amounts were $300,000 for the harmonic telegraph and six million dollars for the telautograph. Even with these large sums Gray did not become an extremely wealthy man. Like Thomas Edison, he invested most of his earnings in further research. Gray moved to Boston in 1899 and continued an active career in invention. He and his son David were working with inventor Arthur Munday on an underwater signaling device. The device was intended to transmit signals to ships to prevent them from running aground at night or in heavy fog. The device received its initial testing on December 31, 1900. Three weeks later, on January 21, 1901, Elisha Gray collapsed of an apparent heart attack and died on the street in Newtonville, Massachusetts.

Chapter 9

Western Union

BY 1876, WHEN BELL GOT his telephone patent, the Western Union Telegraph Company was 20 years old. It had been organized by Hiram Sibley to end the hopeless confusion that existed in the early days of the telegraph industry. Sibley, an astute businessman, was the one who had successfully negotiated with Russia to build the trans–Siberian telegraph line. This project, of course, was abandoned when the Atlantic telegraph cable was completed in 1866. One result of Sibley's negotiations with Russia was his recommendation to the United States to purchase the territory of Alaska in 1867.

Small telegraph companies, competing for traffic, ran lines at random and there was little effort to coordinate their activities. Sibley realized that consolidation of the small companies was the only answer, and he quietly bought up stock until he had the basis for his "New York and Mississippi Valley Printing Telegraph Company." The company intended to exploit the newly invented House printing telegraph, but it soon changed over to the simpler and more reliable Morse equipment. Joined in the venture by Morse's former associate Ezra Cornell, the company was rapidly extending its lines to the Missouri River. At Cornell's suggestion the company was renamed "Western Union."

By 1876, the idea of instantaneous electric communication was well established and telegraph traffic reached levels that taxed the available facilities. This is why both Bell and Gray were in pursuit of methods to increase carrying capacity of telegraph wires. In the process they invented the telephone. Western Union became one of the most powerful and wealthy corporations in America. The company had built the transcontinental line in 1861, and in 1866 the Atlantic cables came into successful operation. There was no real competition, as Postal Telegraph did not enter the field until 1881. With this background of success it is not surprising that Western Union displayed little interest in a potential competitor, the telephone, even though it seemed to be the ideal company to take over the new method of electrical communication. Western Union had the wires, the franchises for rights of way, and the skilled electrical technicians who could easily adapt to telephone work.

The problem was that no one, even Bell himself, had a true appreciation of the tremendous profit potential of the telephone business. Anxious for some quick return on his invention, Bell offered all rights to the telephone for sale to Western Union for a mere $100,000. A curious minute survives of the meeting in which Western Union considered the Bell offer:

> The telephone is so named by its inventor A.G. Bell. He believes that one day they will be installed in every residence and place of business. Bell's profession is that of a voice teacher. Yet he claims to have discovered an instrument of great practical value in communication which has been overlooked by thousands of workers who have spent years in the field. Bell's proposals to place his instrument in almost every home and business place is fantastic. The central exchange alone would represent a huge outlay in real estate and buildings, to say nothing of the electrical equipment. In conclusion, the committee feels that it must advise against any investments in Bell's scheme. We do not doubt that it will find users in special circumstances, but any development of the kind and scale which Bell so fondly imagines is utterly out of the question.

This should go down in history as the world's dumbest committee report, but it was not too surprising, considering the prevailing attitude about the telephone: Many considered it a mere fad that would soon be forgotten. How wrong they were! In a year's time, Western Union would decide that the telephone was a business in which it very much wanted to be involved. Western Union jumped in with both feet and was soon giving American Bell some real competition. In fact, with their comprehensive wire network already in place, Western Union established some of the first telephone exchanges.

Western Union also had a remarkable asset, a young inventor named Thomas Edison, who was a full-time consultant for the company. It would be hard to characterize Edison as an unknown inventor, yet he is probably better remembered for his invention of the incandescent lamp and the phonograph than for his contribution to the telephone. Everyone in the business, Edison included, realized that Bell with their strong patents still did not have a satisfactory transmitter. The Bell sound-powered phones, in which the transmitter was merely a duplicate of the receiver, worked well enough over short ranges but they were hopelessly inadequate for much expansion. By acquiring the Berliner patents and through some devious shuffling of patent applications, the Bell Company managed to extend their patent protection for another 17 years. They also acquired the patent of Francis Blake, who had invented a variation of the Berliner transmitter.

Working together, Berliner and Blake perfected a transmitter that served the Bell System for several years. The Blake transmitter was a good one, but weak in output, and it was housed in a bulky wooden box. Edison decided there must be a better way, and started on one of his famous "campaigns." The term "campaign" was used around the Edison laboratories to describe the period when Edison was in hot pursuit of a new invention. He was fond of saying that "Invention is about 2 percent inspiration and 98 percent perspiration." One of Edison's first inventions was an electric vote recorder for legislative bodies. When he tried to interest the U.S. congress in the device, he was told, "if there is any invention on earth that we don't want down here, it is this."

Apparently, the legislators preferred the leisurely process of balloting in the traditional manner. It offered more time for last minute "arm twisting" to influence the vote. In spite of this put-down, Edison had the satisfaction of seeing similar devices come into widespread use during his lifetime. When Lee De Forest sought an interview with Edison there was some doubt whether the two would meet, as the "old man" was on a campaign and didn't want to be interrupted. He did relent, however, and the two inventors had a pleasant visit.

Edison knew that a successful transmitter would have to work on the variable current principle. Bell's first successful speech transmission was with a variable current transmitter, the famous needle dipping into a conductive solution. The liquid transmitter was soon recognized as not being suitable for commercial use. Edison discovered that powdered carbon was the ideal material if actuated by a diaphragm. His transmitter was the first good one to come along and was the forerunner of most of the telephone transmitters in use today. The new electronic phones do use the "electret" type of transmitter, which is a variation of the capacitor, or condenser, transmitter invented by Dolbear many years ago.

When Edison showed his new transmitter to President Orton of Western Union he was asked, "What do you want for your transmitter?" Edison, who was determined to get at least $25,000, said, "What offer will you make?" Orton exclaimed, "We will give $100,000." Edison, needless to say, accepted the offer, but stipulated that the payment was to be at the rate of $6,000 a year for 17 years. Edison explained this arrangement by saying, "I knew what I was doing. I always had an ambition about four times too large for my business capacity. If I got all that money at once, I would spend it on experiments. By this stroke I saved 17 years of financial worry."

Edison is easily America's most prolific inventor, with 1,093 patents to his credit. His work with the telephone transmitter probably enabled telephone improvements that otherwise would not have occurred until 10 or 20 years later. When Edison invented the incandescent lamp he realized that some type of mounting would be needed that would not only bring the operating voltage to the lamp but would allow ready means of replacing burned out lamps. He invented the screw base, which is so simple and practical that no one has been able to come up with a better idea in the last 100 years. Another Edison contribution to telephony that has lasted to the present was his suggestion that the word "hello" be used when answering the telephone. Bell had used "hoy" but the public liked Edison's word better and was soon using it exclusively.

With the Edison transmitter, the Western Union company was in a good position to compete with Bell. Bell had the electromagnetic receiver, which was vital. As Edison once humorously said, "We stole the receiver from them and they stole the transmitter from us." It should be explained that what in telephone parlance is called a transmitter is what is more familiarly known as a microphone today. In fact, many of the early carbon button telephone transmitters were used as microphones at pioneer radio telephone stations. The carbon button transmitter invented by Edison was eventually acquired by the Bell System when a settlement was reached with Western Union in 1879. Bell perfected a transmitter known as the White "solid back transmitter." The White transmitter, or copies of it, were standard in the telephone industry until the modern, interchangeable capsule, carbon button transmitters were perfected.

Hammond V. Hayes was an engineer with Bell in 1885, and he was in charge of their mechanical and testing department. His testimony at a court case in 1908 offers a glimpse of the transmitter problems experienced by Bell:

> In the early days, 1879 and 1880 or thereabouts, we had two forms of telephone transmitters, the Blake transmitter and the Edison transmitter. These two were both objectionable. The Blake transmitter was unsatisfactory, for the reason that if you tried to make it powerful and spoke closely to it the instrument broke, rattled, was indistinct. The Edison transmitter was objectionable, because you could get very little volume from it except when you spoke with your lips pressed directly against the mouthpiece, which was a condition very hard indeed to get subscribers in the field to do . . . the Hunnings transmitter had a difficulty inherent to it, which rendered it uncommercial.

Hayes commented further on the problems with the transmitters:

> Several men competed in an effort to produce a workable design. The other experimenters' results did not compare with those that Mr. White got. White produced this instrument, which we called a solid back instrument to distinguish it from the pivoted instrument which had a loose back, which the other men had in competition with White. White's instrument proved to be all right. We made the instrument up in the model form, and it has been in use from that day until the present time with practically no change whatever in design or proportions.

With their Edison transmitters, the Western Union Company proceeded to give Bell some real competition—they were starting to cut in on Bell's profits. The name of Peter A. Dowd would be unknown today except for one thing. He was the Western Union man selected by the Bell

Telephone Company to be the target of their suit against his company. The suit was filed September 12, 1878, in the Circuit Court of the United States for the District of Massachusetts. It charged infringement of the two Bell patents, No. 174,465 and No. 186,787. It named Dowd not only as the agent for Western Union, but for the Gold and Stock Telegraph Company, the American Speaking Telephone Company, and the Harmonic Telegraph Company. Dowd and the named companies were charged with putting out telephones in the state of Massachusetts that infringed on the Bell patents.

Western Union conducted a vigorous defense, citing the alleged priority of inventions by Elisha Gray, Thomas A. Edison, and Amos E. Dolbear. Western's attorney, George Gifford, even went back to the work of Philipp Reis and also pointed out that the instruments described by Bell in his first patent were not capable of transmitting articulate speech. One of the landmark cases of the telephone legal wars, the Dowd case dragged on for months with lengthy depositions taken from all sides. Finally, Gifford became convinced on the basis of the evidence heard that his client could not win the case. He advised Western Union to negotiate a settlement with Bell. The agreement between Bell and Western Union was signed on November 10, 1879, and was to be in effect for 17 years. The terms granted Bell a license to use any of the Western Union telephone patents for 17 years, not only for the present patents but for any Western Union might acquire during the life of the contract. The telephone company agreed to purchase the telephones and telephone exchanges of Western Union and to pay a percentage of the future telephone rentals or royalties. The final decree officially ending the case and issued by Judge Lowell was dated April 4, 1881.

Thus was ended the confrontation between Bell and Western Union. The agreement was apparently honored by both parties. There is no record of Western Union ever again attempting to sell telephone service. Bell never offered any public telegraph service, although it derived a substantial income from the use of its wires for telegraphy by private users such as the Associated Press. Western Union, of course, became a good customer of Bell Telephone. Most deliveries of telegrams in rural areas were by telephone and many telegrams were filed that way as well.

Even though Western Union and the Bell Company reached an agreement of sorts in 1879, they were to continue on a more or less adversarial basis for years to come. One can truly appreciate the magnitude of AT&T by looking at some of their statistics during the mid–1960s, long before the ugly word "divestiture" was heard. Never before had a company made so much money—profits in 1964 were a cool $1.76 billion. This was greater than the combined income of the thirty poorest American states, or the five richest. The net profits of AT&T after taxes were said to equal roughly the national income of Sweden. The company owned approximately $3.5 billion worth of securities and cash at the end of 1964. The capital expenditures were greater than those of most European governments. Even with all these big numbers, the company headquarters at 195 Broadway in New York was a relatively modest building. Yet, it was the master control center for a vast complex of associated companies. These included Western Electric, the world's largest manufacturer of telephone equipment, Bell Laboratories, and the 21 regional telephone companies throughout the 50 states. American Telephone & Telegraph was once defined as a "quasi-political state." Bell System executives were always active in local community affairs. For example it was pointed out that almost every important chamber of commerce has one or more Bell executives in its organization.

The Bell System held the telephone industry in a death grip. It owned at least 92 percent of all the telephones used in the United States. The company had continued the early practice of only renting telephones—none were ever sold. The small percentage of non–Bell telephones were mostly what the company would call "illegal." These were, for the most part, telephones that had been acquired by private individuals and hooked to the Bell lines. This was strictly against company rules and the illegal phones would often just be confiscated by Bell. The president of AT&T had coined the slogan, "One System, One Policy, Universal Service." In 1912 Clarence Mackay of Postal Telegraph, joined by a group of independent telephone companies, protested to the Department of Justice that AT&T was operating in violation of the antitrust laws. In January 1913, Attorney General George W. Wickersham advised AT&T that certain of its proposed acquisitions of independent telephone companies in the Middle West would indeed be a violation of the Sherman Antitrust Act. This was followed in 1913 by a report from President Wilson titled "Government Ownership of the Electrical Communications Industry." This was enough to send cold shivers through the offices at 195 Broadway. At this time, AT&T had two choices, one of which was just to stonewall it and depend on legal action. This would have probably meant years of litigation. Also, it would not enhance the public image of the company, which was already perceived as a bloodthirsty monopoly by many. The second choice was to make a few concessions to keep everybody happy. This was the ultimate decision, and it was hailed by President Wilson as an act of "business statesmanship."

One of the factors influencing the decision was the death of J. P. Morgan, who had always pressured Vail and AT&T to grab all they could. A letter dated December 19, 1913, was sent by Nathan C. Kingsbury to James McReynolds, the attorney general who had succeeded Wickersham. In part, Kingsbury wrote: "AT&T and its associated companies, wishing to put their affairs beyond criticism and in compliance with your suggestions formulated as a result of a number of interviews between us during the last sixty days," agreed to dispose of its Western Union stock, and to cease its practice of buying out independent companies. An important part

INDEPENDENT TELEPHONE LINE.

Connecting the Village of Olivet with the Western Union Telegraph Company, at Olivet Station, on the Chicago & Grand Trunk Railway.

Rates for all Messages of Twenty-five Words and under.

Local Message to Olivet Station and Reply, - - - - 5 cents.
Message to Olivet Station to be transferred to the care of the Western Union
    Telegraph Company, - - - - - - - - 10 "
Message taken from W. U. Telegraph Co. at Olivet Station, and delivered
    within one block of the Village Office, - - - - - 10 "
For a greater distance, and within the Village Limits, - - - - 15 "
    All Messages repeated to avoid errors.

Dated *Chicago, June 19th* 1882
Received at *Olivet, June 20th 8 30 a.m.*
To *Hamilton King*

*Hope to see your
44 Candidates for
Chicago Tuesday
afternoon,*

Daniel T. Curtis

10 P¼ Night Rate

Typical example of written messages transmitted by telephone during 1880s. (Courtesy of Stephen Prigozy.)

of the Kingsbury Commitment required AT&T to grant connection to its long-distance lines, so that independent companies could accept toll calls from their customers. The overall cost to AT&T to implement the agreement was around $10 million—$7.5 million lost in the sale of Western Union stock, plus another $2.5 million to pay J. P. Morgan & Company for losses sustained when contracts to buy independent telephone companies were cancelled.

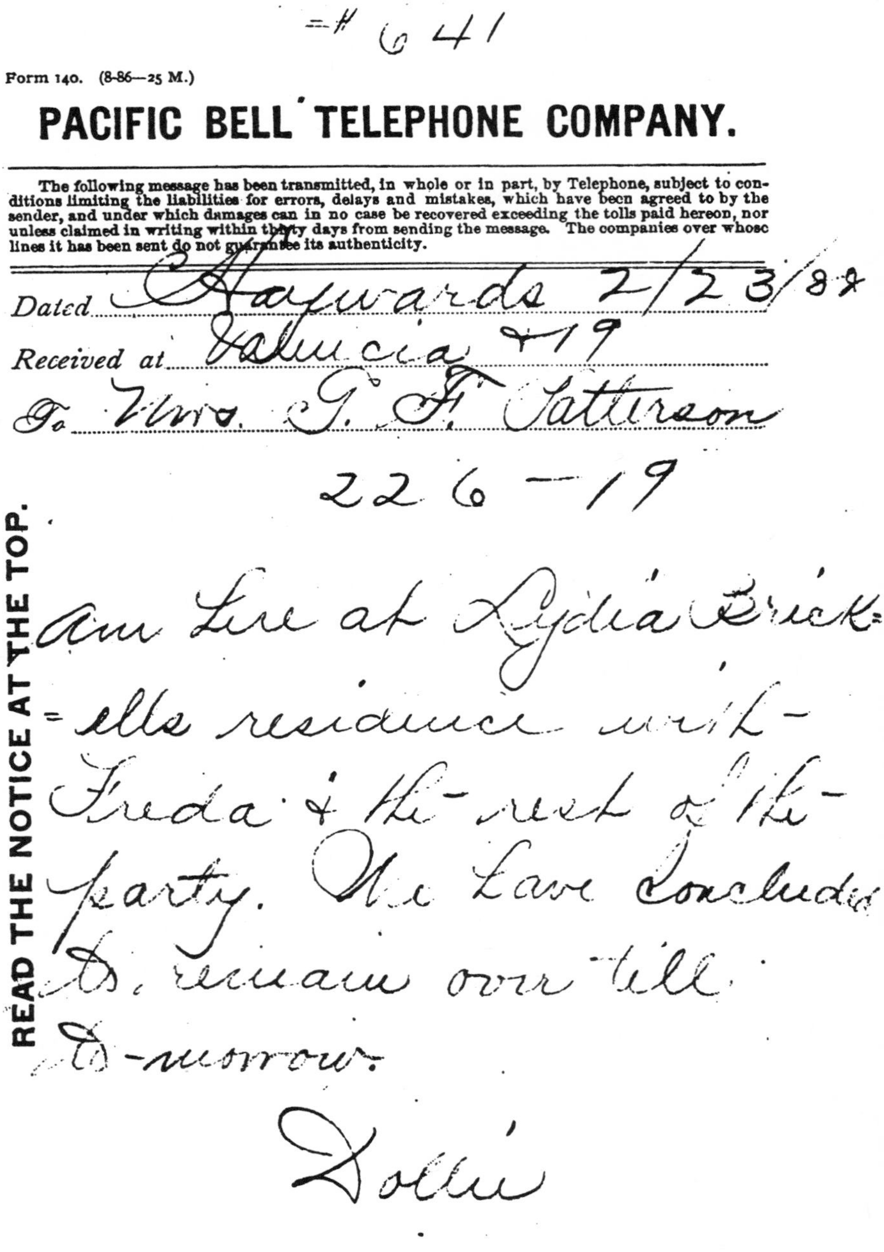

=# 6 4 1

Form 140. (8-86—25 M.)

PACIFIC BELL TELEPHONE COMPANY.

The following message has been transmitted, in whole or in part, by Telephone, subject to conditions limiting the liabilities for errors, delays and mistakes, which have been agreed to by the sender, and under which damages can in no case be recovered exceeding the tolls paid hereon, nor unless claimed in writing within thirty days from sending the message. The companies over whose lines it has been sent do not guarantee its authenticity.

Dated *Haywards 2/23/88*

Received at *Valucia ×19*

To *Mrs. G. F. Patterson*

226 – 19

READ THE NOTICE AT THE TOP.

Am Live at Lydia Brick= =ells residence with Freda & the rest of the party. We have concluded to remain over till to-morrow.

Dollie

Typical example of written messages transmitted by telephone during the 1880s. (Courtesy of Stephen Prigozy.)

Although Kingsbury ended many of the monopolistic features of the Bell System, the company still remained a huge money-making entity, and it retained much of its old power to dominate the communications industry. Compared to the monster AT&T, Western Union seemed like a pygmy. It was not always so. By the time of the Civil War, Western Union was considered one of the largest and wealthiest corporations in America. It held a virtual monopoly on all forms of electrical communication. Telegraph traffic was peaking by the time the telephone was invented, and it was not affected by telephone competition for many years.

The situation began to change as the telephone company improved their technology and Western Union, on the other hand, neglected technological progress. By the time Western Union woke up it was too late. Without even trying, AT&T eroded Western Union's traffic base. The public started increasing their use of the telephone, resulting in a corresponding decrease in what Western Union called its "social telegram" service. Western Union had long catered to the business user in preference to serving private users. Even their business customers were being lured away by AT&T's TWX service, which leased telegraph printers for use over the telephone lines. Western Union's domestic telegraph revenues slumped from 35.2 percent of the total revenue in 1926 to 18 percent in 1943.

The only real competitor that Western Union ever had in its own field was Postal Telegraph, which started operations in 1881. Postal was an active competitor, but it never had more than about 17 percent of the total telegraph traffic that was available. Postal was faced with revenues declining even more steadily than Western Union's. Finally, in 1943, the two companies were allowed to merge. This was not a positive thing for the public, since Western Union promptly closed several hundred public telegraph offices. Far from being an attempt to create a telegraph monopoly, the merger was merely an attempt to dispose of the already decomposing corpse of Postal and set the stage for a revitalized Western Union.

After World War II, Western Union made a valiant attempt to stay alive. Its cross-country microwave system, automatic switching message centers, and later a modern satellite system were all state-of-the-art. With all the technical improvements the company was still on a slow, downhill descent into troubled financial waters. The plain fact was that the telegraph industry, based on the principle of written messages delivered in person by messenger to the addressee, was simply outmoded. The public and business alike demanded faster and faster service. People quickly decided that if they had to telephone their messages to Western Union and then have the telegraph company telephone them to the addressee, they might just as well telephone the addressee themselves. Improved telephone services were also a big factor.

Western Union went into a financial nosedive from which it never recovered and finally called it quits in 1989. The name Western Union is now used by a money transfer company. It has no connection with the former Western Union Telegraph Company. When Western Union folded it sent all of its archives to the Smithsonian Institution, where they are available to serious students by appointment. These archives include photographs, business records, and copies of patents. Western Union also had maintained a sizeable collection of historic telegraph apparatus. This was given to the National Museum and is now held by the Division of Electricity and Modern Physics.

Chapter 10

The Military Telephone

WORLD WAR I PRESENTED an enormous problem for the U.S. Army Signal Corps. The very magnitude of the fighting, the terrain and climate involved, all presented unique problems that had to be solved in a relatively short time. Radio was just emerging as a practical communication device, but it was very primitive compared to the equipment used by the armed forces today. The old reliable heliograph, that had proved itself in the Indian wars and the Spanish-American War, saw little, if any use. The heliograph instrument uses mirrors in precisely adjustable mounts to send the reflected rays of the sun to a distant point. Keying in Morse code is accomplished either by mirror deflection or a small shutter similar to those used on marine searchlights. The heliograph, which sends the most powerful visual signal known, is entirely dependent on sunlight for its successful operation. The report of the Chief Signal Officer, issued after the war, mentions heliographs, but it does not recount any instance of their use in the field. Trench fighting and the generally cloudy weather ruled out the heliograph.

In addition to radio, the army had the Morse telegraph, earth telegraph equipment, blinker light signals, pigeon message carriers, and ground panels for signaling to aircraft. The real workhorse of the campaign was the field telephone. The army had adopted the telephone with enthusiasm. As early as 1879, only three years after Bell's patent, experiments had been conducted at Fort Sill, Oklahoma Territory, using existing Morse telegraph lines on a temporary basis.

General A. W. Greely, when he became Chief Signal Officer in 1887, sponsored the development of field telephones. Greely encouraged Captain James Allen to continue work on improved field telephones, which were announced in 1897. The Chief Signal Officer's report of 1895 spoke with enthusiasm about the telephones equipped with the new "Blake" transmitters. The Blake transmitter was a bulky, six-pound unit with relatively low output, and it is hard to imagine it being used except for fixed locations. The Blake was the first successful transmitter acquired by Bell to replace their sound-powered instruments. By 1901, the army was equipped with fairly modern field telephones using transmitters of the Edison type. By 1917, there was a full complement of lightweight field telephones, portable switchboards and field wire.

In the period after 1900, the Signal Corps had developed some very effective field telephone sets. The Field Artillery Telephone Model 1910 was designed for the needs of artillery observers. Built on a compact aluminum and fiber chassis, the set had a transmitter on a folding arm, headset receiver and a buzzer for signalling. This compact telephone equipment was hung from the operator's neck, leaving both hands free for writing or using binoculars. One of the minor problems encountered was that the instrument swung about wildly when the operator was on horseback. A simple strap around the waist solved this problem. Other field phones were electrically similar to the ones used today, except for being mounted in wooden cases and thus being heavier and bulkier than the current models. Great improvements in various materials have made modern phones more efficient than their predecessors. Also much progress has been made in wire manufacture for use in combat areas.

When the United States entered the war the main problem was to procure the large quantities of equipment required on very short notice. Orders for wire involved lengths sufficient to go around the earth 14 times. Forty million dollars' worth of field glasses were purchased. One hundred thousand field telephones were needed. There were orders for 200,000 pairs of lineman's pliers. A total of 43,000 wristwatches was needed for Signal Corps operators.

One of the cleverest communications devices used during World War I was the Fullerphone. Invented by Captain (later Major General) A. C. Fuller of the Royal Engineers of the British army, the device was not a telephone at all. Rather it was used for Morse code signalling over wire lines. The name "phone" probably evolved from security considerations, much as the term "tank" was used to try to disguise the real nature of the first armored vehicles. The Fullerphone was so useful that it was used in both world wars by the British and Canadian armies. The American counterpart of the Fullerphone was the "buzzerphone" EE-1-A, and a later version known as the TG-5. The Fullerphone and its American counterparts used the principle of putting only a weak DC voltage on the line to prevent inductive pickup. The operator, of course, heard a tone signal sending Morse code.

The army had used "buzzer" signals for years as an adjunct to field telephones. The original buzzer sets applied the pulsating signals directly to the line. Monitoring by earth currents did not become practical until sensitive electronic amplifiers became available during World War I. Buzzer signals would carry over very poor lines—lines that would be useless for telephone communication. Furthermore, these buzzers were very simple devices, no more complex than a doorbell. The pulsating signal

U.S. army TG5-B telegraph set, used until World War II. (Photo by Lewis Coe.)

produced by the vibrating contact was stepped up through an ordinary telephone type induction coil. This gave great carrying power, and although the messages were limited to Morse code, this was no handicap in a day when all Signal Corps operators were required to be proficient in Morse. The British army had what they called a "power buzzer." As the name suggests, it was designed to have a much higher output and consequently longer range than the standard buzzers. This power buzzer had an output of 80 to 100 volts of pulsating current. The high voltage output brought its own disadvantages of interfering with other communications channels and also was more readily detected by enemy listening stations. During the Philippine campaigns, buzzers enabled advancing columns to keep in touch with their base. As the troops advanced, hastily laid field wire worked fine with the buzzer signals. The very efficiency of buzzer signals became a doubtful asset during World War I. With most of the action taking place

between prepared positions close to each other, it was soon found that opposing forces could eavesdrop on the enemy by earth currents induced by the buzzers. Pickup loops connected to sensitive amplifiers gave frequent access to the enemy's signals.

In addition to field operations, the army was confronted with the problem of point-to-point communication between the key French cities involved in the war effort. Existing French facilities did not even approach the capacity necessary to handle the huge volume of wartime traffic. It soon became apparent that large numbers of soldiers were being diverted from field operations to act as operators of the many new switchboards that had been added to the French system.

Accordingly, it was decided to recruit American women to act as telephone operators in France. In response to a cable from General Pershing in November 1917, the first contingent of 33 women operators left New York on March 6, 1918. They were in charge of Grace Banker, Chief Operator. Miss Banker later received the Distinguished Service Medal for her work during the war. Recruitment of women to serve in France was complicated by the necessity that the operators be fluent in both French and English. In some cases it was easier to train women fluent in both languages in telephone procedures than it was to find bilingual operators with telephone experience.

In all, the female contingent numbered 233 and their presence added materially to the efficiency of telephone communications as well as releasing male operators for duty at the front. It was noted in official reports that the arrival of the women operators resulted in a marked increase in efficiency of operations. Not only were women more efficient in the operation of the switchboards, there was a psychological advantage as well. The official report explained it this way: "Officers were inclined to put up with vexatious delays, because of the fact that women were on the board, and that feature alone has much to do with the smooth and efficient functioning of a telephone system."

When the first "telephone girls" reached Paris, they had little idea of what was expected of them. They were given a three-day course of lectures and were quartered at the Hotel Petrograd. They received their first real taste of war when the Germans staged a three-day series of air raids on Paris. As the American operations in France increased, more of the telephone traffic was between American bases and the need for French-speaking operators declined. Then it was possible to enlist operators who were experienced in toll operations without the French-speaking requirement.

Opposite: The first contingent of American "telephone girls" in Paris, 1918. (Photo courtesy of the National Archives.)

Lieut. Col. R. D. Garrett, Chief Signal Officer, 42nd Division, testing a telephone left behind by the Germans in the hasty retreat from the salient of St. Mihiel, Essey, France, September 19, 1918. (Photo courtesy of the National Archives.)

The heroics of the military operators in the field rivaled and exceeded anything we have read about the exploits of the Morse operators in the American Civil War. Just as the Civil War made use of the Morse telegraph to a degree hitherto unknown, field telephone operations during World War I set new records for personal heroism and technical achievement. In spite of the fact that field telephones were widely used, they had to be closely supervised.

The close proximity of the enemy at all times made security the prime consideration. Monitoring stations watched the Allied field telephones just as closely as the enemy's. There had to be constant vigilance against careless conversations on the telephones. Officers who discussed vital information on the telephone were severely reprimanded. Near the front lines every message had to be encoded. One of the codes used to confuse the enemy was the employment of American Indians speaking in their native tongue, which was absolutely baffling to the Germans. Captain E. W. Horner enlisted the services of eight Choctaws of Company D, 141st Infantry to transmit orders over the field telephone. This idea carried over to World War II, where Navajo "code talkers" performed brilliantly. The Navajos were chosen primarily because there was a larger group to choose from, and because the Navajo language is considered the most difficult of the various Indian languages. The Japanese were thoroughly confused by this method of sending orders over the radio.

The idea of using the Navajos was conceived by Philip Johnston, son of a Protestant missionary. Johnston had grown up on a Navajo reservation and was fluent in the language. Johnston took his idea to Major General Clayton B. Vogel, Commanding General of the United States Marine Corps, Pacific Fleet, in 1942. Johnston brought four Navajos to Vogel's headquarters and had them stage a demonstration of translating from English to Navajo and back again. Vogel obtained permission to recruit 30 men for a pilot project. A virtually unbreakable Navajo code was developed, taking advantage of the complexity of the Navajo language. Many arbitrary code words for military items were assigned. "Dive bomber" became *ginitsoh* (sparrow hawk). Grenades became *nimasii* (potatoes). Adolph Hitler was dubbed "Moustache Smeller," and Mussolini became "Big Gourd Chin."

The program was so successful that unlimited recruitment was authorized and the code talkers grew to a unit of 420 men. White recruits from the Navajo reservations could not be accepted because they spoke what was called "trading post language," which was not the same as the pure tribal Navajo tongue. One of the problems that developed was the fact that due to the extreme secrecy of the mission the Navajos were not allowed to communicate with their families. This precipitated many anxious inquiries by parents who could not understand why they had not heard from their son in the Marines. The Navajo "code talkers" were a proud group. They had contributed to the tribal history and greatly to the war effort in the Pacific. The code was highly effective against the Japanese, most of whom had never even seen an American Indian, much less heard one speaking his native tongue.

Earth telegraph systems proved very useful during the trench warfare of World War I. The earth telegraph worked on the principle of induction. Pickup loops or ground plates were placed to cover as wide a baseline

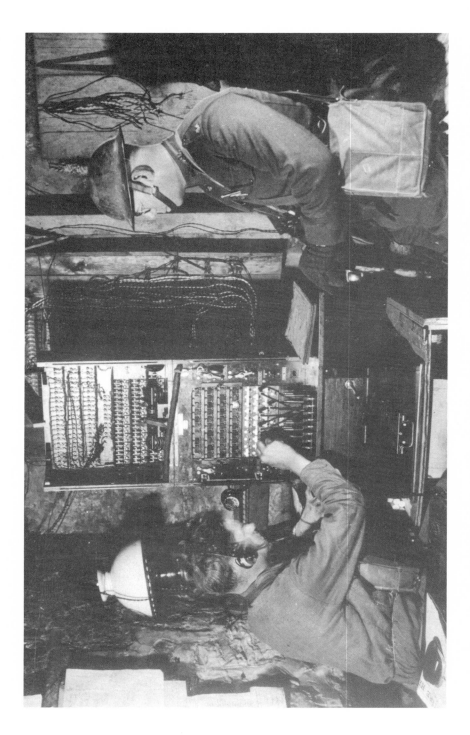

distance as possible. Sensitive amplifiers connected to the pickup wires detected both telegraph and telephone messages that were induced in the earth. For telegraphy, buzzer sending sets were employed and the messages were sent in Morse code. A maximum range of about one mile could be obtained, and this was enough to be useful in the closely spaced trenches.

Of course, messages sent by telegraphy had to be encoded. Occasionally false or misleading messages were deliberately transmitted in the clear, with the full knowledge that the enemy would intercept them. In this way, it was sometimes possible to decoy the enemy into responding to some imaginary attack. Both the U.S. army and the German army used the inductive pickup loops to monitor telephone and telegraph conversations. The problems in maintaining field wire in heavily shelled areas often resulted in the earth telegraph being the only useful means of communication.

Blinker lamps using Morse code were a favorite means of communication when all other modes were unavailable or not working. Blinker lamps would work day or night regardless of weather conditions and could not be knocked out except by a direct hit on the station. Advanced light signalling systems were developed using high intensity lamps for sending and telescopes on the receiving end. These had a range of as much as 25 miles over suitable terrain.

World War I probably had more intense artillery fire than any other conflict. "No Man's Land" was just a barren wasteland, pocked by shell holes. Over this terrain Signal Corps men had to string vital communication lines, often under heavy fire. It was soon found that lines laid on the ground were constantly broken, and the men laying the lines were often killed or wounded. One officer found a young soldier flat on his stomach in the middle of a wheat field. Since the man did not seem to be wounded, the officer asked him what he was doing there. The soldier replied, "Fixin' this wire, Lieutenant, that the damned Boche keeps a breakin' all the time."

The only technique that seemed to counteract the frequent breakage of wire was the so-called "ladder line." In this method two or more wires were laid to the distant objective. Then cross lines were laid at frequent intervals. In this way the chance of a breakage by shell fire was minimized. This was a laborious procedure for the men involved, but it was sometimes considered the only way to protect an important line. Even so, in the heavily shelled areas, telephones could not be depended on, and it was necessary to resort to blinker lights or earth telegraph for communication. Radio was in its infancy during this war. Sometimes it filled a vital need and worked well, but the radios of 1917 were not the slick, transistorized, digital equip-

Opposite: Operating a telephone switchboard in a dugout, France, 1918. (Photo courtesy of the National Archives.)

Attaching message to a Signal Corps carrier pigeon, 1917. (Photo courtesy of the National Archives.)

ment used by the armed forces today. The 1917 radios worked on a lower frequency part of the radio spectrum and were thus subject to atmospheric disturbances.

One of the earliest methods of communication, the homing pigeon, played an important role in World War I. At the outbreak of the war, pigeon experts in the United States were recruited and sent to Europe to organize the service there. Homing pigeons have the uncanny instinct of returning to their home loft if taken to a distant point and released. Advancing units carried pigeons with them. Temporary lofts were set up at strategic points behind the lines. These temporary lofts had to be set up at least a week in advance of the anticipated use. Otherwise, the pigeons might not return to it when used to carry messages.

Although they seemed like a hopelessly archaic method of communicating in 1917, the pigeons nevertheless performed efficiently. They had an overall record of 95 percent in delivering the messages entrusted to them. One bird, "Cher Ami," actually received the Distinguished Service Cross for its services. Even though wounded by enemy fire en route, the plucky bird had carried a message to the 77th Division headquarters from the famous "Lost Battalion." Even the pigeons had their limitations. During the battle of Passchendaele in 1917, the birds were so frightened by the heavy gunfire that they refused to fly and fluttered helplessly near their handlers. Experimental use of homing pigeons had started as early as 1878, and the faithful birds continued to be a part of Signal Corps planning until they were retired for good in 1957.

Radio, or wireless as it was still called, was only in the primitive stages of use in airplanes. Visual communication with airplanes had to be relied on in many cases. For this purpose, the so-called "ground panels" were extensively used. Ground panel stations received information by wire, radio, or other means and communicated it to the aircraft by laying out cloth strips on the ground in various configurations. By this method, the planes could be advised of bombing results and their activities coordinated with the troops on the ground.

Members of the Signal Corps earned 55 Distinguished Service Crosses and 40 Distinguished Service Medals, plus numerous foreign decorations for their services. The Corps received a commendation from General Pershing in these words: "I desire to congratulate the officers and men of the Signal Corps in France on their work, which stands out as one of the great accomplishments of the American Expeditionary Forces."

During the war the Signal Corps had constructed a total of 2,000 miles of pole lines using 28,000 miles of wire, 32,000 miles of line using existing French poles. Field combat lines totaled 40,000 miles. Twenty-two thousand miles of French line were leased and 134 permanent telegraph offices established. There were 273 telephone exchanges and multiplex printing telegraph equipment linked Tours, Chaumont, Paris, and London. At war's end, the Corps had grown to 50 battalions comprising 1,462 officers and 33,038 enlisted men.

From a very early date, the armed forces tried to improve their methods of communication. The White House and the office of the president are generally thought to be the command center for the whole country.

As such, it is usually assumed to be on the cutting edge of technology as far as communications are concerned.

This may be generally true now, but it was not always so. In fact, the higher government departments have always exhibited a reluctance to depart from traditional methods. For example, even though typewriters had been invented several years earlier, the State Department was still insisting that official documents be handwritten as late as 1900. The Civil War is often referred to as the "first modern war," due to the intensive use of the Morse telegraph and railroad transportation of men and materials. Yet, there was no telegraph office in the White House during the Civil War. When President Lincoln wanted to see the latest dispatches arriving from the field of battle, he had to leave his office and go across the street to the telegraph office. It seems incredible that a telegraph instrument and operator were not brought into the White House at that time.

After the invention of the telephone in 1876, one might think that the president, the commander in chief, would be one of the first persons to have one of the new instruments. Actually, a telephone was installed in the White House in 1877, during the administration of Rutherford B. Hayes. This doesn't mean that the president had a phone. The phone was not even in his office, and it was used mainly by staff members and news reporters.

Until 1898 chief executives rarely used the telephone, and none had an instrument in his office. When the president wanted to make a phone call, he had to leave his desk and go down the hall to the phone, just like everyone else. This situation changed abruptly in 1898 when war broke out with Spain. With action on two fronts, in Cuba and the Philippines, the president was suddenly faced with the need for more rapid communications than could be effected by the old methods.

Accordingly, Lieutenant Colonel Benjamin F. Montgomery of the Signal Corps was brought to the White House to install a communications center. Montgomery transformed a second-floor office into a military information center. In this "war room" were installed 25 Morse telegraph operating positions and 15 telephones. There were also large wall maps showing probable battle areas in Puerto Rico, Cuba, and the Philippines as well as the adjacent ocean areas. The installation provided President McKinley with private telephone lines to the War and Navy departments plus other key officials in Washington. There was also a direct line to Tampa, Florida, which was the primary staging area for the amphibious invasion of Cuba. In the field there was a telephone network that gathered information for transmission to Washington.

President McKinley took an interest in the war room, spending many hours there amid the chatter of the telegraph instruments and the constant ringing of the telephones. In this way he must have had a much greater sense of being in command of the situation than any previous president. It is said that McKinley even issued orders to his commanders in the field through the telegraph and telephone facilities installed in the war room.

As the years passed there was slow progress in upgrading the White House telephone and telegraph facilities. President Theodore Roosevelt was supportive of improved wire facilities but is said to have used the telephone little himself, and there was still no telephone on the president's desk. When the 300-pound William Howard Taft assumed the presidency a special telephone booth had to be installed to accommodate his portly figure. Taft apparently used the telephone for personal calls to friends and relatives, but not much for official business except when it was necessary to pressure some congressman whose vote was needed on a critical bill.

Surprisingly, President Wilson did not use the telephone much, even when the war created an intensive demand for speedy communications. Wilson still relied mainly on written and personal contacts to transact the business of his office. The first president to have a telephone handset installed on his desk was Herbert Hoover, and this probably marked the beginning of the modern era of White House communications.

Of course, one reason that the early presidents did not have a phone on their desks was the fact that the freestanding telephone for desk use did not come along until around 1897 and these were of the "candlestick" type. Modern handsets of the type we use today came in around 1927. Prior telephones were designed for wall mounting and were normally used in the standing position. During the Cold War period it was found that it took 12 or 16 hours to contact the Kremlin. The first "hot line" came into use to enable immediate contact with Russian leaders. President Kennedy later had second thoughts about this arrangement and decided that voice contact might not be the best thing when critical decisions about nuclear war might be involved.

From the humble beginnings of McKinley's "war room," the president and the military are served by an ever increasing amount of high-tech communications equipment. The Pentagon, for example, boasts what is said to be the world's largest telephone switchboard. There are 25,000 lines connected through 100,000 miles of cable, and 25,000 calls a day are handled.

The British army was traditionally very cautious about adopting telephone communication. They tended to rely on Morse code instruments of various kinds for communication. There was some basis for this, as the early telephones were not always capable of good speech transmission. Writing in the *Journal of the Royal United Service Institution* in 1892, Major Beresford of the Royal Engineers said in reference to the telephone:

> There may be drawbacks to the discovery, for however well established the fact may be that the more perfect the means of communication, so the greater are the chances of success in any operation of peace or war, it is not so well established that the human voice is, under all circumstances, the medium most to be

desired for arriving at a satisfactory result. Experience, in fact, may have taught some of us that any contrivance for transmitting the voice itself might very easily pass from a blessing into a curse, and that, while considering to what use we could put the telephone, we should not shut our eyes to its possible abuse.

Major Beresford commented further in reference to the telephone:

Its development in England was long delayed by the fact that the patent rights were all in the hands of one company [Bell], but, now that these rights have mostly expired, we may hope for rapid improvements and simplifications both in the instruments themselves and in the methods of using them. This view of the matter is of special importance to the growth of Army telegraphy, where simplicity for the soldier and economy for the exchequer are the two things needful. The telephone in its complete form with microphone and call apparatus is a more or less delicate instrument, and requires an intimate acquaintance with its idiosyncrasies to keep it in good, working order. If we propose to extend the telephone for field service, and introduce it as an article for general use in the hands of the soldier, some simpler form is necessary; in fact, we may not hope to introduce any such apparatus which does not combine extreme simplicity with extreme cheapness. . . . Even the best telephones are not, as yet, perfect mediums for speech. The clearness with which words are reproduced depends to a great extent on the quality of the speaker's voice, if not also on the quality of the listener's ear. The softer or sibilant sounds are transmitted with difficulty, causing delays and errors in the messages, and telephone circuits are peculiarly affected by disturbing influences, such as are produced by neighboring telegraph circuits and earth currents. . . . It might appear at first sight that, in the matter of pace, a telephone used for speaking had great advantage over one used for Morse signals, or over a telegraph instrument. But practically for written messages the pace is limited to the writing pace of the receiving clerk. . . . The telephone, as a speaking instrument, in its present state, is rather more suited for conversation than for the transmission of important military orders; at any rate in the field. Its importance in this respect is most marked under circumstances where queries on minor details demand immediate replies, as in the case in local transactions with our supply services; and here comes the advantage of a telephone exchange. But for use on the main line of communication, or for outpost duty, except under exceptional circumstances, the effective use of the telephone for speaking is doubtful.

These comments are typical of the skepticism that greeted the telephone in the early days. The points are well taken, and for the most part true. The debate about speed of transmission of the telegraph versus the telephone was the same as the one that occurred in the United States when railroads started using telephones for train dispatching. Here, the requirements were essentially the same as in military applications. Written train orders had to be handled with absolute accuracy, and even when given over the telephone their speed was limited to the writing speed of the receiving operator. This meant that the speed was around 25 to 30 words

Portable telephone made by Kellogg Switchboard & Supply. Similar instruments were used by the U.S. army as "camp telephones" before World War I. (Photo by Lewis Coe.)

per minute, the same as it would be using the Morse telegraph. For the railroads the main advantage of the telephone was in the training of operators. It was a lot easier to teach a man to write down messages received over the telephone than it was to teach him Morse telegraphy. In the military the same considerations were not so important. They had plenty of manpower, and most Signal Corps men were trained in Morse code.

The mission of the Signal Corps is the same as it has always been, "get the message through." Only the techniques and equipment have changed; from the Morse telegraph of the Civil War, the heliographs of the Indian Wars, the field telephones and primitive radios of World War I, the advanced radio sets of World War II, Korea and Vietnam to the sophisticated techniques of Desert Storm. Currently, the army's mobile subscriber equipment (MSE) brings complete telephone and data service to all parts of the battlefield. Multichannel satellite systems connect expeditionary forces

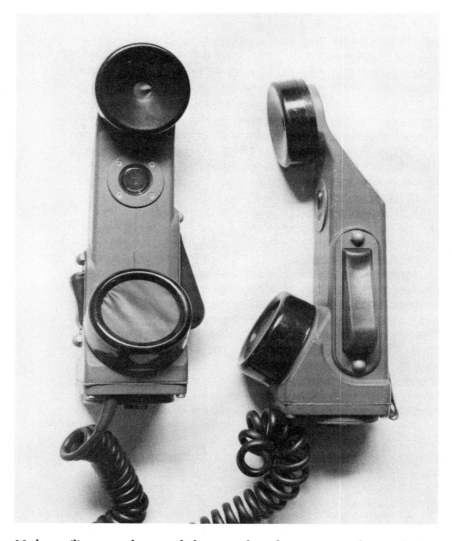

Modern military sound-powered phones work on the same principle as Bell's first phone. (Photo by Lewis Coe.)

with the Pentagon wherever they may be located in the world. The ground communication systems will soon be able to utilize fiber-optic links to further expand their capabilities. Methods are being developed which will allow fiber-optic cables to be plugged into equipment in the same manner that coaxial cable is presently used.

Morse code, once so important to the Signal Corps, is now almost a thing of the past. Some military personnel are trained in its use for special assignments, but the rank and file of the Signal Corps no longer is so trained. Communication equipment now employs secure voice channels, high-speed telegraph and facsimile equipment. When written messages are received they are printed out by automatic equipment instead of the word by word reception used by the former telegraph and radio operators.

Chapter 11

Down on the Farm

GERTRUDE STEIN ONCE SAID: "In the United States there is more space where nobody is than where anybody is. That is what makes America what it is." Such logic might be lost on the harried New York commuter trying to board the subway in Times Square during rush hour. Yet, when we look at the great expanses of America's heartland, especially in those states west of the Mississippi River, Stein's description, even today, is pretty accurate.

Now we have improved roads, electric power distribution, radio, satellite television and of course telephones, so the old isolation has pretty much disappeared. Younger persons now can scarcely appreciate the utter isolation of farm life around the turn of the century and until well after World War I. Even in states like Illinois, within 100 miles of Chicago, life was pretty elemental for the farm population.

There were few improved roads and during the spring thaw the roads became mostly an impassable morass. Horses could get around but sometimes just barely, and the first automobiles had hard going in winter. The Model T Ford came as near as anything to solving the transportation problem. On many rural roads the winter time ruts were cut to the exact gauge of a Model T's wheels. At intervals, turnouts were laboriously created in the mud so two vehicles could pass.

There was no rural mail delivery until 1896, when three routes were opened in West Virginia. The rural mail delivery system spread through most of the country quite rapidly. Yet as late as 1926, new routes were being added. For many years, most families could only expect to get mail on the weekly trip to town, providing the roads and weather permitted.

Against this background of utter isolation in the late years of the 19th century, the telephone came as something created in heaven. By the late 1890s the stranglehold of the Bell Company on telephone communication was beginning to relax, and small groups of individuals could buy the instruments they needed to construct telephone systems. In the far West, the lines could even be strung on fence posts, sometimes using the fence wire itself for the conductor.

Only one wire was needed, worked against ground, a method pioneered by the Morse telegraph. In fact, all the early telephones, wherever located, at first used the single wire system until it was discovered that much better results could be obtained by using two wires. The problem in metropolitan areas was that as telephones multiplied there was bad cross talk between adjacent wires of the grounded lines. In the rural areas, where there was usually only the one wire running along the road, cross talk was not a problem.

The standard subscriber instrument in the early days was the wooden box wall phone with a local talking battery and magneto calling and ringing. These are the phones that are so eagerly sought by collectors today. Quaint as they may seem now, they were the ideal instrument for the times in which they were used. The local battery gave each subscriber his own talking power so that two stations could converse with each other even if the line to the central office was down. The instruments were comparatively simple and rugged. Maintenance could be handled by relatively inexperienced persons.

Most rural telephone companies started on a very informal basis. A group of farmers would get together and decide to build a line. By the late 1890s, as Bell control gradually waned, telephones and associated supplies could be purchased from a number of suppliers, including mail order houses. At one time, through advertising in such publications as *RFD News*, rural letter carriers were offered generous rewards if they would send in the names of farmers who might be thinking of starting a telephone cooperative.

The men would get together and share the work of erecting poles and stringing wire. Usually, there was one individual who had "studied up" on the art of telephony, and he would provide the technical support needed. Otherwise, do-it-yourself books were available and the participants learned as they went along. If the system was large enough to require a switchboard, it was usually placed in one of the farm houses, and the lady of the house acted as operator during daytime hours. Small switchboards were usually not attended continuously at night, but were provided with a "night bell" to summon the operator in emergencies.

Telephone companies in small towns were usually organized on a more formal basis, with stockholders and full-time employees. The small farm cooperative groups eventually extended their lines into the nearest town. Many of the small town companies made agreements with neighboring towns to interconnect. Usually each company involved paid half the cost of erecting and maintaining the line. Such interconnections enabled calls to be handled between the respective communities and in turn to the individual farm subscribers who were connected to the system.

Before the Bell System relaxed its rules on interconnection in 1913, there were no long-distance calls possible from these small local companies.

Telephones introduced the rural population to the complexities of modern life. The farmer could call the elevator in town and get the latest quotations on farm products. Parts could be ordered for machinery and help summoned in emergencies. In those days, doctors made house calls, and the country doctor of old considered it his duty to hitch up his buggy and drive to help in some medical emergency out in the country. Fire calls were dreaded, and without tank trucks there was usually not much that could be done in farm fires except to save as much as possible.

Rural phone lines were invariably party lines with often as many as eight or more subscribers connected to the same line. Each party could hear all the conversations on the line, so it was not a place to discuss confidential matters. Calling of the different parties was accomplished by a coded ringing signal. Long and short rings in various combinations were used. Each party was supposed to answer his own ring, but for most the temptation to "listen in" was almost irresistible.

Farm wives on the same line loved to spend a great deal of time talking with each other. On one line it was always possible to tell when a certain lady was listening in. She had a clock in her kitchen with a very loud tick. It was easily heard through the sensitive transmitter of the old wall phone! There were no daytime soap programs on television or radio and talk on the party line was the only diversion available. When a receiver was off the hook on a local battery telephone, there was a steady drain on the batteries whether anyone was talking or not. Long periods of listening ran the batteries down pretty fast. Then the telephone would not talk very well. When a certain party could not be heard with normal volume it was common to hear the expression, "she must have listened her batteries down!" Many times it was hard to "get the line" for a legitimate call when the gossipers were hard at it. There was not much local news that escaped the attention of these party line hangers-on, and sometimes even the switchboard operator in town, "central," as she was usually known, would join in with her latest news as well.

The old wooden box phones that appeal to many collectors today were actually a well designed and efficient instrument for the purpose. Handmade of quality hard woods, with all the parts mounted and wired by expert technicians, they were almost indestructible unless hit by lightning or destroyed by fire. The relaxation of the Bell patent limitations enabled many companies to get into the telephone manufacturing business. The transmitters employed the latest type of carbon button design first invented by Thomas Edison. There was an induction coil to amplify the voice currents that were generated by the local battery housed in the phone box.

At first, these batteries were the so-called "wet cells" using carbon, zinc

Six-line switchboard of the type often used on farm lines. Made by Williams in 1895. (Photo courtesy Museum of Independent Telephony.)

and a sal ammoniac solution. The "dry cell" was listed for the first time in the Western Electric catalog of 1891 and gradually the messy wet cells disappeared from service. A good phone was marvelously sensitive, much more so than the phones of today; room noise could usually be heard. The standard way of testing an old phone for sensitivity was to hold the receiver up to the transmitter. A loud howl was heard if the phone was up to par.

This test not only revealed if the batteries were good but checked the transmitter as well. One man decided his transmitter was not up to par. In dismantling it he spilled the carbon granules. Deciding that gunpowder looked the same, he refilled the transmitter with black powder. When the battery current hit the powder the results were spectacular!

On farm party lines it was often the custom for everybody to get on the line and listen to some impromptu entertainment from a neighbor's house where there was a piano player or other talented performer.

Most telephone companies bought the No. 6 dry cell batteries by the barrel. Replacing batteries was the common remedy when a subscriber complained of poor talking performance.

Rural telephones came in two types. Technically described as "magneto ringing, local battery telephones" they were either "series" or "bridging." Series type instruments employed low-resistance ringers, usually 80 ohms, and were connected so that the entire line current, talking and ringing, passed through each instrument on a party line. Thus, if the line was broken at any point, all of the phones were out of service.

Bridging type instruments used high-resistance ringers, usually around 2,500 ohms, and as the name implies were connected across the line conductors, or in most cases on the early lines, from line to ground. Bridging type phones had the advantage that if the circuit was broken at one station it did not affect the other phones on the line. A disadvantage of the bridging system was that where there were a large number of stations connected, the ringing load was heavy.

The series phones worked fine as long as there was no line trouble, but bridging systems were considered to be more reliable and were the favorite type in most areas. In the later days of the local battery type phones, manufacturers succeeded in putting all of the components of a wooden box phone in a modern-looking desk set mounting. In many communities the local battery phones were phased out in the 1930s, but they lasted for many more years in some remote areas.

A local battery system at Roxbury, Kansas, was finally taken out of service in 1977. This was one of the last of the local battery systems. If any are still in operation they are probably small private networks without outside connections. Although the local battery phones worked well, they could not keep up with the rapid pace of technological progress. Patrons were starting to demand dial type phones and other services that could not be furnished on the old phones.

Sooner or later, as they grew in size, the small rural telephone companies using local battery phone systems were converted to the common battery system. This was a major decision for most small companies. It involved a large investment, extensive overhaul of the outside plant, and an

One of the last local battery, magneto switchboards. This Monarch board was taken out at Roxbury, Kansas, in 1977. (Photo courtesy Museum of Independent Telephony.)

educational program to acquaint the subscribers with the differences they were going to find in a new system.

Conversion of the local battery system at Galva, Henry County, Illinois, was typical of the process. Galva, a small farming community, 140 miles west of Chicago, had a population of 2,800, and there were about 700 subscribers to the local phone exchange. The telephone company had been organized around 1898. Farm lines extended from town along the roads in all directions, and there were some toll lines to several nearby towns that were operated on a cooperative basis with the other local telephone companies.

After 1913, long-distance connections were available through the Bell System. Since small companies such as the one at Galva did not have technical personnel capable of planning a new installation, this service was usually provided by engineers from the major supply companies. Galva decided to buy its new switchboard and other central office equipment from the Stromberg-Carlson Company of Chicago.

Stromberg-Carlson had been a leading supplier of equipment to independent telephone companies for many years. They were noted for high-grade equipment, whether it was central office items or subscribers' telephones. At Galva, the conversion to the common battery system occurred in 1930. After placing the main order with Stromberg-Carlson, a decision was made to use the subscriber telephone sets manufactured by the Leich Electric Company of Genoa, Illinois. The Leich telephones were of good quality, although not on the same level as Stromberg-Carlson, and were correspondingly less expensive to buy. Once the equipment was ordered, work started immediately on overhauling the outside lines. Some of the lines had been in service for over 30 years with little maintenance work.

A common battery exchange demands a much higher standard of line construction than usually was the case with the local battery systems. The central office battery, usually around 50 volts, is applied to the subscribers' lines at all times. Any leakage causes the switchboard to indicate a calling subscriber, what is usually called an "off hook" condition. Many of the farm lines were still using the single wire ground return system. These had to be rebuilt to use two wires, or what is called a full metallic system.

Meanwhile work was progressing on the installation of the new switchboard. The installation work required the services of 20 technicians from Stromberg-Carlson for two months. The old switchboard had to be kept in service while the new one was being installed to avoid any disruption of service. This involved a very simple item not usually associated with telephone technology. Wooden toothpicks? Yes, toothpicks were inserted in the line protective devices known as "heat coils" on the distributing frame of the new switchboard. This opened the connection and effectively isolated the

Kellogg 1901 single box phone. (Photo courtesy Museum of Independent Telephony.)

old board from the new one until the moment of "cut-over" arrived. Cut-over is normally scheduled for the wee small hours of the morning when telephone traffic can normally be expected to be light in a small town the size of Galva.

Finally, the great day arrived, and at 2 A.M., the technicians started pulling the toothpicks. In the words of one of those present, "the board lit up like a Christmas tree." After all the systematic work on the lines there were still plenty of loose ends to take care of. Then began the painstaking process of dealing with each defective line and clearing the trouble. The real problems came later when subscribers, accustomed to using the local battery type phones, started using the new ones. Many still reached for

Buy Telephones

THAT ARE GOOD--NOT "CHEAP THINGS."

The difference in cost is little. We guarantee
our apparatus and guarantee our customers
against loss by patent suits. Our guarantee and instruments are both good.

WESTERN TELEPHONE CONSTRUCTION CO.
250-254 South Clinton St., Chicago.

*Largest Manufacturers of Telephones
exclusively in the United States.*

Ad in 1898 *Scientific American* **offers wall phones for sale. Cut shows the "Blake" transmitter.**

the generator crank handle, thinking that was the only way to reach the operator. In Galva, as late as 1953, there were still some of the old local battery, magneto ringing phones still in service, mainly on some farm lines that were owned by the farmers themselves. The final evolution of the Galva system came with the installation of the dial system in 1957. The equipment was furnished by the Automatic Electric Company of Chicago.

Users of the old phones were often careless about replacing the receiver on the hook switch. They did not seem to understand that taking the receiver off the hook on the new phone would immediately signal the operator. If the subscriber did not respond to "number please" after a protracted interval, the operator would report the line as out of order. Wire chiefs had "howlers" which they could place on a line, hoping it would signal the errant subscriber to hang up the phone.

On party lines there was always the necessity of selectively ringing the different parties on the line. On most of the early rural lines this problem was solved by coded ringing signals which actually were heard by all the parties on the line. A more sophisticated method involved splitting up the line for ringing purposes. Half of the parties were rung by sending the ringing signal over one line wire with ground return. The other half were signalled using the other line wire. Thus, a subscriber only heard his own ring, plus the rest that were on his half of the line. Four party lines in town could be signalled by using tuned ringers in the telephones. They would only respond to the right frequency so that the subscriber heard only his own ring.

Opposite: **Local battery, magneto ringing switchboard of the type used in rural communities. Made by the Suttle Equipment Company of Lawrenceville, Illinois. (Photo by Lewis Coe.)**

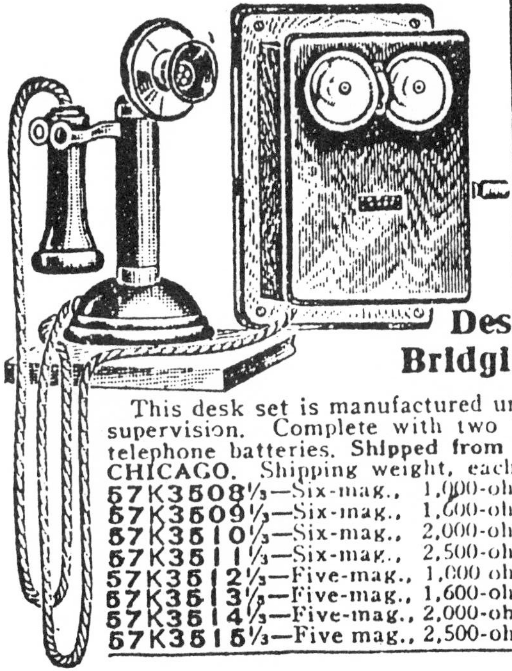

Chicago DeLuxe Bridging Telephones

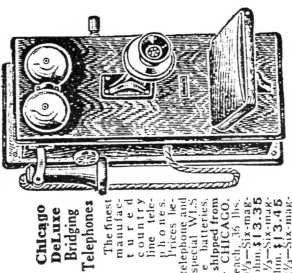

The finest manufactured country line telephones. Prices below include telephone and set of two special WLS telephone batteries. Phones are shipped from factory near CHICAGO. Shpg. wt. each, 36 lbs.

57K3500⅓—Six-magnet, 1,000-ohm..$13.35
57K3501⅓—Six-magnet, 1,600-ohm..$13.45
57K3502⅓—Six-magnet, 2,000-ohm..$13.60
57K3503⅓—Six-magnet, 2,500-ohm......$13.70
57K3504⅓—Five-magnet, 1,000-ohm......13.30
57K3505⅓—Five-magnet, 1,600-ohm......13.35
57K3506⅓—Five-magnet, 2,000-ohm......13.45
57K3507⅓—Five-magnet, 2,500-ohm......13.75

Service

We are in a position to give you figures on a switchboard ranging from six to three hundred lines. Send in your requirements. We will forward an estimate, showing necessary equipment at lowest prices.

Desk Phone Bridging Type

This desk set is manufactured under our own supervision. Complete with two WLS special telephone batteries. Shipped from factory near CHICAGO. Shipping weight, each, 33 pounds.

57K3508⅓—Six-mag., 1,000-ohm..$15.10
57K3509⅓—Six-mag., 1,600-ohm.. 15.20
57K3510⅓—Six-mag., 2,000-ohm.. 15.25
57K3511⅓—Six-mag., 2,500-ohm.. 15.30
57K3512⅓—Five-mag., 1,000-ohm.. 14.95
57K3513⅓—Five-mag., 1,600-ohm.. 15.10
57K3514⅓—Five-mag., 2,000-ohm.. 15.20
57K3515⅓—Five mag., 2,500-ohm.. 15.25

The problem of selective ringing on party lines received much attention from inventors, and during the period 1879 to 1891 at least 161 patents were issued for selective ringing alone. Party lines held on in general use for a long time, not only because they were cheaper, but due to the fact that telephone companies in rural areas did not actually have the lines available to give private circuits to all who wished to have them. When telephone lines changed from open wire lines to multiconductor cable, either aerial or underground, circuits were usually available to all who wanted private line service.

One of the big problems with party lines was human, not electrical. There were always long winded talkers who had the line tied up when someone else wanted to make a call. In most states it was illegal to refuse to yield on a party line for emergency calls.

In 1903 it came as a shock to independent telephone company executives to discover that one of their principal suppliers, Kellogg Switchboard and Supply Company of Chicago, was being subjected to a buyout campaign by the Bell System. Bell, always looking for ways to fight the independents, figured that by controlling Kellogg they could control the independents at will. Such an outcry over this practice was raised that by 1909 a court decision compelled Bell to relinquish their Kellogg stock. Kellogg could now resume their former status as a favorite supplier of high-grade equipment to the independents.

Prior to about 1893, the telephone business in the United States was under the absolute control of the Bell System. There was no way that anyone could buy or manufacture telephones or offer telephone service to the public without a license from Bell. Only a favored few got these licenses and most of them became millionaires in the process. All of this changed with the expiration of the Bell patents. Now the way was clear for small rural telephone companies to spring up, and there were dozens of manufacturers ready to supply them with equipment. One of these was the Suttle Equipment Company of Lawrenceville, Illinois, whose products included switchboards for the local battery, magneto ringing telephones usually found in rural areas. Still in business today, Suttle makes equipment for the modern telephone industry.

By 1910, the number of telephones in the United States had increased about ten times from the 1893 total. Of these, probably half were telephones connected to independent telephone companies. The Bell System had concentrated its efforts on telephone service in metropolitan areas. This gave the independents an unparalleled opportunity in the rural areas. For example, starting with almost no farm telephone lines in 1893, rural service in

Opposite: **1927 mail order catalog offered choice between wall-mounted and desk set local battery, magneto ringing phones. (1927 Sears Roebuck catalog.)**

Indiana had grown to at least 20,000 lines by 1910. Many small independent companies were the outgrowth of the original farmers' cooperative lines, where the subscribers owned and operated the equipment. Some of these companies grew and were the foundation of local success stories. The owners of some of the independent companies profited handsomely when they eventually sold out to the Bell System.

One example of a little telephone company "that could" is the Northwest Indiana Telephone Company of Hebron, Porter County, Indiana. During the depression years, this company had a few run-down rural lines, using local battery, magneto ringing equipment. The company had deteriorated to the point where it no longer was capable of furnishing adequate service to the community it professed to serve. Offered for sale at a bargain price, there were no takers until a young engineer working for AT&T became interested and bought the company. Slowly, through the years, the system was upgraded, first to a common battery exchange and finally to fully automatic switching equipment. The enterprise and foresight displayed by the young engineer have paid off. Now the company is a thoroughly modern plant with a handsome headquarters building. In addition to telephone service the company furnishes cable television service to the community it serves. The cable TV fills a vital need, since Hebron is too far from Chicago to get quality reception over the air with conventional home antennas. The company is affiliated with GTE and offers every modern type of telephone service to a growing community.

In Alaska, where rural isolation was a way of life, the first phone service was provided by a single vehicular radiotelephone set bolted to the wall of the town hall or other easily accessible location. The first improvement in rural service came when the White Alice radio network was established in connection with the DEW line during the Cold War period. Now every village of over 25 persons can have modern telecommunication service. A satellite orbiting over the Pacific Ocean relays calls from small earth stations in the various locations. Also, fiber-optic technology and microwave networks are used to give the 49th state a communication system that is a far cry from Billy Mitchell's first Morse telegraph network.

In the lower 48 states, as recently as 1986, it was estimated that about 16 percent of the rural areas did not have access to modern telecommunications. Since 1986, the situation has changed rapidly, and by the time of the 1990 census the reports showed that only about 5 percent of the total households lacked basic phone service. Actually, most of these no-phone households were in the metropolitan areas. In the truly remote areas of the country, much progress has been made with radio links, fiber-optic cables and other advanced technologies. Aiding the process is a financing program known as Universal Service Fund, which allows telephone companies to get assistance if they can show that it would cost

15 percent more than the national average to furnish service to certain subscribers.

Typical of the trend toward universal coverage by telecommunication services is the program currently under test by MCI. Highly sophisticated handheld devices will allow communication by both voice and data signals at any geographic location. Persons with these new instruments will get a single phone number and calls to their home phones will be automatically forwarded to the portable unit. The new units are said to be superior to the current cellular service, and they will operate in tunnels or inside buildings. According to MCI, this service should be available by 1996.

Chapter 12

Collecting Telephones

TELEPHONE COLLECTING IS PROBABLY not our oldest hobby. It may have started as far back as 1877, but probably did not. Outside of metropolitan areas, many people had probably never even seen or used a telephone until the late nineteenth century. In those early days, telephone collecting would have been an almost impossible hobby. There just was not enough material available to make it interesting for the average collector. For one thing, the greatest percentage of telephones was owned by the Bell Telephone Company. They only rented phones—they didn't sell them. The situation had improved somewhat by the turn of the century. The original Bell patents had mostly expired and many competing manufacturers entered the field. Anyone could buy a phone and many did, but there was a catch; unless you used it on a non–Bell telephone line there was a problem. Not until as recently as 1969 did the Bell Company allow anything except their own instruments to be used in the Bell System. This, of course, meant manufacture by Western Electric. Now, Western Electric made some of the best telephones there were—and priced them accordingly.

Perhaps the greatest shot in the arm for the telephone collecting hobby came in the early years of the 20th century, when many rural telephone companies converted from the old local battery, crank type phones to the common battery system. Many small telephone companies ended up with warehouses full of the old phones, for which there was virtually no market at that time. Today's collectors can weep real tears when they hear stories of how whole truckloads of the old phones were hauled to the city dump just to get rid of them. Many rural phone subscribers owned their own instruments, dating from the earliest days when telephone companies were organized. These still show up at estate auctions and are eagerly snapped up by collectors. In fact, that is about the only source of the old phones. The telephone companies themselves have long ago disposed of whatever they had by one means or another. A few speculators may have bought some telephone company stocks of old phones. Those who did have probably reaped a handsome profit on their investment. Another source of the old phones might be from industrial plants, where they were used for intercom purposes long after the general conversion of the public telephone system to the common battery type.

The old local battery, magneto ringing telephones are mostly of the wooden box type, although in later years some were made in desk set type. The wooden box types are broken down into one- or two-boxers. The one-box type, as the name implies, had a single wooden box which contained the telephone apparatus and had a separate compartment for the batteries. Two-box types had an upper box which contained the bells and magneto generator along with other components. The lower box contained the batteries. The lower boxes were sometimes extra wide to accommodate the wet cell batteries that were originally used. In the final days of the local battery system, the standard battery was the No. 6 dry cell, which had a nominal voltage of 1.5. Most phones used two batteries, but there were some models using three. The No. 6 dry cells, which were once carried at any hardware store, are now just about extinct in store stocks. They can still be ordered from Radio Shack, and probably other sources. A less expensive alternative to power up an old phone for demonstration purposes can be had by securing one of the little plastic holders for two "D" size flashlight batteries. These flashlight cells will not have the long-term capacity of the No. 6 dry cells, but for intermittent use will energize the old phone for testing purposes. No attempt should be made to use lantern batteries in an old phone. The lantern batteries are rated at 6.0 volts, which is too high and might damage the phone. An easy way to tell if the old instrument is performing is to hold the receiver up to the transmitter. A loud howl should be heard. To perform this test, the line terminals should be connected together if the phone is not actually connected to a working line. This completes the circuit to the receiver which is usually in series with the line.

Two old phones that are complete and in working order make an excellent intercom, for example between rooms of a home, or between house and outbuildings. Unless modified for the purpose, an old phone will not work on the public telephone system. In the past, many of the old phones have been modified by installing new internal parts and rewiring the instrument for use on the public telephone system. Serious collectors think this procedure is sacrilegious, yet it is the owner's privilege. It doesn't seem to make much sense, however, to destroy a valuable antique that is worth several hundred dollars in its original state. Another thing that disturbs serious collectors is the outrageous prices being paid for phones that are incomplete, or in such poor condition that it would be difficult to restore them to working order. Part of the problem is that old phones have come into favor with decorators. Commercial dealers exist who specialize in supplying quaint items to professional interior decorators. These dealers can

Glass bells were issued for the 1976 Telephone Centennial. (Photo by Lewis Coe.)

afford to outbid anyone else at an auction, as they simply pass along the inflated price.

It seems that any telephone instrument in a wooden box starts the dollar signs dancing in the eyes of auction sale buyers. Persons buying old phones should check them carefully to make sure they are complete. Mouthpieces for transmitters are often missing. Receiver housings are often cracked. Cranks for generators are often bent or missing. Battery compartments can be badly damaged by corrosion if old batteries are left in place for years. Various parts are available but will be expensive, whether they are original old parts or new replicas.

Along with the telephone instruments themselves, there are other items connected with the industry that add to a collection. Porcelain signs with the Bell or other company logo are much in demand. Glass paperweights in the shape of a bell are prized. Several were issued in 1976, the centennial of the Bell company. Aside from the wooden box phones some very desirable collectibles exist in the form of imported "French" style phones. These are very distinctive in appearance and bring high prices. At a 1994 auction held in Cologne, Germany, an Ericsson telephone made in Sweden in 1890 fetched a price of $4,300. At the same auction an 1881 German wall phone brought a bid of $3,750. Collectors dealing in these kinds

Stromberg Carlson telephone has all the components of a wooden box phone in a modern desk set style telephone. (Photo by Lewis Coe.)

of telephones have to be very knowledgeable and above all have plenty of money!

More modest in price are some of the early Western Electric desk phones of 50 to 60 years ago. Some of the most expensive and desirable of the desk phones are the early Automatic Electric dial phones. Thirty or more years ago there were several metropolitan dealers who specialized in exotic phones for those willing to pay the price. The buyers of these phones had problems, as the general policy of the Bell System was to refuse connection to any telephone instruments not furnished by Bell. Now the problem is simpler—the phone company does not care what kind of telephone you use as long as it does not pose any threat to the service.

For a complete list of telephone manufacturers, see Appendix 5. This list is fairly complete, but there are probably some rare specimens that are not listed. For the most part, these old makers are no longer in business. Some of the phones made in the United States that are most likely to be encountered include:

Automatic Electric
Kellogg Switchboard & Supply Co.
Leich Electric

Circa 1900 Bell System candlestick phone. (Photo by Lewis Coe.)

Monarch
Stromberg Carlson
Western Electric

All of the above are of high quality and usually represent a good investment if the price is within reason. Of the U.S. manufacturers of telephone
equipment, one name that might confuse collectors is "Federal." Several
companies have used this name. Federal Telegraph Company of California
was primarily a manufacturer and operator of radio telegraph equipment.
It became an affiliate of ITT in 1928. Federal Telephone Company was

Western Electric extension ringer in oak case. (Photo by Lewis Coe.)

a New Jersey holding company. Federal Electric Company was a manufacturer of electrical devices used in industry. The Federal Telephone and
Telegraph Company of Buffalo, New York, is known as a manufacturer of
radio broadcast receiving sets. Not so well known is the company's involve-
ment with the telephone industry. The company was formed in a 1908
merger of Century Telephone Construction Company, Frontier Telephone
Company, and Inter-Ocean Telephone & Telegraph Company. Prior to
1920, Federal Telephone and Telegraph and the other companies joining
in the merger were active in the telephone market, both in operating exchanges and the manufacturing of apparatus. After 1920, the company concentrated on the radio receiver manufacturing part of its business, taking
advantage of the boom in public broadcasting that started at that time.

   Determining a reasonable price is the number one problem for the collector. About the only way one can acquire a sense of value is to attend auctions and keep track of the prices realized for the various items. At some
auctions there will be a bidder who refuses to concede defeat and will keep
on bidding until the price exceeds any reasonable estimate of value. At such
an auction, just pack up and leave, as there is no way you can win. At other
times, there may not be any other interested buyers, and you can get some

real bargains. Of course, you have to do your homework and be able to recognize a real value when you see it. Curiously, some of the old wooden box phones are not marked with any maker's name whatsoever. Sears Roebuck explained it this way in their 1908 catalog:

> Our name does not appear on our telephones in any way. We find that occasionally customers who would like to take advantage of the low prices and high quality of our telephones, hesitate to do so because of the antagonism of local companies or other interested parties and for this reason we do not put any nameplate or identifying mark of any kind on our telephones. You can send us your order for telephones with perfect assurance that the transaction is in every way confidential, and that no marks will appear on the telephones inside or outside to show where you bought them.

Most telephones sold to the public now are actually of foreign manufacture, and while some of them are adequate for use they have little collectible value at present. Probably some of the most affordable phones for the collector of average means, assuming that a lot of us cannot shell out $300 to $500 for a wooden box phone, are the "modern-looking" phones made 60 years ago. These include the desk set versions of the local battery, magneto ringing phones by Stromberg Carlson and others. The Western Electric E1A and 202 desk set phones from the late 1920s have become very popular. Unfortunately, the popularity has been accompanied by a price rise, so that mint specimens may be priced over $200. With any phone, whether wooden box or the more modern sets, the key consideration is condition. Phones that are dirty, or missing parts or cords, should be considered mostly for parts or extensive restoration and priced accordingly.

In the last years before deregulation the Bell System seemed to become very casual about accounting for company owned phones. Remodeling of buildings, changing tenants and other causes seemed to leave a lot of phones as orphans that nobody wanted. This accounts for many of the good Western Electric sets that show up at auctions and flea markets. So, even if the phone says "property of AT&T," do not worry—it is very unlikely that anyone is going to dispute ownership of your new collectible. Telephone advertising signs are now in great demand, everything from the tiny signs that warn about digging due to underground cables to the larger signs marking pay telephones and business offices. If it is blue and white with the familiar Bell logo it probably is a good investment and highly collectible.

Telephone collectors have their own organizations that welcome membership from any interested person. Actually, collectors of telephones come from all walks of life. The Antique Telephone Collectors Association has its headquarters in Abilene, Kansas. One of its yearly shows is held there, and members can also enjoy visiting the Museum of Independent

One of the last of the good ones, a "design line" set made by Western Electric. (Photo by Lewis Coe.)

Telephony as well as the Eisenhower Library, all in close proximity. Telephone Collectors International also holds regular meetings in different parts of the country. Both organizations publish newsletters and other information for their members. These collecting groups are unanimous in feeling that their activities help preserve many historic artifacts that might otherwise be lost or destroyed. In the past, much historic telephone equipment has been simply scrapped to make way for new and more modern equipment. Collectors and a few company museums are about the only hope for preserving these items for future students. The Smithsonian Institution in Washington, D.C., is, of course, a large repository of historic telephone equipment. Unfortunately, the Smithsonian collections are so large that only a fraction of them can be publicly displayed. Even so, the Smithsonian is a priceless resource, and its collections are always available to serious students who need primary sources.

Although the "French" style handsets that are standard today were known for many years previously, they were not adopted by the Bell System until the late 1920s. There were a couple of important reasons for this. First, the transmitter output varied widely according to the way the instrument was held. Second, there was a tendency for acoustic feedback between the transmitter and receiver, the phenomenon known as "singing" or "howling." Subscribers were using the telephone for communication over ever longer circuits and it was thought that the handsets would not deliver adequate performance. In time, improved transmitter buttons came along to solve the first problem. Next, the material of the handle itself was examined to find a material that would be a poor conductor of sound waves. Reduction in "singing" was also obtained by the anti-sidetone circuits that became standard in all phones. Sidetone is the reproduction of the subscriber's voice in his own receiver. If the sidetone is too loud the user tends to speak more softly, resulting in hearing problems at the other end of the line. Sidetone that is too weak tends to make the user talk too loud, with resulting distortion. Sidetone reduction is obtained by a balanced bridge arrangement, usually involving windings on the induction coil. A portion of the output of the local transmitter is balanced out at the local receiver. At the same time, the full output of the transmitter is sent to the line and the distant receiver. At first sidetone reduction circuits were used only on the operator's positions at switchboards. The extra expense and complication of the talking circuit were thought to be justified by more efficient speech circuits for the operator. Eventually, it was found that anti-sidetone circuitry would be worthwhile on subscribers' sets and ways were found to reduce the complexity and cost of the equipment. Although it became standard on common battery subscribers' sets, the anti-sidetone feature was never used to any extent on local battery sets in rural use. Here the subscriber set had to work through long loops of varied length. Users learned to hold the receiver away from their ear slightly if the sidetone was too loud.

The final studies involved the physical measurements of the handset. It was necessary to come up with dimensions that would be optimum for the average user. This study of physical dimensions included measurements of 4,000 adults in 1919. After the results of the measurements had been analyzed a standard ear to mouthpiece dimension was adopted. The final dimension was said to be close to optimum for all but 3 percent of the adult users.

The transmitter button problem was more complex in nature. The standard "solid back" transmitter delivered good performance in its normal vertical position on a desk stand, but suffered decreased performance in other positions. The solution came with the "barrier button" transmitter devised in 1921. This transmitter was capable of good performance, except when turned face down, a position that would not normally be used. The final result was the E1A handset and the A1 handset cradle introduced in 1927. Even after the handset was introduced, many desk stand sets remained in use. They were falling out of style however, and none were manufactured after 1940. The handset is now the universal telephone instrument.

The only variation currently in use is the headsets with a boom microphone used by telephone operators and others who need both hands free.

The handset type of instrument was once referred to as a "French" phone. There was a good reason for this. In 1878, R. G. Brown was head operator of the Gold and Stock Exchange in New York. He designed a handset and received a patent in 1879. Brown eventually went to France, and in the course of his work as electrical engineer for La Société Générale in Paris, introduced the French to his handset. The instrument was widely used in Europe, where the telephone officials did not have the same reservations about using it that prevailed in America. Most of these early handsets used transmitters based on the Edison patent. The cumbersome Blake transmitter used by the Bell System for many years was obviously not suited to the handset type of instrument. Photos do exist of operators wearing a six-pound Blake transmitter on a complicated shoulder support—pity the poor operator who had to wear one of these monstrosities!

Big users of telephone communication were the nation's railroads. Introduced to the miracle of instantaneous communication by the Morse telegraph in 1851, the railroads kept a close eye on the development of telephone communication starting with Bell's 1876 patent. By 1882, some telephone dispatching systems had been placed in service and the trend continued. By the time of World War II, about half of the track miles in the country had been switched to telephone dispatching. Even though the telephone was used for train dispatching, the Morse telegraph remained an important part of railroad communications until it was finally phased out in the 1950s.

The telephone possibly increased the ease of communication between the dispatcher and the individual station operators. However, in the case of formal train orders, the speed was limited to how fast the receiving operator could write. Also, the receiving operator was required to repeat the order back to the dispatcher word for word before the order was marked complete. For these reasons there was little gain in speed of operation by using the telephone. The real reason the telephone was so widely adopted seems to be that it simplified the training of railroad operators. It was easier to teach a man the railroad procedures than it was to teach him to telegraph, and this gave the railroads a wider choice in filling positions. *Scientific American*, in its issue of May 14, 1898, commented on the railroad use of telephones:

> The Pan Handle Railway is putting in telephones at points where improvements are in progress, and in this way furnishing a means for facilitating the movement of trains without the expense of telegraph operators, which has been the custom heretofore. This is only one of the many cases in which the telephone is crowding out the telegraph, and we may expect many more such.

Kellogg candlestick telephone used on the long-distance lines of the Postal Telegraph company. Pictured is the switchboard of a Mackay Radio station in 1933. (Photo by Lewis Coe.)

Today, any telephone equipment used by the railroads is sought after by collectors. The basic telephone set used at railroad depots was the candlestick type phone mounted on a swinging scissor arm. Included with this equipment was a foot switch to activate the talking circuit. There was also a small wooden box containing the induction coil and other components of the talking circuit. The receiver was the headband type so the operator had both hands free to write. Railroad dispatching circuits were a long party line with many stations connected. The dispatcher had a signaling device called a selector. This enabled him to call any station on the line individually, or any combination of stations. The individual stations did not need any calling equipment because the dispatcher wore his headset constantly while on duty and thus heard immediately any station that called in.

Trains were sometimes equipped with portable phones to use in an emergency. These were supplied with jointed bamboo poles equipped with wires and metal clips at the top. Using these the train crew could tap the overhead wires without having to climb a pole. There were often telephone boxes located at long track sidings and other places where trains might have

Opposite: **Typical operating position in the bay window of a railroad station showing candlestick phone used on dispatcher's wire. (Photo by Lewis Coe.)**

NEW YORK, N.Y.
SEP 11
7 30 PM
1905

The Henry Co. Telephone Co.,
Leatherwood, Va.

If not delivered in 5 Days return to

ERICSSON TELEPHONE CO.,
296 Broadway, NEW YORK CITY.

The EE-8 field telephone was the workhorse phone of the U.S. army during World War II. (Photo by Lewis Coe.)

to wait for orders. Using these trackside phones the train crews could communicate with the nearest operator. Practically all of these railroad telephones used local battery circuits, and all except the main dispatchers' lines used magneto ringing generators. The closing of hundreds of railroad stations released much of the railroad telephone equipment for collectors. Especially prized are the swinging scissor arm candlestick phones. These should not be considered complete unless they include the headset, foot switch, and a small wooden box containing the induction coil and other items associated with the talking circuit.

Opposite: **Postal cover featuring telephone company logo in 1905.**

Typical stamps once issued by telephone companies to pay for written messages sent over telephone lines. (Photo by Lewis Coe.)

Railroad telephone lines paralleling the Hudson River were used in a unique way in the days before radio. College boat races were held on the Hudson, and there was much public interest in these events. Reporters with portable telephones perched on the river bank and tapped into the convenient railroad wire that was temporarily diverted for this use. In this way, progress of the race was reported at different points along the river by a process which anticipated modern live coverage by radio and television.

When radio had progressed to the point where it could be considered for operation aboard moving railroad trains, it was thought that the new medium might in some way end the possibility of train collisions. Much progress has been made along these lines. Yet, even with the most modern signal equipment, two way radio, and automatic trackside reporting devices, accidents happen that are no different than those that occurred 100 years earlier. In 1991, two Norfolk & Southern freight trains were involved in a head-on collision near Knox, Indiana. The trains had somehow been switched to opposite directions of travel on a single-track line. The result, as the oldtimers used to call it, was a "cornfield meet." The trains met on an absolutely straight stretch of track, during daylight, in clear weather. All of the most modern electronic devices, including instantaneous communication with the dispatcher, could not avoid this tragic accident which killed one man and critically injured another, not to mention the total loss of two locomotives and a large amount of rolling stock. When experienced

Opposite: "Fullerphone" of World Wars I and II was not a telephone, but was intended to send Morse code signals over wire lines. (Photo by Lewis Coe.)

railroad men commented on the accident, they shrugged their shoulders and said, "somebody must have been asleep."

Starting around the turn of the century, a large user of telephones was the U.S. Forest Service. Most of these phones were of the local battery, magneto ringing type, the same used on typical farm lines for many years. The phones of the forest service were often worked on one-wire, grounded circuits. These worked just as well as full metallic circuits in the remote areas where there was not much possibility of cross talk or earth current interference. Aside from lines built by the army, the forest service lines were often the only communication service of any kind in some of the western areas. The prime purpose of these phones was to link the fire lookout stations so that forest fires could promptly be located and reported. Long before the days of broadcasting and two-way radio sets, the telephones in the ranger stations made life a little less lonely for the rangers and fire lookouts who might not see another human being for weeks at a time.

U.S. postage stamps commemorate many aspects of telephony and are of interest to telephone collectors. They include Alexander Graham Bell, of ten cents denomination, issued in 1940; Telephone Centennial, of 13 cents denomination, issued in 1976; Progress in Electronics (Lee De Forest), of 11 cents denomination, issued in 1972; Thomas Edison, of three cents denomination, issued in 1947; Atlantic Cable Centennial, of four cents denomination, issued in 1958; Communications for Peace, of four cents denomination, issued in 1960; International Telecommunications Union, of 11 cents denomination, issued in 1965. Of these, the Bell stamp is the most expensive. The reason for this is that when it was issued the Bell Telephone Company bought large quantities of the stamp to use on their parcel post mailings, making mint specimens of the stamp scarce today.

One of the classic military field telephones is a nice addition to any telephone collection. Telephones of World War I and earlier are pretty hard to find today. One that is readily available is the EE8, introduced after World War I, and heavily used in World War II and in the postwar years. Telephones in the EE8 series are basically local battery, magneto calling and ringing telephones, very similar in operation to any of the old wooden box phones. The EE8 has a feature not found on the old wooden box phones, in that it can also be used on a common battery system. A hook switch is provided and when switched in to the circuit it functions just like a conventional common battery phone. However, even if the phone is being used on a common battery line, the talking power is provided by the local battery, consisting of two "D" size flashlight batteries. The first of the series, the EE8, was built on an aluminum chassis. Later models, designated EE8A and EE8B, used a steel chassis but were identical to the original model except in minor details. Either canvas or leather carrying cases were issued.

HELLO, DEARIE

Typical humorous postcards featuring the telephone.

Large quantities of these phones were sold as surplus after World War II, some brand new in the original military packaging. They have been widely used ever since by civilians needing telephone communication — between buildings, on rifle ranges, and on construction jobs.

Not a telephone, the "Fullerphone" of World Wars I and II is nevertheless an appropriate addition to a telephone collection. Fullerphones were designed to eliminate eavesdropping by enemy operators on conventional buzzer telegraph systems. The Fullerphone does not generate any ground current signal that can be detected by inductive pickup devices. They are an interesting example of 1917 design methods and construction that survived until after World War II. Used by the British and Canadian armed forces, large quantities were sold as surplus by the Canadian army, and many have found their way to the United States. The chassis of these instruments is nicely crafted in sheet metal, and includes a buzzer-chopper module and a heavy duty telegraph key. The carrying case is rather crudely made of ⅜″ plywood painted in olive drab color. The complete Fullerphone set includes the basic chassis, telegraph key and a pair of headphones.

Wiring diagrams and instructions are inscribed on metal plates attached to the inside of the box. These outfits were powered by two small 1.5-volt batteries, for which there is no source today. However, they will work just fine on "D" flashlight cells, which can be mounted in the plastic battery holders sold by Radio Shack. When attempting to test a Fullerphone, be sure to short-circuit the line terminals, otherwise no tone will be heard in the headset when the key is operated.

Aside from postage stamps, other paper collectibles might include sheet music with a telephone theme. Examples are "Hello Central, Give Me Heaven," and "All Alone by the Telephone."

The telegraph companies issued large numbers of stamps. These were used to pay for telegrams in lieu of cash. The telephone companies issued stamps too, but here the application was limited. When the telephone was new, not everyone had one. Yet it was possible to send a message to a distant point by telephone. The message was phoned to a point near the addressee where it was written out and delivered much as a telegram would be. In some cases, the addressee might be summoned to the telephone office where he could converse directly with the other party. The telephone stamps were used as payment for such services. Around the turn of the century, when the telephone was still a comparative novelty to many people, humorous postcards with a telephone motif were popular, and they can still be found at paper collectible sales.

For many years, the telephone was like the Model T Ford automobile. You could have any color you wanted as long as it was black. Then the telephone company introduced colored telephones. These could be had at an extra charge. Otherwise, the basic black was the minimum cost instrument. One subscriber was surprised to learn that his "black" telephone was actually a colored model that had been repainted! There is an almost unlimited variety of specialized telephone instruments that the collector may encounter. Among these are the explosion proof mine telephones. These are normally mounted in heavy cast iron cases and are sealed so that explosive gases cannot reach the contact points and cause an explosion. Outdoor telephone sets are also mounted in heavy metal cases but do not meet the criteria for "explosion-proof" service. Telephones used on navy ships are of extremely rugged construction to withstand hard use and battle conditions. Large passenger ships once carried telephone systems that were the equivalent of those found in a small city. These shipboard systems could be connected by a cable to the shore telephone system when the ship was in port. Oddly enough, some of the latest merchant ships, carrying every electronic communication device known, still have the traditional voice tubes installed for communication between the bridge and engine room.

Chapter 13

Hackers and Phreaks

IN A 1915 ADVERTISEMENT by the American Telephone and Telegraph Company appearing in the *National Geographic*, the question was posed as to what would happen if all telephone service suddenly ceased. The accompanying illustration depicted a mighty hand with a pair of pliers cutting all the wires in the country with one clip. The ad was titled "If a Giant Cut the Wires." The ad went on to explain, in the usual pious attitude assumed by the telephone company in talking down to its customers, that this was not going to happen. They were right, of course, because the original phone system was a physical system, that is, all connections were made by actual copper conductors. Outside of an occasional local outage caused by weather, or manmade accidents, there was no possibility that the entire country could be affected.

What was true in 1915 is not necessarily true in the 1990s. The telephone system now is almost completely electronic and controlled by computers. The old reliable plug and jack switchboards that needed a direct lightning hit, fire or earthquake to stop functioning, no longer exist to any extent. Electronic switching centers now do the work of the old switchboards, and as long as they are working well they do the work far better than it was ever done by the "number please" operators or the electromechanical automatic switchers. All computer owners, however, know that computers sometimes have a mind of their own. The computers used to control electronic switchers are no different.

The stage was set, and it finally happened: the AT&T crash of January 15, 1990. A software problem instantly disabled phone switching equipment in many cities, including Atlanta, St. Louis and Detroit. It was suggested that computer hackers might have somehow gotten into the system and caused the crash. This was possible, but highly unlikely, and finally the software company that supplied the telephone company admitted that it had found a "glitch" in the software used in the electronic switchers.

Then, in 1991, there were further software problems involving the switchers in Washington, D.C., Pittsburgh, Los Angeles and San Francisco.

This crash affected the service of about twelve million people. In September 1991, a spectacular crash shut down the service to all three of the New York City airports: Kennedy, La Guardia, and Newark. This was not caused by computer failure, however; instead the electrical power at the switching stations failed and the backup power systems did not function. The power failure alarms were not heard by the three technicians supposed to be watching them. These employees were on another floor of the building, attending a training class at the time — a training class devoted to power failure alarms!

After the first crash, AT&T's CEO, Bob Allen, issued a statement:

> AT&T had a major service disruption last Monday. We didn't live up to our own standards of quality, and we didn't live up to yours. It's as simple as that. And that's not acceptable to us. Or to you.... We understand how much people have come to depend on AT&T service, so our AT&T Bell Laboratories scientists and our network engineers are doing everything possible to guard against a recurrence. We know there's no way to make up for the inconvenience this problem may have caused you.

As soon as the telephone company grew large enough to become a visible corporate identity, it became the target of every kind of fraud that the larcenous public could think up. At first, these fraudulent capers were technologically simple, such as attacking pay phones with crow bars and screwdrivers. Sometimes the whole phone was just carted away to be opened at leisure. In the process, designers kept improving the security of the coin phone until it was as nearly theft-proof as any device could be and still be accessible enough to perform its intended function. Even the handset cords had to be armored to discourage thieves, who used to snip the cords and steal the handsets with impunity. Handset cord cutting was probably done partly out of the mindless vandalism that is often seen in public facilities of any kind. Otherwise, many handsets were probably stolen by people seeking an extra extension phone for their home, or by young experimenters who wanted them for some electronic project. Handset theft was probably never considered a very serious crime by those who did it — after all, what was a handset to a wealthy corporation like AT&T? Probably none of the guilty parties ever stopped to consider the predicament of the poor fellow who wanted to make an emergency call from a pay phone, only to discover that the handset was missing. Pay phones seemed to present a particular challenge to the light-fingered community — the thought of that box full of money was just too tempting.

Regular hangers-on around railroad stations, airports, and other public places where there were numbers of pay phones could often be observed routinely checking all the coin return slots for coins that the patrons might have forgotten to retrieve. This, of course, was legal, but would not yield more than the price of an occasional cup of coffee. A more profitable, and strictly illegal, activity was practiced by the persons known as "stuffers." These miscreants made a practice of stuffing the coin return slots of pay telephones with tissue paper. Returning later, they could collect any coins that had been intended as a refund for legitimate users of the phones. Some college boys devised a way to get free phone calls at a group of coin phones that were mounted side by side. They were smart enough to figure out that the gong that signalled the dropping of coins was purely acoustic in operation. If they were going to make their call on phone No. 1, they held the handset near the phone box of No. 2 phone and dropped the coins in it. The operator heard the normal sounds of the coins dropping and completed the connection. Now, all these petty crooks had to do was hang up the No. 2 phone, and the coins were automatically returned to them.

Pay telephones have recently come under scrutiny for another reason. It is alleged that many of these phones are now the favorite means of communication for drug dealers and other unsavory characters. The city of Chicago recently has taken steps to limit the number of public pay phones in neighborhoods where illegal activities are common. This move has been opposed by those who say that in poorer neighborhoods many families cannot afford their own phone, and thus depend on the public telephone when they have to make calls.

Residential subscribers had their own forms of larceny. Unauthorized extension phones and ringers were the most usual methods of "screwing the phone company." Before divestiture, the telephone company had very strict rules about unauthorized equipment. If you wanted an extension phone, you called the company and they came out and installed it and you paid so much a month for each extension. The same applied to extra ringers, typically installed on the outside of the home. Extension phones and ringers were a fairly safe form of larceny unless the phone company decided to check your line. Wire chiefs could take readings that indicated the number of ringers connected to the line. The safest method of using extension phones was to disconnect the ringers so that the wire chiefs got the normal reading for the equipment that you were actually paying for. Telephone servicemen were notorious snoops when they visited a home. They were trained to look carefully for unauthorized extensions, non-standard wiring, or anything else that indicated the subscriber was trying to get away with something. In today's telephone climate, the company does not seem to care what you do. As long as you pay your monthly bill and do not connect any dangerous voltages to the lines you will not be bothered.

As telephone technology got more complex, so did the methods of stealing. The famous "blue boxes" of 30 years ago, before the breakup of the Bell System, involved circuitry that would send certain tone signals over the line. These signals were those used by the telephone company to route long-distance calls. The phone phreaks, having discovered this, could bypass regular switchboards and talk long distance for free. The phreaks would often route these calls initially to "information" in the distant city. Then they would seize control of the line with their blue box and call anywhere they pleased. With improved recording equipment the phone company soon discovered calls to "information" that might last a half hour or more, not a normal thing in ordinary telephone usage. The telephone company finally had to admit the existence of their "AMA" (automatic machine accounting). With this machine, even local calls were automatically recorded. The company had denied existence of the machine, as they realized it would create a flood of paperwork initiated by police seeking to establish evidence, or by customers who wanted to complain about their bills.

The first blue boxes were built using vacuum tubes that required rather heavy, bulky batteries to function. When transistors became available, the blue box became highly portable and could be used on a public phone or any other handy location. Illegal calls placed from public pay telephones have always been the hardest to detect. However, improved monitoring enabled the phone company to catch most of the illegal calls. If they couldn't trace the originating location they could tell where the call was going, and often the people at the receiving end would tell all. Blue boxes gradually disappeared when electronic switching centers came into use. The old tone signals had no effect on the new switchers.

Along with the blue box came the "red boxes." Red boxes were comparatively simple, but they enabled two cooperating parties to talk for free. They worked on the principle that the circuit between two telephones is established by the ringing signal. The calling party gave a one-ring signal to the distant party and then hung up. This notified the called party to get his red box ready. Then when the phone rang again, he punched a button which, in effect, notified the calling office to discontinue the ringing signal. The military EE8 field telephone was often used in lieu of building a "red box." These EE8 phones had the necessary circuitry already built in. Since the circuit was still complete, the two parties could then converse to their hearts' content. Here again, the only giveaway was that the phone company records showed that the calling party had first given the one-ring signal, and then allowed the phone to keep ringing without an answer for extended periods.

The "one-ring" signal has long been used by travelers to call home and report that everything is fine. A one-ring signal that is expected by the called party can convey the essential message without any toll charges. It has also often been used by amateur radio operators to signal another operator with whom they have such an arrangement that he should turn on his radio and converse on a prearranged frequency. Of course, such use of the phone lines for signalling is strictly illegal, yet the phone company is almost powerless to prevent it. Oddly enough, most of the people that pull these tricks can well afford to pay for phone services. It seems that getting something for nothing is irresistible to many people. Also folks who otherwise would not steal an apple are perfectly at ease with their consciences when they steal from a big corporation like AT&T!

As the phone companies installed better and more sophisticated monitoring equipment they were able to detect any unauthorized tone frequencies such as those sent out by the blue boxes. This also enabled the companies to detect unauthorized use of Touch Tone service. When they detected that a subscriber was using Touch Tone without paying for the service they would call him and give him the choice of paying or having the tone service discontinued. Now, nobody seems to care. Most subscriber phones are now arranged for either tone or pulse, and the system does not care which method of dialing is used. It is rather remarkable that the phone company has been able to design a dialing system that will accept either tone or pulse. This accommodates the many old rotary dial phones still in use. Tone signalling is now the preferred method. It is the only way that many telephone services can be accessed.

More innocent and harmless was the discovery that a Touch Tone pad could be used to make calls from an older dial phone that did not have push buttons. Most of the early hacking was not really intended to steal anything of value, even though it was technically defrauding the telephone company.

Now hacking has taken on an ugly image, as it is being used to steal valuable information from the telephone company and other large corporations. Some hackers will go to any lengths to get the information they need. Individuals known as "dumpster divers" make a practice of systematically searching dumpsters near telephone offices and large corporate offices. They hope to find carelessly discarded documents that will contain confidential information. An elemental form of stealing is just looking over someone's shoulder while he punches in his phone ID code. Large numbers of these ID codes are stolen and used to make free calls at the expense of the legitimate owner of the number. With the popularity of cellular phones, a regular cottage industry has evolved in stealing user ID codes and selling them to persons who can then use a cellular phone without paying the charges. In one method of stealing cellular codes, hackers station themselves at the exit of a busy metropolitan automobile tunnel. As each vehicle that has a cellular phone in service comes out, the phones have to reestablish their ID code with the base. The hacker with sophisticated monitoring equipment copies these codes, which are readily sold and used to clone cellular phones. Many of these "cloned" phones are used by drug dealers and other criminals who understandably do not want a phone that can be traced to them.

Phone phreaks and hackers were originally just young people who delighted in circumventing the "system" and did not fit the usual classification of criminals. Typically they were young, extremely brilliant persons who seemed determined to show that they could master any technology that the telephone company could dish out.

The telephone companies have become increasingly aware of the fraud problem, and are using very sophisticated equipment to detect anything unusual. They have software that will make systematic searches for unusual calling patterns such as many calls to certain 800 numbers, or to foreign cities. Sprint says that as many as 70 percent of its illegal calls originate in New York City. Sprint has also stepped up monitoring of Los Angeles calls. All of these illegal calls are charged to someone's phone number and unless some kind of a deal is worked out, that subscriber is liable for the charges. The telephone companies do realize that many of their subscribers are innocent victims. Sprint and AT&T will cover losses over $25,000; MCI says it will cover 30 percent of the first loss. These figures offer small consolation to the subscriber for whom a phone bill of over $100 would be catastrophic.

One form of telephone theft that still goes on involves misuse of PBX (private branch exchange) systems operated by business offices. Many of these systems can be accessed by anyone having the proper password. Hackers obtain the passwords and sometimes access the PBX switching equipment by dialing an 800 number, which is a free call from anywhere in the country. Once in, the hacker can then call anywhere in the world, and the call is charged to the owner of the PBX system. How do hackers get the passwords? Sometimes by over-the-shoulder monitoring of a legitimate employee of the company in question, sometimes by the activities of the "dumpster divers," and sometimes by programming their own computers to try thousands of number combinations until they hit one that works. Fraud of this kind has cost U.S. companies as much as $1.25 million dollars in a typical year. Telephone company suggestions to PBX owners include: longer and more complicated passwords to make access more difficult; blocking the PBX from making international calls if such ability is not needed on a regular basis; shutting off remote access to PBXs during non-business hours. In general, courts have ruled that owners of the PBXs are responsible for the fraudulent calls, but no set policy prevails. For example, the Christian Broadcasting Network was not required to pay for $40,000 worth of fraudulent calls charged to its PBX in 1987.

Computer hackers are a little more sinister than the phone phreaks. They can do a great deal of harm by getting into computer systems and manipulating transactions for their own benefit. They can obtain information that is supposed to be confidential. There is, however, a widespread misconception on the part of the public as to what a computer can do. A computer by itself cannot interconnect with anything. It must be connected to a working telephone circuit. To connect with another computer, a number must be dialed. In metropolitan areas, where thousands of numbers can be called without toll charges, a hacker can have a field day. To call distant computers where the telephone call is a toll call can soon pile up astronomical phone bills. The only way to beat the toll charges is to use radio to link the computers. This involves having an amateur radio license. Amateurs regularly send messages throughout the country by packet radio links using legal amateur operations. For the most part, amateur radio links are not used by criminally minded hackers, just by people who enjoy mastering the technology involved.

The privacy of a telephone conversation, or lack of it, has been a subject of discussion since the telephone came into general use. Party lines, of course, were never private, but how about the so-called "private lines"? The answer is, they are not very private. Wiretapping has been practiced since the earliest days of the telephone. Many telephone users have fancied that their phone was tapped because they heard clicks or other strange noises. A normal tap is done in such a manner that it gives no trace of its existence. Wiretapping by the police is subject to strict regulations and must be authorized by a court order if the evidence is to be useful in court. There are private investigators however, who specialize in wiretaps and often do it surreptitiously without the knowledge of the police or the phone company. Often these investigators are former telephone employees or persons otherwise knowledgeable in the cable routes and wiring practices of the telephone company. In this way, they can tap a specific line at any location where they can gain access to the terminal strips, for example, the basement of a building, or in a manhole. This kind of tap may be discovered by a telephone employee in the course of routine work, but not usually as the result of a search for taps. Such professional wiretaps are expensive — they are usually used to acquire confidential business information or as a part of investigations involving marital problems.

There are other ways of tapping a phone without actually connecting to the circuit involved. One clever gadget is a tiny FM radio transmitter. It is built to look like the standard transmitter button of a telephone and interchanges with the regular unit. Of course, it requires that someone have access to the phone involved long enough to unscrew the normal transmitter button and insert the FM transmitter. These units are powered by the normal line current of the telephone and are activated whenever the phone is taken off the hook. The range of the transmitter is several hundred feet, enabling someone in a parked car outside the building to monitor the conversations. It is also possible to wire a phone so that the transmitter is always in the circuit. This allows monitoring of conversations in the room even when the phone is on the hook. Apparently it has been a common practice in some totalitarian countries to have all subscriber phones wired in this manner to catch persons who might say something against the regime.

The least private of all phones are those that use some form of radio transmission. This includes the popular cellular and cordless phones. Anything said over these phones is literally broadcast to anyone who wants to listen in. It is illegal to listen to these radio conversations, especially if the listener makes any use of the information heard. That does not stop the listening, and it is difficult to enforce the no listening regulations. Telephone employees are sometimes suspected of eavesdropping on conversations. Of course, the telephone technicians and operators have occasion to tap into various circuits in the performance of their duties, and the courts have held that they are legally permitted to do this. It is unlikely that many telephone employees ever listen to conversations other than to check that a circuit is operating normally. The best proof of this comes from telephone people themselves. They will tell you that other people's phone conversations are incredibly boring to listen to for any length of time.

Early on in its history, the telephone was recognized as an invader of personal privacy. In fact, the gradual invasion of personal privacy is a price we are paying for the electronic age. A vast database exists and it is virtually impossible for an individual to avoid being a part of it if he wishes to lead a normal life. You cannot rent a house, use electricity, drive a car, subscribe to newspapers and magazines, own property, receive mail, and of course not have a telephone without your life being on record somewhere. Aside from junk mail, the most common annoyance is telemarketing phone calls. They usually start out by mentioning the subscriber by name. This guarantees them a few minutes of the answering party's time, because no one wants to hang up on a worthwhile call. Otherwise, once you have determined that the caller is trying to sell something, just hang up. Remember, the person calling is running through hundreds of numbers; he would rather you just hang up than waste his time if you have no intention of buying anything. It is hard to believe that there are people whose lives are so dull that they are just sitting by the telephone waiting for a call that will tell them about something they cannot live without. Yet the telemarketers stay in business, and they would not do so if they were not finding a high percentage of suckers. Getting an unlisted number may help, but it will not eliminate the annoyance. Some telemarketers use machines that are computer controlled to just dial numbers in numerical order. In a relatively short time these machines can dial every working number in a good-sized town.

Telemarketing calls are surely annoying to most telephone users, but unfortunately they are not yet illegal. In some jurisdictions it is illegal to make these calls after certain hours, such as 8:30 P.M., local time. Even this does not help the worker on a midnight shift who may be trying to get a little sleep in the early evening hours. A much more insidious, and still legal, aspect of telephone service is the proliferation of "900" numbers. Calling a 900 number inflicts a perfectly legal charge on the caller's telephone bill.

Services offered are seldom worth anything—it is just a racket, and has become a cottage industry for a certain caliber of business entrepreneurs. Little investment is required, and the telephone company collects the money for you. Fortunately for parents whose children may have run up astronomical phone bills calling 900 numbers, the telephone company can lock out your phone so it will not have access to the 900 numbers. The next time your television screen invites you to make a call to a 900 number just ignore it—all it is after is your money. On the other hand, "800" numbers are a useful service and cost nothing to call. They save you money when there is occasion to call the company or person having this service.

A much greater abuse, one that is strictly illegal, is the calls made to harass or threaten the person answering the telephone. Such calls seem to flourish in metropolitan areas. There are thousands of numbers for creeps to call, and the very complexity of a big city gives them a certain anonymity. In the past it was very hard to catch and prosecute the perpetrators of these illegal calls. Now improved telephone technology has made it a little easier. Answering machines do serve to isolate the subscriber, and other services are now available in certain areas. In New York, where the problem is understandably severe, the telephone company is offering a "call trace" service. This service automatically traces the most recent call and logs the information with the phone company. In New York, the call trace information is not revealed to the subscriber unless there is also a police complaint and investigation of the circumstances. Caller ID, now available in many areas, identifies the calling number automatically. This is an extra charge on the telephone bill, and the subscriber must also purchase his own unit to display the information. For the person who is really being harassed by unwanted calls, one security expert advises getting a new line and leaving an answering machine on the old line. In this way, the creepy caller may soon decide he can never reach his intended victim and give up. It becomes more difficult to catch offenders who call from pay phones and cellular phones, or from points outside the local area. The best defense against any bad phone call is still just to hang up—hopefully not on your mother-in-law or some good-hearted person who is trying to do you a favor!

Chapter 14

Over the Waves

JUST AS THE TELEPHONE followed the telegraph, it was inevitable that thoughts would soon turn to transmitting the voice through the air without wires. The first attempts involved simple induction systems which actually worked, but were too limited in range to be practical. The first wireless, or radio, transmitters used the discharge of high voltage across spark gaps to create hertzian waves. For a long time, this was the only known method of communicating without wires. This worked fairly well for the dot and dash transmission of messages by Morse code. It was definitely not the answer for speech transmission. In the transmission of speech a process called modulation is used. Modulation imparts the speech to the basic carrier of the radio frequency energy. Attempts were actually made to modulate the spark transmitters with voice. This was not satisfactory, due to the character of the spark transmission of hertzian waves. Spark transmitters generated what was called a damped wave, that was very irregular in form. What was needed was an undamped wave of regular wave form that could be modulated by the speech transmission.

The first successful speech transmitters did not come along until the carbon arc method of generating radio waves was discovered. Arc transmitters employed carbon electrodes operating in a magnetic field with hydrogen present. The wave they generated was a constant undamped wave not unlike the vacuum tube transmitters that came later. While the arc was widely used for telegraphy, it was not too practical for telephony, even though the carrier wave was suitable. The problem was that there were only a few methods available for speech modulation of the arc. Typically the method used was to connect a carbon microphone directly in the antenna lead of the transmitter. The varying resistance of the carbon microphone caused changes in the antenna current corresponding to the speech pattern. This worked fairly well on low power transmitters, but was not suitable for high power. All sorts of heavy duty carbon microphones were devised, some even water cooled to prevent overheating. At best these were makeshift systems and very limited in power handling capability.

Another early method of generating radio waves was the high frequency alternator as developed by Alexanderson and Fessenden. These generators produced an undamped wave suitable for telephony. The problem of how to apply speech modulation was subject to the same kind of limitations that applied to the arc. The real breakthrough in radio telephony came when De Forest invented the vacuum tube. As research continued, the original audion was scaled up to larger sizes of tubes suitable for producing larger amounts of radio frequency power. Thus it was De Forest's genius that originally made long-distance telephony by wire possible, and later the miracle of transmitting the voice through the air. Strangely enough, De Forest, who had contributed so much to the art of the radio telephone, was treated like an outcast by some of his peers. When he sought to visit the station at the Eiffel Tower in Paris, where some of the first transatlantic radio telephone tests were underway, he was refused permission to enter the station as a spectator.

In 1915, the Bell System decided that the time had come to explore the possibilities of transatlantic transmission. The U.S. navy cooperated by allowing the use of its huge transmitting antenna at Arlington, Virginia. The French government allowed the use of the Eiffel Tower station on a limited time basis. Even this was quite a concession, since the French were then in a fullscale conflict with the German army. The vacuum tube had been the subject of much improvement since De Forest's original audion. Yet there were still no large size power tubes such as those that came a few years later. The largest tube available was the type "W," which had an output of 25 to 50 watts. To obtain the power necessary to span the ocean, large numbers of these small tubes were connected in parallel. This technique could be used because of the low frequency employed, around 50 kHz. At higher frequencies, connecting large numbers of tubes in parallel presents insurmountable problems. Even at low frequencies, the problem is to get each individual tube to carry its share of the load, and this requires careful matching of tubes. The transmitter used at Arlington had an output power of between two and three kilowatts and this required from 300 to 500 of the small power tubes. Observers were sent to Panama, Mare Island, California, Hawaii, and Paris to listen for the signals. The receiving sites other than Paris were at the various naval radio stations.

On August 27, 1915, phonograph music and live speech were heard at Darien, Panama. On September 29, 1915, speech was received at Mare Island, and the following day the signals were heard in Hawaii. Time at the Eiffel Tower was severely limited by the French military, but scraps of speech were heard in the period October 12–21. On October 23 a demonstration was arranged and a number of listeners heard the transmissions from Arlington, 3,600 miles distant. The Paris transmissions were also heard several times in Pearl Harbor. Thus ended the first transatlantic tests.

The increasing demands of war-related work put an end to further developments for several years. Still, the point had been proven and several important facts had been learned.

Public reaction to the transmission of voice by radio was almost the same as that which greeted the first transmission by wire. The first experimental broadcasts were only heard by a few shipboard wireless operators and amateur experimenters. It seemed positively uncanny to these early listeners to hear voices and tinny phonograph music coming out of nowhere. At first, no one knew exactly what to do with the new medium. Finally, a few pioneer stations began broadcasting programs of public interest. One of these was KDKA in Pittsburgh, Pennsylvania. Originally, there were no commercials, except that broadcasters would call attention to the company that sponsored them. Radio station KDKA was an unabashed scheme to sell the receivers manufactured by Westinghouse.

It was not long before AT&T and the Bell System began to speculate on the possibility of using radio for long distance circuits. Especially needed was a means of extending the telephone to distant offshore islands and across the Atlantic. The first commercial application of a radio link occurred in 1920. The Pacific Telephone Company had requested that AT&T develop the link between the California mainland and Catalina Island because suitable underwater cable could not be procured in the period immediately after World War I. This circuit covered a distance of about 30 miles. The equivalent of a four-wire telephone circuit was obtained by employing widely separated frequencies, 638 kHz from the mainland to Catalina and 750 kHz in the opposite direction. The radio transmitters were of nominal power, about 100 watts output, but in general they were quite adequate to cover the distance involved. Of course, the frequencies used were right in the middle of the frequencies used for public broadcasting. Anyone with a suitable radio could eavesdrop on the telephone conversations, and most everyone did.

Eavesdropping on radio telephone conversations is a custom that flourishes today. It cannot be done with a simple broadcast receiver anymore, but the eavesdroppers use sophisticated scanners to monitor cellular phone calls, cordless telephones, and ship-to-shore telephone services. Monitoring cellular phone calls is illegal, and it is now forbidden to manufacture and sell scanners that will receive the cellular transmissions. This does not stop the monitoring. The FCC has no way, actually, to catch anybody doing this. Every radio magazine carries advertisements offering instructions for "unlocking the cellular channels" and for the services of individuals who will do it for you.

By 1923 the government was requesting that the Catalina service be terminated because the frequencies were needed for the rapidly growing public broadcast service. The radio system was closed on August 1, 1923, and service was then provided by two submarine cables. The Catalina system, although primitive compared with later practice, provided AT&T with valuable experience in using full duplex systems, multiplexing, signaling, and privacy. It also demonstrated the utility of radio circuits in providing temporary service under emergency conditions.

Starting in 1922, the telephone company was actively investigating low-frequency transmission problems with the ultimate goal of providing a telephone circuit suitable for commercial service across the Atlantic. Arrangements were made to use the RCA transmitting antenna at Rocky Point, Long Island, New York. This was a truly giant antenna, supported on six steel towers 400 feet high. The flattop antenna consisted of 12 parallel wires stretching out for one and one-half miles. The receiving antenna was located at Houlton, Maine. This antenna was of the long wire Beverage type. It consisted of four parallel pole lines, separated by a considerable distance and each about three miles long. These antennas were built using conventional telephone line construction, and their effectiveness was due to the long length and not to height above ground. By spacing the antennas and combining the output at the receiver it was possible to compensate for phase shifting of the signal in transmission. The new systems gave an improvement over the 1915 experiment by about a factor of six. It was decided that a commercial service was practical. The operating frequency was nearly 60 kHz and the transmitter used 150 kilowatts of output power. Commercial service was initiated on January 7, 1927, with a charge of $75 for a three-minute call.

Improvements in high-power transmitting tubes using water cooling made the new transmitting power possible, but still required a number of tubes to generate the required output. In 1929 work was started on an improved low-frequency system. It was planned to locate the transmitter in Maine, which would bring it closer to receivers in Scotland. This work was interrupted by the stock market crash and the subsequent deterioration of business conditions. The low-frequency system was continued in operation as late as 1939. The system had pioneered the use of the single sideband method of modulation, which contributed a lot to the successful operation. Conventional amplitude-modulated radio telephone consists of the carrier wave and an upper and lower sideband, both of which actually carry the speech information. By eliminating the carrier and one sideband, all the speech power is carried by the remaining sideband. The carrier is reinserted at the receiver to make the speech intelligible. To provide privacy, the original system used speech inversion. This meant that a given low frequency component was automatically shifted to a given high frequency and vice versa. Unfortunately, the privacy feature was of little value because eavesdroppers quickly learned how to build simple converters that would re-invert the speech.

By the time that business conditions had improved, it was decided not to resume work on the low frequency system. New developments in high frequency, or shortwave, had made further work on the low frequency system inadvisable.

When radio first came into use, around the turn of the century, it was thought that only the low frequency, long wavelength portion of the radio spectrum would be useful for communication. This belief, of course, was reinforced by the fact that the first generators of radio frequency energy, the spark gaps and the carbon arc, would not function efficiently at the shorter wavelengths. About 300 meters, or 1,000 kHz, was the limit for efficient operation. Consequently, when radio acquired its first regulatory laws, the lower frequencies were reserved for commercial applications. Amateurs and experimenters were limited to frequencies above 1,500 kHz (200 meters) in the belief that these channels were worthless for commercial use. The amateurs, not knowing any better, started experimenting with higher and higher frequencies. First they went down to 80 meters (3,750 kHz) and achieved spectacular results. They were soon spanning the Atlantic with frequencies as high as 14,000 kHz, using very low power compared to the existing commercial services.

Needless to say, these amateur achievements did not go unnoticed in commercial circles. The Marconi Company in England was particularly active in this regard. They recognized the possibilities of a system to connect the far-flung British empire with shortwave service that would be less expensive and more reliable. The spectacular results on shortwaves were due to reflection of the signals off of a layer of ionized gas above the earth's atmosphere. This phenomenon had been earlier predicted by Oliver Heaviside of loading coil fame. The Marconi "beam system," using transmitters of relatively modest power, and directive antennas, was soon spanning the globe with ease. This was a radio telegraph system, handling messages in Morse code with high speed sending and receiving machines.

Early in 1927, the telephone company had started up an experimental high frequency channel between Deal, New Jersey, and New Southgate, London. By 1930, stations were in operation at Lawrenceville, New Jersey, for transmitting and Netcong, New Jersey, for receiving. These facilities provided three channels to London and one to Buenos Aires. Initially, these shortwave systems used conventional amplitude modulation in which both the carrier and the two sidebands were transmitted. Eventually, it was found that the added complexity of single sideband paid off in superior performance, just as it had on the low-frequency systems. Operation on shortwaves required that the transmitters have two or three alternate wavelengths available. It had been found necessary to change wavelength over most of the circuits due to changing conditions between night and day.

As the radio art developed, many different ways of conveying the voice without wires were discovered. One of the first was the so-called "wired wireless" invented by George O. Squier in 1910. Although this did involve wires, the speech was carried by radio waves. Squier discovered that low frequency radio waves could be coupled to a wire line and would follow the wire rather than be radiated into space. There was some radiation from these wires, but the main energy was directed along the wire. This method of communicating found several useful applications. Perhaps one of the most outstanding was the application of radio carrier telephones to high-voltage power transmission lines. In the late 1920s the public utilities were starting to build cross-country lines to bring power from large hydroelectric generators to distant points. Communication was needed between the various switching stations involved. Radio carrier telephones solved the problem and eliminated the need for expensive telephone lines. At first these power line carrier installations consisted of more or less conventional radio transmitters using amplitude modulation. They were used primarily for voice communication. The frequencies used were usually in the range below 100 kHz. Power line carrier sets kept pace with the latest technology and eventually used single sideband for voice transmission. The carrier sets were also eventually used for telemetering and relay control.

Squier, who held a Ph.D. in electrical engineering, served as Chief Signal Officer during World War I and held the rank of Major General. Lee De Forest had been associated with Squier in the development of wired wireless, and he gave Squier as a reference when he applied for a job with the Marconi Company. Even with this good recommendation, De Forest's application was ignored by Marconi.

Today's cordless telephones are another form of voice transmission without wires. Cordless telephones are nothing more than a low-powered FM radio transmitter and receiver. The base unit interfaces with the telephone system and transmits the speech and ringing signals to the remote handset. The handset receiver is tuned to the frequency of the base transmitter. The handset, in turn, has a small transmitter that carries the speech and calling tones to the base receiver. Cordless phones have considerable radiation outside of their normal working distance. They can sometimes be heard up to one-half mile or more. For this reason, cordless phones do not offer much privacy, as they can be monitored by anyone with a scanner. The newer cordless phones are becoming more sophisticated in design and presumably offer more privacy to the user.

Cellular phones use radio frequencies in the 800–900 MHz range and can readily be monitored by anyone with a suitable scanner. Such monitoring has been declared illegal, and newer scanners have the cellular frequencies locked out, but this does not really stop the monitoring. Cellular phones employ base stations geographically located to give good coverage of certain areas. Each base or "cell" is designed to cover a certain area, and as a mobile unit moves along the signal is automatically transmitted to the cell that is getting the best signal. Cellular phones have assumed a new role in making people feel safer on the highways. Industry sources estimate that there are about 16 million of the cell phones in use, and of these some 70 percent of the users have them for safety reasons. Police in general are enthusiastic about the new uses of cellular phones in spotting dangerous drivers, the prompt reporting of accidents, and other aspects of public safety that have been enhanced by the proliferation of telephone-equipped cars on the road. It is estimated that presently people with car phones make as many as 600,000 calls per month to emergency numbers.

Since there is no actual privacy of communications using conventional FM radio equipment, the current trend among services requiring privacy is to use some form of digital modulation. This type of modulation, already in use by police departments and the military, is virtually free from unauthorized monitoring. It will probably be used eventually by all radio common carriers of speech communication.

By 1876, when the miracle of transmitting the voice over wires had been proved possible, the Atlantic telegraph had been in successful operation for ten years. The telegraph cable, first proved possible by the ill fated cable of 1858, was now a fact of everyday life for those who could afford to patronize it. It was inevitable that thoughts should turn towards the possibility of transmitting the human voice across the Atlantic by means of the cable. In December 1877, a lecture on the new art of telephony was given before a military group by W. H. Preece, the British Post Office expert on electrical communication of all kinds. After outlining in great detail the principles of the telephone as then known, Preece took questions from individuals in the audience. Captain Mayne, R.N., asked, "I should like to ask you how far the voice will go, and whether you have any idea of being able to communicate in this way across the Atlantic?" Preece replied:

> I am not prepared to say that there is much hope of our talking across the Atlantic, but I think it possible to talk to distances greater than the distance across the Atlantic. The reason we cannot talk across the Atlantic is because there is a peculiar electric effect in submarine cable called induction; it is as though the electricity were absorbed by the gutta-percha, and small currents sent at one end never arrive at the other. They get rolled up as it were into one, so that on a long submarine cable, instead of getting the finer sounds when the vibrations are rapid, they would all come out as one current, not producing any sound at all. It does not seem at present practicable to apply to a greater distance than 200 miles, but in the present day that man would be a very rash man who would affirm that it is impossible to do anything.

Preece's theory of submarine cables was a little muddled, but he was right about one thing: It would be many years before voice would be carried by an Atlantic cable. Radio telephone across the Atlantic came first. The

Atlantic cable was, in effect, a big condenser, or capacitor as we term it now. The capacity of the cable effectively soaked up all the electrical energy put into it, except the slow reversals of Morse code telegraphy. The cable simply would not transmit the complex wave form of telephony which consisted of alternating current frequencies up to 3,000 Hz. The efficiency of the telegraph cable had been increased by duplexing, which permitted messages to be sent in both directions at the same time, but that was about the limit. Thus it was that the newer medium of radio gave the first commercial overseas circuits for telephone.

Telephony by cable remained an impossible dream for many years. Then Western Union laid the first permalloy cable in 1925. Permalloy added a value of inductance to the cable, distributed over the entire length. This canceled out the old bugaboo of capacity and made high-speed telegraphy by Atlantic cable possible. The permalloy cable, while permitting a great increase in telegraph speed, still did not meet the requirements of telephony. A 2,000-mile telephone circuit, even with the most efficient line wires, would not function without intermediate repeater stations. At least six repeaters were required to put the transcontinental line in operation in 1915. Repeaters in mid-ocean seemed like a ridiculous suggestion. Then, finally, advancing technology made the idea of underwater repeaters feasible. These repeaters were carefully constructed for long life and reliability. They were housed in sealed containers and lowered with the cable at the required intervals. Power supply for the repeaters was obtained by applying a high voltage to the same conductor that was carrying the messages. The repeaters were assembled to very high quality standards, under conditions of surgical cleanliness which were reminiscent of later space technology.

The first transatlantic system went into operation on September 25, 1956, and continued in successful operation until 1979. It was then taken out of service, having exceeded its 20-year design life. Other cables, of course, had augmented the original one, and repeatered telephone cables are now common. One way in which the carrying capacity of telephone cables has been increased is by the use of the so-called "TASI" equipment (Time Assignment Speech Interpolation). This device takes advantage of the fact that most telephone conversations have long gaps — as much as 60 percent silence according to the statistical studies that were made. By a miracle of electronics, the conversations are interleaved with each other — a circuit with a gap is switched to a conversation in progress. This is done so quickly that the talkers are unaware of it and it has the effect of increasing the carrying capacity of the cable channels. All of us could probably cite persons who talk continuously, but apparently they are not numerous enough to cause the TASI system to fail.

The first interruption of service on the 1956 cable occurred in February 1959, when it was apparently snagged by a fishing trawler. Along the main Atlantic cable routes there was a concentration of cables in the shallow coastal waters and breaks due to deep sea fishing trawlers began to occur frequently. Part of this was due to the fact that postwar fishing trawlers were larger and more powerful than any previously used. An effort was made to inform the fishermen of the location of the various cables. Also, fishermen were even offered financial compensation if they would cut loose from their underwater gear after snagging a cable. It was finally decided that the only solution to the problem was to bury the cables on the sea bottom.

A machine called "Sea Plow IV" was capable of laying cable at a depth of 500 fathoms and burying it two feet below the sea bottom. Burying the cable in this way effectively solved the problem of breakage by fishing trawlers. Another machine was developed that could be maneuvered by remote control on the bottom. It was equipped with television cameras and greatly facilitated the problems of working with the cables at great depths. The Sea Plow buried cables in essentially the same way as they were done on land. All of these machines can trace their ancestry to Samuel Morse's original cable plow in 1844. Morse's plow worked well enough, but the cable he was trying to bury was defective. This led Morse to give up on buried cable, and for almost 100 years communication lines went overhead on poles.

Wartime security of submarine cables was a subject that received much attention. Col. John J. Carty, formerly of AT&T, was delegated to study the matter. After careful study Col. Carty decided that it might be entirely possible to tap submarine telegraph cables without being detected. He submitted a suggested plan to the engineers at AT&T and they thought it would work. Accordingly, a special ship was outfitted with the necessary apparatus and put to sea with the express purpose of tapping one of the Atlantic cables. With this apparatus a cable was successfully tapped without giving any indication to the shore ends, and a clear record of the passing messages was obtained. After this proof of vulnerability it was quickly decided that all cable traffic must be encoded. No longer could the supposedly secure Atlantic cables be used for plain English messages. During World War I it was rumored that the Germans had laid their own cable across the Atlantic for the purpose of having an uncensored line to the United States. Since the report came from what was considered a responsible source a careful investigation was made. The work was done by telegraph and cable personnel who were familiar with the entire New England coastline and the various cables that existed. After careful searching, no such cable was ever found.

At this time the cables were still using the slow-speed DC current transmission in Morse code that had been in use since the beginning. Later types of loaded telegraph cables using high-speed transmission apparently cannot be successfully tapped. The same thing can be said of modern repeatered telephone cables. When overseas telephone conversations became rather common, many persons who had not followed technical matters assumed that the conversations had been carried by undersea cables. For example, there was the German spy who claimed he had eavesdropped on a conversation between Roosevelt and Churchill by tapping submarine cables. The first telephone service across the Atlantic was provided by radio in 1927 and it was not until 1956 that the first telephone cable went into service.

This does not mean that cables cannot be cut by enemy forces, and they have been in all modern wars. The meanest trick is to cut the enemy's cable in several places, making it a very tedious job to find and repair all the breaks. In both World Wars, enemy ships shelled cable stations on remote islands to interrupt the service. During World War II, a Japanese battleship shelled the cable station on Cocos Island in the Pacific. The station was damaged, but the cable circuit was not interrupted. This fact was concealed from the Japanese for the duration of the war and they never came back to finish the job.

One of the longest submarine telephone cables is the ANZCAN, which runs from Port Alberni, Canada, to Auckland, New Zealand, and Sydney, Australia, via Hawaii, Fiji, and Norfolk Island. The total distance is 15,000 kilometers. The cable was placed in service on October 1, 1984. This cable is a coaxial type cable and can carry 1,380 telephone conversations. Planning for this cable started in 1977, when fiber-optic technology had not advanced to the present level. It was known even then that vastly increased message capacity would be available with the fiber-optic cables of the future. However, it was decided to go ahead with the $500 million investment in a coaxial cable, as its message capacity was adequate and could also be augmented by improved terminal equipment to reach a capacity of at least 4,000 telephone circuits.

By the end of ANZCAN's design life of 25 years, there will be many of the new fiber-optic cables in place. Nevertheless, ANZCAN can stand on its own record of being the largest project of that type ever attempted. Preliminary work involved extensive ocean surveys to determine the best route. A ship from the New Zealand navy, HMNZS *Monawai*, spent five months in a careful survey of the ocean bottom to determine the best route. It was especially important to avoid areas where breakage from deep sea fishing trawlers, ships' anchors, and undersea earthquakes could be a problem. The cable rests on the ocean bottom even in areas where the sea is five kilometers deep. Modern cable ships have developed the technique of finding and repairing these deep sea cables to a fine art. There is none of the uncertainty that prevailed in Cyrus Field's day. Grappling for the cable at the deepest parts takes longer than in shallow water, but it is done with certainty by the modern cable ships.

All undersea telephone cables, no matter the type, require repeaters at regular intervals to overcome the losses inherent in these very long circuits. The ANZCAN repeaters are housed in torpedo-shaped cases that are laid along with the cable. They are spaced about 13.3 kilometers apart. In addition to the repeaters, so-called "equalizers" are used to adjust the electrical characteristics of the cable for optimum performance. In all, there are 1,124 repeaters and 75 equalizers. The repeaters are built to high standards of workmanship, with many gold-plated parts. They cost nearly $100,000 each, accounting for the immense investment in a cable of this length. Power to operate the repeaters is transmitted from the shore terminals in the form of relatively high voltage direct current, which travels over the same conductor that carries the voice circuits. The design is so carefully worked out that each repeater receives exactly the right voltage to operate it at maximum efficiency—no more and no less. Although this cable has since been eclipsed in message carrying capability by the newer fiber-optic links, it represents an outstanding achievement in providing a needed communications link over the vast reaches of the Pacific.

Part of the $500 million investment in ANZCAN is represented by new shore station construction at Port Alberni, B.C., and Keawaula, Hawaii. These facilities had to be upgraded to accommodate the additional apparatus required for the new cable. Like most long undersea cables, ANZCAN depends on satellite links to provide alternate communications routes when cable trouble occurs. Present-day international communications are provided by a mix of high-capacity cables and radio satellites. Satellites are extremely costly to launch and maintain. Cables are costly too, but they tend to be more cost effective in many situations. In spite of the marvels of satellite communication, it appears that cables will continue to be important for a long time, carrying on from the first Atlantic telegraph cable laid in 1866.

Developments have been rapid since 1984. The Pacific is now spanned by a number of the new fiber-optic cables that have a capacity of 57,000 telephone channels. Fiber-optic technology has advanced so rapidly that the latest cables only require repeaters every 150 kilometers as against 75 kilometers with previous systems. On the Australian continent an investment of 20 million pounds is being made to link all the capital cities with fiber-optic cable. Australia, New Zealand, North America and Asia are now linked by fiber-optic networks that have tremendous capacity for both voice and telegraphic communication.

One fiber-optic cable that links the United States with Japan went into service in 1991. The landing points of the cable are at Pacific City, Oregon, Seward, Alaska, and Miura, Japan. The connection to Seward originates at an "undersea branching unit" located at mid–Pacific that is located 551 nautical miles from Seward. The Alaskan part of the route, running from Seward via the undersea branching unit to Pacific City, is 1,458 nautical miles in length. Repeaters are spaced 32.4 nautical miles apart. Power is fed to the undersea repeaters through copper conductors in the fiber-optic cable. One thousand four hundred volts of direct current is applied at Seward and Pacific City, and the line current is 1.4 amperes. A total of 17 repeaters is installed on the link from the branching unit to Seward, and from the branching unit to Pacific City there are 28 repeaters.

This cable has six color-coded glass fibers, each about the size of a No. 22 AWG copper wire, surrounding a copper center conductor which is part of the DC power supply circuit. The glass fibers are protected from being crushed by three steel bands, which in turn are covered by steel armor wires to provide tensile strength. A copper sheath over the armor wires provides the other side of the DC power circuit. The outer cover is of polyethylene, which has succeeded the old gutta percha for this purpose. Only two of the six glass fibers are being used in the section of the cable between Seward and the branching unit. The other four fibers are not being used at present and are not connected through the repeaters. Of the two fibers being used, one carries westbound traffic and the other eastbound.

The two fibers in use constitute a 420-megabit digital system with a nominal capacity of 6,048 voice channels. However, advanced techniques at the terminals have increased the capacity far beyond the 6,048 channels, and this has been achieved without noticeable degradation of the circuits. The Alaskan telephone system known as ALASCOM maintains a satellite communication link with the lower 48 states that is instantly available in case of interruption on the vital fiber-optic line. This has actually happened twice since the undersea cable went into service. Earth stations at Eagle River, Alaska, near Anchorage, and on Vashon Island, Washington, are kept in operation, ready to go into action immediately when needed. While on standby, the satellite link is used to carry miscellaneous traffic, such as video feeds for television broadcasts. These auxiliary services help pay the cost of the standby link and can be interrupted at will when it is necessary to provide "restoral" service on the fiber-optic cable.

Chapter 15

The Singing Wires

BY THE TIME THE TELEPHONE was invented in 1877, the Morse telegraph was well established, having been in operation for over 30 years. Line construction, such a mystery to the early telegraph workers, had pretty much been standardized. Once the principle of earth conductivity had been discovered by Steinheil of Germany in 1837, all telegraph lines were operated in the single-line ground return mode. Indeed, it was alleged that for telegraphy, the ground return was superior to a metallic conductor. Many of the early telephone experiments over appreciable distances had involved telegraph wires since they were the only lines readily available. With this experience as a background it was only logical that when the telephone company started to build its first lines the ground return system was used. A ground return system by itself worked fine, just as well as a two-wire circuit.

Unfortunately, as the telephone system expanded and ended up having a complex system of circuits in metropolitan areas, the limitations of the ground return system were all too apparent. The problem was that the ground return lines interfered with other such lines in close proximity. Old Mother Earth is a great conductor of electricity, and it was not unusual for a person to find himself in conversation with someone on a completely different line. The U.S. Army Signal Corps used this principle for "earth telegraphy" during World War I. Ground return circuits were also subject to picking up all sorts of random noises generated by electric street cars and other electrical devices that were starting to come into widespread use by the turn of the century. It was soon realized that the two-wire metallic circuit was the only answer to these problems, even though it was more costly and increased the wire congestion on main line poles. The first demonstration of a two-wire line took place on January 10, 1881, between Boston and Providence. The two-wire lines offered immediate improvement, but it was also noticed that there was still some cross talk on long lines. In 1886, a telephone company official commented:

> We found that between metallic circuits with wire connected straight through, there was a very considerable amount of crosstalk, not quite as much perhaps, as there would have been on grounded circuits, but not materially less. We have entirely removed that by securing a balance between circuits.

Balance was achieved by a practice known as "transposition." Transposition reverses the physical position of the wires on a cross arm at regular intervals. It has the effect of canceling out the interfering signals.

Another early problem was in selecting the right wire. Telegraph practice had been to use iron wire, galvanized to prevent rusting. It was realized that copper wire would offer the advantage of lower circuit resistance. This was relatively more important in telephony. In telegraph practice it was only necessary to increase the line voltage to overcome the resistance of the iron wire. This could not be done on telephone circuits and copper wire seemed to be the answer. Yet it could not be adopted immediately because the only copper wire available at the time was so soft that it could not be stretched tightly between poles. A man named Thomas Doolittle had been working on a better copper wire as early as 1877. It was first tested by the telephone company in 1881 under the supervision of none other than Thomas A. Watson. It was one of Watson's last activities before he left the telephone company for good in the same year. The telephone company placed an initial order for 500 miles of the new wire, and it was tested on a circuit between New York and Boston on March 27, 1884. The adoption of copper wire by the telephone industry was resisted by some engineers who objected to the higher cost per pound, not yet realizing that the copper was actually cheaper for a given line resistance.

With the adoption of hard-drawn copper wire, cross-country telephone lines began to take on the standardized form of construction that was to continue until World War II. Transposition patterns became increasingly complex on long lines involving a large number of circuits. These patterns were carefully worked out by the engineers. Special brackets and insulators were developed to meet the needs of transposition. A carefully constructed open wire line was a very efficient medium for transmitting voice signals. The open wire lines had some disadvantages. In wet weather there was considerable leakage, even with the best insulators available. Even in the dry desert country, leakage could be a problem due to the alkali dust containing chemicals that were good conductors of electricity that adhered to the surfaces of the glass insulators. The Mountain States Telephone Company, operating in the region of the Great Salt Lake, once used steam from the boiler of a Stanley Steamer automobile to clean insulators. Insulator leakage was a particular concern to the telephone industry, where there was no good way to compensate for the losses. In contrast, Morse telegraph circuits would work on lines of heavy leakage by merely readjusting the instruments or applying higher line voltage. There was even some evidence to suggest that Morse lines worked better with a little leakage present.

Fortunately for telephony, the basic problems of insulators had been pretty well worked out in the telegraph industry long before the telephone was even invented. Glass emerged as the most economical and efficient insulator. The Cauvet patent of 1865 had ended the former nuisance of insulators pulling off the pins. This patent specified coarse threads cast into the insulator to fit mating threads on the hardwood mounting pins. Most of the subsequent developments in insulators were related to designing efficient machinery to produce glass insulators in the large quantities needed by the telegraph, telephone and electric power industries. An early writer on the subject of insulators once commented: "The invention of insulators is a kind of scientific measles through which all telegraph managers pass with more or less danger." A typical line on an important route might require as many as 1,200 or more insulators per mile. The enormous quantities of insulators required were supplied by several large glass companies who produced insulators exclusively (see Appendix 4).

Communications lines started going underground after World War II and the demand for glass insulators was gradually reduced so that by 1975 there were no glass insulator factories in production in the United States. By that time there were virtually no open wire lines still in use, except along some railroad right-of-ways that still had the traditional pole lines in operation. The relatively small quantities of insulators they needed for maintenance purposes could be met from existing stocks, or salvaged from abandoned lines. The public utilities still used insulators on their open wire lines, but these were mostly of the porcelain type and these are still manufactured. Insulators were once the favorite target of roadside marksmen. This was an entirely thoughtless practice — those who did it had no idea of the expense and inconvenience they were inflicting on the owners and users of the lines involved.

The electric power industry and the telephone were rapidly expanding in the same time period. It soon became apparent that a high degree of cooperation was going to be required between the telephone and power companies. Electric power lines generated inductive fields that were a serious problem to nearby phone lines. At first, the power and telephone interests tried to put the burden of interference on each other by means of litigation. Then, finally recognizing that this negative approach was no longer going to work, they started to work together in a cooperative manner to solve the interference. The problems got worse as both services proliferated, the electric lines becoming more powerful and the telephone equipment becoming more sensitive. The first group to study the problem was formed in 1921 and was known as the "Joint General Committee of the National Electric Light Association (NELA) and the Bell Telephone Sys-

Typical two-groove insulators, for transpositions on open wire lines. (Photo by Lewis Coe.)

tem." One of the original committees was headed by R. F. Pack of the NELA interests, and in 1931 Pack issued a statement, saying:

> Today inductive coordination as between the Bell Telephone System and the power companies is no longer a problem but only a routine day-to-day job of cooperatively continuing research work and developing the art of both systems to eliminate as far as possible causes for inductive interference.

There are still problems of inductive interference, but the means for solving the problems are much better now with improved measuring equipment and the expertise gained through years of practice. Furthermore, the problems are fewer now that most of the telephone system is underground. Yet even an underground telephone cable can be subjected to interference from an electric power line running parallel and in close proximity to it.

It was inevitable that insulator collecting would become a popular hobby. The diversity of types from different manufacturers gave the collectors great incentives to assemble collections, some dedicated to a particular manufacturer, color, or other distinctive classification. The hobby really took off after World War II, when lines started going underground. When open wire lines were dismantled, there was some market for the wood poles and the copper wire. Insulators, however, had no market value and were usually free for the taking. Most of the insulators from a dismantled line tended to be of the same common type, but occasionally a rare one could be found. Collectors overlook no possibilities when searching for different specimens. Particularly interesting are the old routes in remote areas, which may yield very rare specimens. Insulator collectors are a very enthusiastic group and have devoted a lot of thought to their hobby. One example is a classification system that makes it possible to identify a particular insulator among the almost endless variety of types and manufacturers that existed.

Insulator collecting is a hobby that can be enjoyed by almost anyone. Thousands of specimens are in existence and the more common types are not expensive. Insulator collectors have their own national organization, The National Insulator Association, which publishes a monthly magazine called *Crown Jewels of the Wire* (see Appendix 3). The association holds several yearly shows at which collectors can buy and sell and see outstanding collections. Membership applications are welcomed from any person interested in insulators and related communications history. Canadian collectors have their own magazine, *Canadian Insulator Collector Magazine*, published bi-monthly (see Appendix 3).

Most insulator collectors feel that by preserving these bits of glass they are helping to save a bit of communications history that is fast disappearing.

The open wire lines were vulnerable to storms and became almost physically unmanageable in metropolitan areas. The line on West Street in New York City once had 25 cross arms on 90-foot poles carrying 250 wires. Even in congested metropolitan business districts pole lines proliferated to meet the ever-increasing demand for telephone and other wire services. The obvious answer to the problems of open wire construction was to adopt cables containing a large number of wires bundled together. Although the use of cable, both aerial and underground, had started in the 1880s, there were severe limitations, some due to the fact that cable manufacturing technique was relatively new. It was immediately discovered that the losses in cable were high compared to the open wire conductors. Improved cable construction, together with the perfection of loading and repeaters, finally made cable a practical method of transmission. Today, almost all telephone circuits, even in rural areas, are underground. The development of plastic sheathed cables, replacing the former lead sheaths, has made underground circuits easier to install and maintain than the open wires.

The linemen who patrolled and maintained the old open wire lines were a hardy lot, closely identified with their brethren of the telegraph lines. Telephone linemen probably worked to a little higher standard than prevailed in telegraph work. The nature of telephone service required lines in good condition. Most linemen were rugged, self-reliant types who faced danger every day as a routine part of the job. They had to climb tall poles in all kinds of weather and at all hours of the night. They were always

Concentration of open wire in the vicinity of the telephone exchange in Pratt, Kansas. (Photo courtesy Museum of Independent Telephony.)

subject to the possibility of serious injury in remote locations where medical help might not be immediately available. Among the hazards were falls due to climbing hooks breaking out in old and rotted poles, electrocution by accidental contact with high-voltage wires, derailment of motor cars used to patrol lines along railroads, and the cuts, bruises and scrapes common to the profession. For these reasons, linemen as a class were not exactly the darlings of the insurance industry. In fact, many could not even obtain life insurance unless they lied about their occupation.

The old time linemen would have marvelled at a modern line truck. Hydraulically operated buckets can elevate a lineman to the desired position, so that pole climbing is now a rarity. Powerful booms now raise poles effortlessly and drop them into the holes drilled by a power augur. The old way of setting poles involved digging the hole by hand. Then the pole was manhandled into position. Once the pole was at a suitable angle the rest of the work was done by "pike poles." These were long wooden poles, maybe 12 or 14 feet long, with a steel pointed spike on one end. Two pike poles with the spikes jammed into the pole would support it in one position. Then two more pikes were put in and the pole was gradually "walked" up until the butt end dropped into the hole. The pole was held in the proper upright

position by pike poles until the dirt was filled in around the pole and solidly tamped. All of this heavy work was done by the "grunts," and that is how they earned their name. The lordly linemen could stand by and watch until it came time to go aloft and attach insulators and wire to the pole.

The individual patrolmen who regularly covered a certain section of line were well known along their routes as they passed through on a regular basis. An AT&T lineman named W. C. Shields regularly patrolled a section of line in Henry County, Illinois. Since he was considered the resident expert on telephones, his services were often sought by small telephone exchanges along his route. Shields was able to augment his AT&T income by doing spare time repair work for the local telephone companies who did not have an employee to do the work. He used to have a standard technique for dealing with these local problems. The problem was usually something simple that he immediately spotted. However, in order to justify his repair charges, he would assume a serious expression and make a multitude of tests. Finally, after a suitable time interval had elapsed, he would grin and announce, "There, that ought to do it," and the customers were happy that their equipment was working again.

While the lone patrolman took care of routine maintenance, replacing broken insulators or downed wires, larger line gangs took care of more extensive construction projects. The journeyman linemen were the elite of the larger gangs. Their most-used tools were climbing irons, known as "hooks" or "irons," safety belt, "come alongs," "Kleins," and splicing tools. Come alongs were self-clamping fixtures that gripped the line wire while it was being pulled up tightly for splicing. The splicing tools had grooves to fit the copper sleeves used for splicing. A splicing tool or clamp was applied to each end of the sleeve. Then by twisting the handles of the splicing clamps in opposite directions a neat and effective splice was made. "Kleins" was the name for the lineman's plier which was used for cutting and manipulating wire. The name came from the manufacturer, M. Klein & Sons of Chicago.

If nothing else, the linemen had to be strong physically. They had to climb a tall pole with nothing supporting them but the spurs of the climbing irons dug into the pole and the strength of their arms grasping the pole. Then, when they reached the desired position on the pole, they had to hang on with one arm while the other arm unhooked one end of the safety strap from the belt, threw it around the pole and re-hooked it into the "D" ring on the belt. This required good coordination and lots of strength in the arms

Opposite: **Concentration of overhead wires always marked the location of a telephone exchange in the late 19th century. Shown is the cable leading to the second-floor office of the telephone exchange at Crown Point, Indiana. (Photo courtesy Dart Koedyker.)**

and legs. The lowest stratum of workers on a line gang was the groundmen or "grunts," as they were usually called. The grunts did the heavy work of digging holes for the poles and attached various items to hoisting ropes to send them to the linemen working overhead. An ambitious grunt might advance to lineman status after he demonstrated his skill at climbing and the other tasks required of a full-fledged lineman.

The first telephone lines in metropolitan areas were strung over the rooftops of houses and other buildings. This method soon became impractical as the lines started to increase in number. Then came the move to poles, and this soon became the standard method of line construction in either city or country. By 1891, standard specifications for poles began to be issued. The specifications called for 40-foot poles of live cedar or chestnut. Minimum diameter at the butt end was 17 inches for cedar and 12 inches for chestnut. Poles up to 90 feet in height had to be used in certain locations. Standard spacing of poles was 130 feet, or 40 to the mile. Ten-foot-long cross arms were spaced two feet apart on the pole. Wire spacing on the cross arms varied from six inches to 12 inches between the individual wires and 16 to 30 inches between the pairs. Wires were normally stretched tightly between poles, becoming even tighter in cold weather as the metal shrunk slightly. Even a slight breeze blowing through the wires was enough to set up a musical hum. Children used to press their ears to the poles and listen to the hum — sometimes there were slight variations in the tone, and it was possible to imagine that actual messages were being heard. The telephone and telegraph companies soon learned the advantages of mutual cooperation in stringing their lines. This led to the practice of renting "pin space" on poles that actually had been erected by another company. This was a good solution for the company that wanted to string wires in a certain location without having to erect any poles of their own. It was also a good deal for the company that owned the poles as it gave them additional income without any expense.

Around 1883, the discovery of phantom circuits and simplexing increased the carrying capacity of circuits and reduced the number of actual conductors needed on a given route. Phantom circuits, obtained by connecting special transformers between lines, enabled three telephone circuits to be obtained from every two pairs of wires. The simplest form of simplexing produced one Morse telegraph circuit for every telephone pair. Another increase in the carrying capacity of telephone lines was obtained by the practice known as "compositing." Compositing will yield two telegraph circuits for every telephone pair. Applying these methods to the transcontinental line in 1915 gave the four-line wires an actual capacity of

Opposite: "Walking up" a pole using pikes to support it. (Photo courtesy Museum of Independent Telephony.)

three telephone circuits and four Morse telegraph circuits, one phantom telephone circuit by simplexing and four Morse telegraph circuits by compositing. These extra telegraph circuits derived from telephone pairs were quite important to the telephone company. They served as communication links between various telephone facilities and could also be rented to commercial customers such as brokers, and newspapers.

Phantom circuits could produce unexpected sources of revenue for small telephone companies. Around the turn of the century, the Postal Telegraph Company was expanding their network of wires around the Midwest. They needed an extension of their Chicago line to Galesburg, Illinois. The Galva, Illinois, telephone company was located on the main Postal line from Peoria to Rock Island and also had a telephone pair between Galva and Galesburg. By placing simplex coils on this telephone pair Postal was able to extend their line to Galesburg. This was a nice source of revenue for a small telephone company like the one at Galva. It cost the Galva company virtually nothing to provide this facility since they had to maintain the telephone line anyway as part of their normal service.

Once the carrying capacity of the open wire lines had been augmented by phantom circuits and composite telegraph equipment, there seemed to be no further room for improvement until around 1910. Then, the discovery of "wired wireless" by Squier and others prompted the telephone company to investigate carrier transmission over the open wire lines. The high-grade toll lines of the period, carefully constructed with heavy copper wire and strung on good insulators, turned out to be the ideal medium for carrier transmission with minimal losses. The first system, appropriately designated Type A, used frequencies ranging from five to 25 kHz. The idea was first tested on an experimental system at Maumee, Ohio, in 1917. Here a carrier was applied to a line going to South Bend, Indiana, and then looped back to Maumee. The first commercial installation was between Baltimore, Maryland, and Pittsburgh, Pennsylvania, in 1918. Successive developments in this type of carrier, labeled Type B and Type C, proved to be very reliable. They continued in use as long as the open wire toll circuits were in use, reaching a peak of about 1.5 million circuit miles in the 1950s.

As the open wire system neared the end of its usefulness, increasing attention was given to the problems of using cables as a replacement for open wire. Cables were used in the open wire days for short connections to offices in metropolitan areas and for river crossings. The frequent outages along the Eastern Seaboard emphasized the need to develop cable circuits that would be immune to the weather. Cables posed problems that had not

Opposite: Lineman, "grunts" and on-lookers pose for picture. Pole is supported by pike poles preparatory to tamping dirt around base. (Photo courtesy Museum of Independent Telephony.)

Linemen having a little fun on an aerial cable. (Photo courtesy Museum of Independent Telephony.)

been encountered in open wire transmission. Increased capacity effects plus smaller conductor sizes made the attenuation in cables extremely high compared to the open wire's. Finally, in 1913, a circuit using cables was opened between Boston, Massachusetts, and Washington, D.C. When this cable first opened there were no vacuum tube repeaters and the early type of mechanical repeater invented by Shreeve was used. The final evolution of cable transmission saw the use of loading to neutralize the capacity of the cable and vacuum tube repeaters at rather closely spaced intervals. The considerably higher cost of cable was offset by the relatively large number of circuits obtained compared to the former open wire lines.

Concurrent with the development of the microwave radio system was the work on coaxial cables. Coaxial cable permitted the use of much higher carrier frequencies and resultant wide band transmission which could accommodate television circuits. The final coaxial system, designated L4, was an incredibly complex system, involving close-spaced repeaters. The repeaters were powered from a central point, using high voltage transmitted over the center conductor of the coaxial cable. This was the same method used to power the submarine telephone cable repeaters. During the 1960s, with the Cold War in progress, attention was being given to "hardened" communication facilities that could function during a nuclear attack. The main station buildings were spaced at 150 miles along the L4 routes and were completely underground. These underground stations were designed to operate for several weeks completely sealed off from the outside world. They were stocked with food supplies and emergency power supply equipment. Fortunately, no nuclear attack ever came, but the underground stations are still there, and they provide a unique work environment for the employees assigned to them.

One of the great line-building feats of the 20th century involved the wartime construction of a telephone line paralleling the Alaska Highway. Rivaling the 1861 transcontinental telegraph line and the 1915 telephone line, this project was considered vitally necessary for the war effort. Not only did construction involve some of the most difficult terrain and weather conditions in North America, it had to combat the typical bureaucracy that characterizes wartime operations. The first snafu encountered was when the initial order for line material was placed with the Graybar Electric Co. This seemed a practical thing to do as Graybar had the necessary material in stock and was prepared to make immediate delivery. The Chief Signal Officer's purchase branch, thinking to spread the work around, let the contract to five other companies besides Graybar. Since none of the five had the material, it was necessary to renegotiate the contract with attendant delays. Construction started on the first 500 miles between Edmonton, Alberta, and Dawson Creek, British Columbia. Everything that could go wrong did. Four hundred miles of poles were set but there were no cross arms for them. The War Production Board would not authorize the all-copper wire that was specified. Substituting copper-coated steel wire introduced more attenuation into the circuit and additional repeater stations were required to maintain the voice transmission at the proper level. Struggling against almost impossible odds, the crews worked to complete the line. It was necessary to drive three-ton trucks over frozen rivers where the ice sagged and swayed under the weight. Icy roads and five-foot snow drifts were common as the men placed cross arms and strung the wire—often working in temperatures of thirty degrees below zero.

On December 1, 1942, a telephone circuit was completed between Dawson Creek and Washington state. This was only a temporary circuit hastily patched together. In some places twisted pair wire was strung on railroad right-of-ways until the permanent pole lines could be completed. Finally, after months of heroic work involving the Signal Corps, the Engineer Corps and several different civilian contractors, the 2,000-mile line linking Fairbanks with the lower 48 states was completed by mid–October 1943. This telephone line served three main purposes: (1) It provided a direct and secure line of communications between the United States and the armed forces in Alaska; (2) it provided telephone and teletype communications between the principal military airfields and weather stations on the Northwest staging route, thus permitting up-to-the-minute weather service and better control of air operations; and (3) it permitted direct and immediate communications between the various points along the Alaska Highway and oil distribution pipelines, thus facilitating administration and control of operations in the Northwest Service Command.

Aside from the overseas circuits radio was not a large part of AT&T operations during the 1930s. However, research was being carried on in many aspects of high frequency operation in that part of the spectrum that was soon known as "microwaves." As early as 1931, International Telephone and Telegraph Company had a microwave circuit in successful operation across the English Channel. All of this work was, of course, known throughout the telephone industry. Practical application of some of the new discoveries had to wait until after World War II. During the war a great deal had been learned in the course of development of radar, which employed frequencies in the microwave range. By the late 1940s the Bell System was committed to building a microwave communication system to augment its long-distance network. Strange-looking towers started appearing across the countryside. Some of the first ones were concrete structures. The transmitting and receiving equipment was placed on the upper floors of the tower to shorten the wave guides necessary to bring the signals from the receiving antennas and send them up to the transmitting antennas. These were radio relaying or repeating stations. The incoming signal from the distant tower was received and retransmitted to the next one in line. Tower spacing varied according to the terrain—averaging 35 or 40 miles in flat country.

Since transmission was in the line of sight, relatively long ranges could be covered in the mountains from one peak to another. The first system went into operation between New York and Chicago in 1950 and the following year a transcontinental system was in operation. The miracle of microwaves was the enormous number of channels that could be handled. The first systems had six channels in each direction and each channel could handle 480 voice circuits or one television program. Advancing technology brought a steady increase in the number of channels that could be accommodated. This capacity was further increased when solid state equipment started to be developed after the discovery of the transistor in 1947. The microwave systems incorporated automatic switching of defective channels. Automatic rerouting was done if there was any problem along a specific route. These developments did much to improve the overall efficiency of telephone communication. The enormous number of circuits available made direct dialing possible on long-distance circuits for the first time.

Along with microwaves, fiber-optics are now leading the way in communications systems. Even in the late 19th century the principle of light transmission through wave guides had been demonstrated. For a number of years, medical instruments have utilized the transmission of light through optical fibers. However, these applications were limited to transmitting light for a few feet. Optical fibers for communications systems could not be used until methods were found for producing fiber that would transmit light waves for many miles with little loss. The first concentrated efforts in this direction started around 1960. Advanced research involved chemistry and the development of machines to draw glass fibers into the long lengths required. Coincidentally, research in lasers gave the kind of light source that was adapted to fiber-optic transmission. Additional problems had to be solved in the splicing technique necessary to create long lengths of fiber-optic cable. The splices not only had to introduce the minimum loss in the circuit, but had to be strong enough to match the basic tensile strength of the cable.

All of these developments came in a 20-year period, and it was possible to make the first submarine lightguide sea trial in September 1982. By the early 1980s, optical communications systems were coming into worldwide commercial use. Intensive and basic research involving semiconductor lasers and diodes and the lightguide media has paved the way for rapidly expanding lightwave technology. Fiber-optic cables have many advantages for the telephone companies in metropolitan areas. It means that they can greatly increase their sevices to certain areas by simply pulling new cables into existing ducts under city streets — no expensive digging is required. As for the ultimate dream of having fiber-optic circuits to every subscriber's home, it appears to be many years away. Japan hopes to accomplish it by 2015. Whether this progress can be matched in the United States is questionable.

Telephone subscribers are already using their lines to perform a variety of chores that would have been unheard of a few years ago. With a computer and a modem, the telephone subscriber can access a variety of services, and do it all over the same telephone pair that has changed little since Bell's day. In some areas, library patrons can use their home computers to access library card catalogs and place holds on books. Home fax machines have steadily declined in price so that anyone needing one can usually afford it. Fiber-optic cable is seen as offering better telephone service to remote areas. Conventional subscriber loops operating on the central office battery of 50 volts are limited in length. Eventually the adoption of the fiber-optic system will enable the rural dweller to have the same telephone service as his city cousin.

Communications satellites have now added new dimensions to worldwide telephony, television and data transfer. Using portable earth stations that are almost suitcase sized, telephone service can be had in the most remote areas of the earth. It appears however, that submarine cables will continue to be an important part of the worldwide system. The new fiber-optic cables are very cost effective compared to the satellite service or the former copper cables. The high-frequency radio links that were the original medium of telephone transmission across oceans are now a thing of the past, except for some limited uses such as to ships at sea.

Chapter 16

How They Worked

ALL TELEPHONES, FROM THE very first to the most modern, work on the principle of what Bell called "undulatory current." This means that however it is done, the sounds of the voice, with all the variations of tone and timbre, must somehow cause an electrical current to vary in the same degree. The instrument for doing this is called the transmitter, or microphone. The first transmitter capable of meeting this requirement was the liquid contact transmitter, probably invented by Elisha Gray, and copied by Bell. It was the liquid contact transmitter that gave Bell his first successful results, on March 10, 1876. Thomas A. Watson once stated, "I have no recollection of having understood anything that was said through the telephone prior to March 10, 1876."

Modern transmitters use carbon granules to accomplish variable resistance. Carbon has the property of undergoing relatively large changes in electrical resistance in proportion to pressure, precisely the characteristic needed in a transmitter. To convert the undulatory currents back to voice sounds an instrument called the receiver is used. The receiver consists of an iron diaphragm operating in the field of a permanent magnet together with a magnetic coil which is connected to the incoming line. The incoming voice currents either add or subtract from the permanent magnet field and thus cause the diaphragm to vibrate and reproduce the incoming voice. For a basic telephone circuit all that is needed is a transmitter, a receiver, and a battery to furnish direct current. In addition to the transmitter and receiver, a practical telephone uses what is called an induction coil. The induction coil is a simple transformer and has a step-up ratio; that is, there are more turns on the secondary winding than on the primary. Induction coil patents were issued in 1878 to Emil Berliner and Thomas Edison. These coils were first called "repeat coils," but the term repeat coil now applies to transformers used in other applications. Induction coils were originally wound on a core consisting of a number of soft iron wires. The core was open-ended and the end piece supporting the core and terminals was a block of hardwood. These are the kinds of coils found in the old wooden box phones.

173

The transmitter and battery are connected in series with the primary. The receiver is connected in series with the secondary winding and the incoming line. In this way, the voice currents generated in the primary coil are amplified and sent to the line. Also, by this connection, the receiver is not influenced by the battery current needed to operate the transmitter. Induction coils for later model common battery phones have extra windings used to produce the "anti-sidetone" feature. Also, the coil and other components are sealed in a single enclosure and called a "network." The network usually includes a capacitor used to isolate the receiver from the line battery current while still allowing it to respond to the voice signals. This is done because direct current flowing through the receiver coils tends to desensitize it.

Also included in most phones is the "hook switch." The hook switch serves to place the phone in standby position when the receiver or handset is placed on it. The early wooden box phones had an actual hook protruding from the side of the box. In modern phones the function is performed by a simple button that is depressed when the handset is placed on it. The terms "off hook" and "on hook" are still used to describe the status of a telephone set. The old local battery phones used to run down the batteries rather fast if the phone was off hook for any length of time. In the modern phone system an off hook condition means that the line will indicate that it is busy to anyone trying to call that particular number. Also, the central office sends a characteristic signal to try to alert anyone who has inadvertently left his phone off hook for an extended period. For what now seems a comparatively simple gadget, the hook switch was the subject of much head-scratching and several patents. The early type of Bell sound-powered telephones did not need a hook switch because there was no battery current to shut off when the phone was not being used. The first Bell phones did not even have a mechanism for calling; they relied on hitting the phone with a small hammer to call the distant party.

Local battery phones require a means of signaling the operator or another phone on the line. This has been done traditionally with the magneto generator first invented by Thomas Watson. The magnetic field of these generators is provided by horseshoe permanent magnets; anywhere from three to six are used. The magnets are mounted on the pole pieces which fit closely around the rotor. The rotor has just one main slot which is wound with fine wire. There is a large step-up ratio between the crank gear shaft and the rotor axle gear. This gives high-speed rotation of the rotor with moderate cranking speed. At maximum speed, most of these generators will develop 75 to 90 volts of alternating current at a frequency of 15 to 30 Hz. The six-bar generators were normally used on long, heavily loaded farm lines where the many ringers bridged on the line constituted a relatively heavy load. The generators are provided with an automatic disconnect switch. This switch operates when the crank is turned to connect the generator to the line. When the crank is released the generator is cut out of the circuit. This is necessary to avoid the generator's relatively low resistance attenuating the talking circuit.

Watson also invented the polarized ringer, which has been standard for over 100 years. The ringer employs a small permanent magnet which acts on the bell armature to hold the clapper to one side. The alternating current supplied by the generator either adds or subtracts to the magnetic field of the permanent magnet and causes the clapper to vibrate with the ringing frequency. Old-time switchboards in small towns had a ringing generator for the operator to use. Larger installations began to use ringing machines which simulated the output of the hand-cranked generators and relieved the operator of cranking the generator every time she wanted to ring a subscriber. Local battery boards had magnetic drops associated with each subscriber's line. These "drops" were released and fell forward when a subscriber rang in. One of the peculiarities of the local battery system was the "ring-off" signal. When a subscriber was through with the call he was supposed to give a quick turn of the generator handle. This triggered a special cord circuit drop and signaled the operator that the call was finished and that particular cord could be taken down. If the ring-off signal was not given, the operator had no way of knowing when the call was completed unless she listened on that line. Common battery systems did not need a ring-off signal because the operator had a supervisory lamp that went out when the subscribers hung up their phones.

Common battery phones did not need a ringing generator. Taking the handset off the hook closed a circuit on which the central office was sending out battery voltage. Closing the circuit activated a signal lamp on the central office switchboard to notify the operator that a subscriber wanted to place a call. Of course, in the modern dial phone, the subscriber no longer hears the familiar "number please" of a human operator. All he hears is a steady dial tone indicating that he has a complete circuit to the switching center and can proceed to dial a call.

Although the ringing generator at the subscriber's set is no longer needed, central offices still need some type of ringing machine to call a subscriber's phone. The ringers in the subscriber's set are virtually the same as those invented by Watson so many years ago. The only exceptions are the modern all-electronic phones in which the ringing sound is made by solid state devices. However, the basic low-frequency alternating ringing current works the new phones quite well and is compatible with the old and new style ringers. The conventional ringers, when used on common battery systems, are operated in series with a small capacitor. This capacitor will pass the low-frequency ringing current quite freely but blocks the direct current line voltage so that the switchboard signals will not be activated in the on hook condition. Local battery phones did not normally use this capacitor in series with the ringer. Ringers for rural party lines came in different resistance values of the magnets, ranging from 80 ohms to 2,500 ohms. The 80-ohm ringers were intended for series party lines, or for single line use from a switchboard. The 2,500-ohm ringers were intended for rural lines where there might be eight or more phones bridged on the line.

The old wooden box, local battery, magneto ringing telephones usually incorporate a lightning arrester. It may take the form of carbon discs separated by mica washers, or it may be merely an air gap between metal plates. The lightning arresters are a very important part of any telephone equipment, but they were especially crucial on the old open wire lines, which were a prime target for lightning hits. The lightning arresters offer some protection to the apparatus, but nothing is going to protect the telephone, or the subscriber, from a direct hit. Modern phones usually have a lightning protector, as well as fuses, where the wires enter the building. The possibility of lightning hits was greatly reduced when telephone lines started going into underground cables. Even these, in rural areas, can pick up considerable charges from nearby lightning hits, as evidenced by the ringer bells tapping during a severe thunderstorm. For this reason, talking on a phone during a local lightning disturbance is not recommended.

By the turn of the century, relatively efficient telephone instruments had been devised. At that time however, the prime consideration of design was to achieve maximum output from the transmitters and maximum sensitivity from the receivers. This was necessary to achieve acceptable levels on long-distance lines, which were more and more coming into use. There were no electronic amplifiers available and loading was widely used on open wire lines. The result was a characteristic "telephone speech" that was accepted by millions of users. The telephone company acknowledged this problem as early as 1877 in one of its first advertising publications:

> The proprietors of the Telephone . . . are now prepared to furnish Telephones for the transmission of articulate speech through instruments not more than twenty miles apart. Conversation can easily be carried on after slight practice and with occasional repetition of a word or sentence. On first listening to the telephone, though the sound is perfectly audible, the articulation seems to be indistinct, but after a few trials the ear becomes accustomed to the peculiar sound.

The obvious advantages of telephonic communication offset the disadvantages of voices that did not sound "normal." In the old days, there were no instruments to make accurate measurements of transmission characteristics. In later years, with improved measuring equipment it has been possible to evaluate the performance of the old phones. These measurements, made on surviving examples of the old equipment, show that the combined transmitter-receiver frequency response peaked around 1,000 Hz, with a rapid falling off on either side of the peak.

The old phones, with their peaked frequency response, were usually quite intelligible, even though the speech was distorted by comparison with later standards. With electronic repeaters gradually coming into use after their debut on the 1914 transcontinental line, the former constraints of design were removed. With unlimited amplification available, the gain of long circuits could be adjusted at will and it was no longer necessary to use high-output transmitters. Also, the new amplification made it unnecessary to use heavy loading values on open wire lines. The new generation of subscriber's equipment had a much wider frequency response, and speech began to sound more lifelike. The changes came so gradually that most users old enough to remember the old phones were not conscious of the changes.

As the name suggests, local battery phones required some kind of battery to supply the direct current needed to power the transmitter circuit. Before the advent of dry cells, about 1891, this need was met by "wet cells," primary batteries using a fluid solution to produce the chemical action needed to generate electricity. The first dry cells were not an unmixed blessing. Dry cells are not actually dry. They are assembled with a moist paste between the elements. Before improved sealing methods were devised, it was quite common for the cells to corrode badly and rapidly lose power. For this reason, the wet batteries continued in use long after dry cells became available. Eventually, of course, the manufacture of dry cells was perfected and they became the standard source of power in the local battery phones. Of the old wet type cells, the Fuller cell was favored. It had a relatively high output of 2.1 volts and had a long life. Not many telephone users today would want to take care of wet cell batteries in their telephone. Consider these instructions for setting up a Fuller cell that appeared in the 1896 Western Electric catalog:

> Make a paste by mixing up pulverized bichromate of potash with strong sulfuric acid in about equal parts by weight. Put about ten ounces of this paste into the outside jar, pour over it two or three ounces of sulfuric acid and fill up with water. Into the porous cell pour a teaspoon full of mercury, put the zinc in place and fill up with water. The zinc should be lifted out occasionally and the sulphate washed off. Keep a supply of mercury in the porous cell, so as to have the zinc always well amalgamated.

As the telephone came into general use, there developed a need for loud-sounding receivers so that the user did not have to hold a receiver directly to his ear. There was little success in this direction in the days before electronic amplification. In 1913, a remarkable feat of loud talking was performed when an audience of 300 people in Tulsa listened to an address by the governor of Oklahoma, who was speaking into a microphone at Oklahoma City, 122 miles away. There was no means of amplification and all the speech energy was generated by the microphone. A special water-cooled microphone was used and was supplied with three amperes of direct current, about 50 times the power applied to an ordinary telephone transmitter. The line used was a pair of No. 12 gauge open wires. This demonstration was said to be successful, but such methods never became popular. The high speech levels required were prone to cause crosstalk in neighboring circuits.

"Public address systems," now usually called sound systems, started to be much more practical when the new audion amplifier tubes became available. Originally, the telephone company led the way in public address systems as they were considered the logical ones to handle speech reproduction. In 1919, an installation was made along three blocks of Park Avenue in New York for a Victory Loan drive. Over 100 loudspeakers were used, driven by high-power electronic amplifiers. Rapid progress was made in the field with the invention of the high quality double button carbon microphone and the volume indicator instruments that permitted precise adjustment of sound levels. A landmark event occurred on Armistice Day 1921, when an elaborate set-up was installed to carry the ceremonies connected with the burial of the Unknown Soldier at Arlington Cemetery. Besides being amplified for a local audience of 100,000, the speech was carried by telephone lines to an estimated 30,000 people in New York City and 20,000 in San Francisco. Progress was rapid after that, and the telephone company gained much useful experience which stood them in good stead when they started handling broadcast program circuits in the late 1920s. Benjamin Franklin once wrote about a preacher, the Reverend Mr. Whitefield, who had an extraordinarily loud and clear way of speaking. One night when the good parson was addressing a crowd in the streets, Franklin checked the power of the speaker's voice by walking away in different directions until the voice faded out. He calculated the area involved and the number of people who theoretically could find standing room in such an area. In this way he came to the conclusion that Whitefield was capable of reaching at least 30,000 listeners using his own lung power alone.

In the last quarter of the 19th century, the characteristics of wire lines, both telegraph and telephone, began to be examined critically. New theories started to come forth, some of which sounded very controversial to the engineers schooled in the old methods. For instance, it had always been assumed that leakage of current on a telegraph line, such as occurs in wet weather, was detrimental to good performance. Then it was learned through practical experience that a line actually worked better when there was some leakage from the conductor. This was contrary to all previous theories, yet it was proved to be true. After adjusting the instruments properly, the transmission rate was actually better on a line with some leakage. Soon it was being suggested that the same principle applied to the voice transmissions of telephony. A line having some leakage was shown to cause less distortion of speech than a line without leakage. One of the leading exponents of this theory was Oliver Heaviside. As usual, Heaviside was impatient with those who disagreed with him. Writing in his book *Electromagnetic Theory*, published in London in 1893, he said:

> Is it impossible to find an insulator of comparatively low resistance which should be suitable in other respects? Telegraph cable manufacturers would probably say, No. That however, need not be considered conclusive, because, as is well known, when an industry or institution is once established, it always gets into grooves, and has to be moved out of them by an external agency, if at all. But should such an insulator be unattainable, then the only alternative is to have artificial leaks, as many as possible. The theory is, I think, quite plain, and I know that the practice is also, up to a certain point. But here be grooves again. For people working in established ways have their own proper work to do, and have no time to waste upon "fads." So much is this the case that it often happens that they have exceedingly little knowledge of how things would work out if they departed from the routes they are accustomed to run along. That is to say, the spirit of scientific research, which was to some extent present in the industry in its early stages, has nearly all evaporated, leaving behind regular rules and a hatred of fads. I am no wild enthusiast, having been a practician myself, but it has certainly been a matter of somewhat mild surprise to me that cable electricians, who have had such unexampled opportunities in the last 20 or 30 years, say, should have done nothing in the matter of leaks. Perhaps there may turn out to be objections, at present unthought of. The same could be said of anything untried. Several cases of resistance to change of established practice, where the changes ultimately turned out to be of great benefit, have come under my personal observation. The proposed changes were (I believe quite honestly) first scouted as fads, and the innovator was snubbed; next, under pressure, they were reluctantly tried; thirdly, adopted as a matter of course, and the innovator snubbed again but this is the nature of things, and can be seen everywhere around — very notably in the political world.

There seems to be no record that controlled leakage on telegraph and telephone lines was ever adopted. However, the idea of adding inductance to lines, another Heaviside idea, was widely adopted and made the first really long-distance telephony possible.

Chapter 17

The New Kids on the Block

PRIOR TO THE DIVESTITURE of the Bell System in 1984, it would have been ridiculous to suggest that we would have much competition in the telephone field, particularly in long distance toll traffic. Of course, GTE had always been there, and since the Kingsbury commitment of 1913 GTE had enjoyed full interconnection with the Bell facilities. It was with some surprise that the public realized that competition was possible in the new state of things. Two lively newcomers, MCI and Sprint, appeared on the scene and were soon busily engaged in laying fiber-optic cables, leasing satellite facilities and putting up microwave routes. Furthermore, they were able to use the facilities of local Bell companies for interconnection and could even have their bills for toll calls collected by the local companies (for a suitable service fee!).

Telephone subscribers were soon being bombarded by the claims of three different long-distance suppliers, each hoping to convince the local subscriber that their service was best. Some of the advertising claims were ingenious, if not logical. For example, Sprint has made much use of its claim that you could hear a pin dropping over a Sprint connection. This particular claim seems to disregard the way pins drop in the real world. They are usually dropped onto thick pile carpet, which makes no noise whatever, and they are usually not found until some incautious person walks over the hiding place with bare feet. If someone actually dropped a pin into a tin cup, then it probably could be heard over Sprint or any other company's circuits. Actually, all telephone circuits are adjusted to state-of-the-art techniques and are carefully standardized by engineers who may have worked for several different telephone companies at one time or other. Even a high-quality telephone circuit is not going to work any better than the terminal set used by the subscriber. This may be a cheap drugstore telephone built to sell at a low price, rather than a high-quality instrument designed to deliver maximum fidelity of reproduction.

The most prominent of the newcomers, MCI (Microwave Communications, Inc.), began in the early 1960s as a scheme to provide two-way radio communication to trucks traveling between Chicago and St. Louis. The range of a mobile radio at that time was limited to about 15 miles. Once a trucker left the terminal he was soon out of communication with his dispatcher. Led by a self-educated engineer named Jack Goeken, a group of radio men based at Joliet, Illinois, decided that by building a group of 11 repeater stations spaced about twenty-five miles apart, continuous radio communication could be obtained over the entire 290-mile route. Not only could the trucks stay in continuous contact with their terminal, but the Chicago dispatcher could speak directly with St. Louis and vice versa without using the services of AT&T. It was soon realized that the radio relay route from Chicago to St. Louis could be the means of offering a competitive long-distance telephone service between the two cities. However, it could not work unless MCI could obtain rights to use the Bell System for connection to local subscribers' equipment. In 1968, William G. McGowan joined the fledgling enterprise and immediately applied his business skills to obtaining adequate financing. McGowan was to continue as chairman and CEO of MCI until late 1992.

Then began a long battle with AT&T, which understandably was not thrilled at having a competitor when previously they had had things pretty much their own way. In 1969, five years after filing an application, MCI was granted a license for a microwave communications link between Chicago and St. Louis. By 1971, MCI was proceeding with authorization from the FCC to compete with AT&T for domestic long-distance telephone calls. From the very first there was a problem because AT&T would not allow the local connections necessary to implement the long-distance service. This led to the 1974 legal action against the Bell System. This hard-fought legal battle finally resulted in victory for MCI in 1980. Resistance by AT&T continued, however, as AT&T imposed unreasonably high access charges to connect MCI toll calls with local numbers. The 1984 divestiture of the Bell System ended AT&T's monopoly for all time and firmly established the principle of equal access to local networks by all competing long-distance carriers.

Both in technology and marketing MCI continued to be very innovative. By 1984, it had already laid 4,250 miles of fiber-optic cables. Today it has more than 32,000 route miles in the United States available in its fiber-optic, microwave, and satellite facilities. International circuits began with Canada in 1983 and now extend to 250 locations on six continents. Operators are available 24 hours a day to handle calls placed in 19 different languages. Alliances with British Telcom, Canadian Stentor, and Mexican Banacci have placed MCI in a very strong position to grow and advance in the international market. The company has now progressed to the point where it can rent channels to such resale carriers as TDX, a subsidiary of British Cable & Wireless. Resale carriers solicit long-distance traffic and then place it with the carrier offering the best terms. Such activities were unheard of in the old monopoly days of the telephone industry. They would have been impossible as well because AT&T was the only game in town.

The key to modern telephone services seems to lie in advanced computerization of every phase of the telephone operation. With a myriad of services available through a multiplicity of carriers, billing becomes a very complicated process. It must faithfully record millions of transactions and accurately bill individual customers using the dozens of varied services being offered by the respective companies. Chairman William G. McGowan of MCI says: "To survive and especially to thrive in this industry, you've got to be completely automated." The logic of this can be seen in some of the innovative services offered by MCI. Their "Friends and Family" service offers a 20 percent discount on calls made to a selected group of numbers. The only way such a service can be implemented is through an advanced computer system that can handle the specialized billing required. One MCI executive describes their phone network as one big "computer with long wires."

With the three major carriers scrambling for long distance traffic, aggressive bidding policies are in effect whenever a major contract comes up for grabs. After AT&T and Sprint won a lucrative government telephone contract, MCI protested that it was being unfairly treated. When its lower rates were cited, the other two said the service being offered was not comparable to theirs. Thus the telephone wars continue, hardly the same as those existing in the early days of the Bell monopoly, yet no less real to those involved. The big dog in the industry is still AT&T, holding approximately 70 percent of the market; MCI comes in for a 15 percent share and Sprint has about 8 percent.

Even though Sprint is No. 3, in market share it is actively competing for the long-distance market. Its all-digital circuits attract customers who want data handling capability. In a deal to be finalized in 1995, Sprint has agreed to sell a 20 percent share of its company to French Telecom and Deutsche Telekom. This $4.2 billion deal is expected to create a telecommunications entity that will rival AT&T in size. The 1993 merger of Sprint and Centel has been a major factor in giving Sprint the local access lines that all long-distance carriers must have to do business.

Like its rival MCI, Sprint had very modest beginnings. It started with the Brown Telephone Company, which was organized by C. L. Brown in 1899 at Abilene, Kansas. An enterprising businessman, Brown operated other businesses in Abilene. At one time he was employing about 25 percent of the wage earners in Abilene, including David Eisenhower and his son Milton, the father and brother of the thirty-fourth president of the United States. Brown's company grew into one of the large Midwestern independents, United Telephone. Centel is the outgrowth of a one-man electrical shop operated by Max McGraw in Sioux City, Iowa, starting in 1909.

It was to become one of the large independent telephone companies operating in the Midwest, gradually buying out many small local companies.

Even though its power base continues to be eroded by very active competitors, AT&T has its loyal customers. One executive said, "If there is a problem with AT&T services, they will just throw people at it until it is solved." All of the new long-distance carriers have catered to the demands of business in a way that was never done by AT&T. Instead of saying, "This is what we have available," the newcomers will likely say, "What do you need?" Since the new companies were starting from scratch, they could put in the latest state-of-the-art equipment. Bell companies have traditionally followed very conservative practices in depreciating existing equipment before installing anything new. Bell's charges for services have always been based on their own cost estimates, which were usually accepted without question by regulatory authorities. The new companies demonstrated that they could provide service at a fraction of the Bell System's charges, which were based on unrealistic cost estimates. It has been said that no one can say exactly what it costs to handle a telephone call. The usual practice has been to charge all the customers will pay and whatever the regulators will approve. This practice has certainly worked for the Bell System and AT&T, placing them among the world's richest and largest corporations, even after the vicissitudes of divestiture.

All of the competitive carriers, along with AT&T, now have their eyes focused on extending wideband fiber-optic facilities to the private homes and offices of subscribers. The technology to do this now largely exists. The main reason for holding back is increased costs. To fulfill the ultimate dream of having a wideband fiber-optic link with an individual home or office requires a terminal set that is far more complex than the simple telephone set used by most subscribers. Right now, the cost of such equipment is prohibitive for the average user, though maybe in time it will come down to affordable levels. For example, MCI has offered a "picture phone" for some time, yet there is little interest in it since the basic set costs $750. This is cheaper than the comparable equipment offered by Bell, but still too much. The picture phone is a terrific novelty, but it may not be what anybody really wants. One advantage of the present telephone is that it gives visual privacy. Users do not have to dress up, or even comb their hair, before talking. One can react with a disagreeable expression when the conversation is less than pleasant, yet talk sweetly. It seems a reasonable guess that many picture phones will be disabled on the video side once the novelty wears off.

Another factor, and an important one, that will delay revolutionary changes in the telephone system, is that the existing local operating companies have a large investment in conventional copper wire cables. To replace these represents a great financial loss. It may be that the cable television systems provide the best way to move into the future. With a wideband cable into the home, the subscriber can get telephone service, television, and other electronic services such as on-line computer operations all on the same cable. Many telephone subscribers, however, are not interested in obtaining sophisticated electronic services. They only want a telephone that works in the conventional manner. This class of telephone user, probably the great majority, would not welcome the sharply increased rates that would come with wideband service. Still, the competitive companies — MCI, Sprint, and others — will continue to work for improved local connections because they know this is the key to full utilization of the technically advanced systems they have built.

The original methods of telephone communication, involving open wires strung on poles and cross arms, were a decided factor in maintaining the monopolistic concept of the industry. After all, there was only so much space along highways and railroads to set poles and string wires. It was bad enough with one company doing it and would have been impossible for three or more competitors. During the years when Western Union and Postal Telegraph were competitors they did manage to get along fairly well. Western Union wires usually ran on the same poles as railroad wires. Postal went on the other side of the tracks or else shared the public highways with electric utility lines. With AT&T, Postal, Western Union, public utilities, and the railroads all vying for pole space there just was not much room left. Yet this was limited competition for space compared with what would have happened with two telephone companies. Open wire lines were very expensive to build. The lines not only had to be built, they had to be maintained very carefully to continue functioning. This meant stationing a routine patrolman about every 50 miles along major routes. Even with the most advanced technology that came along, open wire lines were limited in message carrying capacity, putting a limit on the revenue that could be generated by a very expensive line. With these considerations in mind, the public and regulators alike accepted the idea of a total monopoly to furnish telephone service. After all, the telephone company had enough to worry about without some pesky competitor showing up to cut rates.

Advancing technology, ironically developed by AT&T, made it possible for competitors to set up intercity routes at a fraction of the cost associated with the old copper wire lines. There was no problem of space, as microwave towers were only required every 25 or 30 miles. Locations for these could easily be obtained as they did not require a large tract of land. In the mid–1940s AT&T started its microwave system. It soon became the prime carrier of telephone circuits, leading to the gradual abandonment of the old pole lines. Besides being more economical and easier to maintain, the new facilities gave hundreds of circuits where there had been only dozens during the open wire days. Also, the new circuits were capable of carrying wideband facilities such as television. The new technology was developed by AT&T, which then showed everyone else how to do it. Then the competitors stepped in and showed AT&T how to do it at low cost. Even for the microwave system, AT&T's costs were relatively high. The company built substantial buildings at the repeater sites and erected complex antenna systems. In contrast, MCI used low-cost prefabricated buildings at its repeater sites, and only bought the very minimum of real estate.

One thing that AT&T considered unfair competition was the fact that MCI concentrated on the routes between major cities where the traffic was heavy. Operating as a regulated monopoly, AT&T was obliged to furnish service over routes that were not especially profitable. This was the same argument that prevailed when radio telegraph service was proposed in competition with the established land wire telegraph system. When radio first became practical for the purpose, many companies proposed circuits between major cities to compete with the land wire companies for telegraph traffic. The FCC turned down many of these early requests for radio licenses because they realized the radio companies were only interested in "skimming off" the profitable traffic between major metropolitan areas. The land wire telegraph companies, by the terms of their franchises, had to furnish service throughout the country.

Predating radio and television were the telephone "broadcast" services that sprang up in Europe around the turn of the century. Telephone subscribers could call a certain number and receive musical programs, news broadcasts, and other informative material. In Budapest, Hungary, there were at least 6,500 users of this wire service during the late 19th century. This idea apparently never penetrated the United States. Only the rural party line gave such service on an informal basis. Before radio, the party line was a valued source of information and entertainment for rural dwellers.

Curiously, the new telephone carriers have revived the term "wireless" to describe some of their new offerings. For example, MCI is currently testing a new personal telephone system. This will allow a subscriber to have one telephone number that will reach him wherever he goes. The new service is said to perform better than the current cellular system. It is all done, of course, by radio, but MCI chooses to call it wireless. "Wireless" was the original form of space communication invented by Marconi and the word is still used in England. The word "radio" (from the Latin *radius*, meaning to emanate from a central point) was first proposed at the International Wireless Telegraph Convention in Berlin in 1906. The scientific community thought that it was a more descriptive term to apply to electromagnetic waves. "Wireless" continued to be used for several years, out of force of habit, but by 1912, when the first law concerning the subject was passed in the United States it was the "Radio Act of 1912."

Chapter 18

Conclusion

AFTER YEARS OF BITTER court battles, charges and counter-charges, Alexander Graham Bell emerged as the legal owner of the title "inventor of the telephone." Whether he is the moral owner of that title has been debated ever since that fateful day when U.S. Patent No. 174,465 was issued. Circumstantial evidence at the time pointed the finger of suspicion at Bell. Bell certainly posed as an upright and honorable gentleman who would not even consider fraudulent practices. Yet, burning ambition can skew a man's sense of values. Bell certainly had the ambition, and early in the game he realized that he had stumbled onto a fortune. In this realization he had the advantage over Gray and the other claimants to the telephone invention.

One can hardly escape the similarity between Bell and Morse, the inventor of the telegraph. Both were non-technical men, Bell a speech teacher and Morse a portrait painter. Neither man had more than a superficial knowledge of electricity yet both essayed inventions which, at the time, were on the cutting edge of electrical technology. Just as Morse had his Alfred Vail so did Bell have his Thomas Watson. It is hard to escape the speculation that maybe these two faithful and talented assistants had more to do with the respective inventions than they ever got credit for. In each case, the assistants seemed disenchanted with the miracles they had helped create. Vail left the telegraph industry after four years, saying in a letter to his brother: "The reason why I must give up remaining here is, that I am wearing myself out in the telegraph, for the interest of the patentees, without compensation, and the care and study is accumulating every day."

Watson, too, left the telephone industry in 1881, only five years after the first patent. He was in a little different situation than Vail, since with his 10 percent share of the telephone patent his financial worries were over. By that time, the telephone industry was growing rapidly. In 1881 the Bell Company's net earnings were over $500,000, and they continued to escalate rapidly in the following years. One would have supposed that Watson, holding many telephone patents in his own name, and steeped in the lore of the telephone, would have wanted to stay. One wonders if, secretly, Watson was fed up with Bell. Consider the famous quotation, "Mr. Watson, come here, I want you!" If the quote is accurate, and there is every indication that it is, does it sound like something that you would say to a coworker with whom you had shared many long hours working shoulder to shoulder? Would it not have sounded more believable if Bell had hollered, "Hey Tom, come here, I need your help"?

Bell, like Morse before him, was involved in an endless series of court battles. If nothing else, Bell was an expert at being an "expert witness." He gave long dispositions under oath and was the lawyers' delight, that is, the lawyers representing the Bell interests. Against a man like Bell, easygoing witnesses like Daniel Drawbaugh didn't have a chance. Even though we have to acknowledge Bell's victories in every major court case, we can still pay tribute to the many who really brought the telephone to life and made it what it is today. These other "forgotten" inventors were just as talented as Bell, some a lot more so, and they labored long and hard to complete the missing links in the Bell invention.

Appendix 1

Cities with Independent Telephone Companies

Anchorage, Alaska	Anchorage Telephone Utility
Long Beach, California	GTE
Santa Monica, California	GTE
Ft. Myers, Florida	United
St. Petersburg, Florida	GTE
Tallahassee, Florida	Centel
Tampa, Florida	GTE
Winter Park, Florida	United
Honolulu, Hawaii	GTE
Bloomington, Illinois	GTE
Des Plaines, Illinois	Centel
Matoon, Illinois	Illinois Consolidated Telephone Co.
Park Ridge, Illinois	Centel
Ft. Wayne, Indiana	GTE
Lexington, Kentucky	GTE
Muskegon, Michigan	GTE
Lincoln, Nebraska	Lincoln Telephone & Telegraph Co.
Las Vegas, Nevada	Centel
Rochester, New York	Rochester Telephone Corp.
Durham, North Carolina	GTE
Hickory, North Carolina	Centel
High Point, North Carolina	North State Telephone Co.
Chillicothe, Ohio	Chillicothe Telephone Co.
Elyria, Ohio	ALLTEL
Lorain, Ohio	Centel
Mansfield, Ohio	United
Hershey, Pennsylvania	Continental (CONTEL)
San Juan, Puerto Rico	Puerto Rico Telephone Co.
Bristol, Tennessee/Virginia	United
Johnson City, Tennessee	United
Charlottesville, Virginia	Centel
Staunton, Virginia, and Waynesboro, Virginia	Clifton Forge–Waynesboro Telephone Co.
La Crosse, Wisconsin	Century Telephone Enterprises

Cities That Once Had
Independent Telephone Companies

Los Angeles, California	Home Telephone and Telegraph Co.
San Diego, California	San Diego Home Telephone Co.
Miami, Florida	South Atlantic Telephone Co.
Chicago, Illinois	Chicago Tunnel Co.
Indianapolis, Indiana	Indianapolis Telephone Co.
Des Moines, Iowa	Mutual Telephone Co.
Sioux City, Iowa	Sioux City Telephone Co.
Kansas City, Kansas and Missouri	Home Telephone Co.
Topeka, Kansas	Independent Telephone Co.
New Orleans, Louisiana	People's Telephone Co.
Portland, Maine	Northeastern Telephone Co.
Baltimore, Maryland	Maryland Telephone and Telegraph
Fall River, Massachusetts	Fall River Automatic Telephone Co.
New Bedford, Massachusetts	New Bedford Automatic Telephone Co.
Detroit, Michigan	Detroit Telephone Co.
Grand Rapids, Michigan	Citizens Telephone Co.
Minneapolis, Minnesota	Tri-State Telephone Co.
St. Paul, Minnesota	Tri-State Telephone Co.
St. Louis, Missouri	Kinloch Telephone Co.
Trenton, New Jersey	Inter-State Telephone Co.
Buffalo, New York	Frontier Telephone Co.
Syracuse, New York	Syracuse Telephone Co.
Akron, Ohio	Akron Peoples Telephone Co.
Cleveland, Ohio	Cuyahoga Telephone Co.
Columbus, Ohio	Citizens Telephone Co.
Dayton, Ohio	Dayton Home Telephone Co.
Toledo, Ohio	Toledo Home Telephone Co.
Youngstown, Ohio	Youngstown Telephone Co.
Portland, Oregon	Home Telephone & Telegraph Co.
Philadelphia, Pennsylvania	Keystone Telephone Co.
Pittsburgh, Pennsylvania	Pittsburgh & Allegheny Tel. Co.
Providence, Rhode Island	Providence Telephone Co.
Knoxville, Tennessee	East Tennessee Telephone Co.
Memphis, Tennessee	Memphis Telephone Co.

Fort Worth, Texas	Fort Worth Telephone Co.
Spokane, Washington	Spokane & Columbia Telephone & Telegraph Co.
Milwaukee, Wisconsin	Northwestern Telephone Co.

Appendix 3

Associations and Publications Related to Telephony

Telephone Collectors International, Inc.

The nature of its business is: to educate the public regarding the history of telephony, the value of old telephones and related items, their collectibility and preservation; to research telephone history and publish and promote literature thereon; to promote the public exhibition of old telephones and related items; to promote the exchange of information about old telephones and related items; and to promote common courtesies and guidelines for use by the public.

Any person or organization sympathetic to the purposes of this corporation may apply for membership. For information regarding membership, write to:

Telephone Collectors International
P.O. Box 124
Newark, IL 60541
(815) 695-5763

Canadian Insulator Collector Magazine

Published bi-monthly, this magazine will be of interest to all persons interested in insulator collecting and the related fields of telegraph and telephone history.

For information on this publication contact:

Mark Lauckner
Mayne Island, BC Canada, V0N 2J0
(604) 539-5937

National Insulator Association

Membership is open to any person interested in insulators, lightning rod equipment or a related collecting or historical activity. Any club of insulator collectors or dealers may apply for a regular membership in the NIA upon approval of its bylaws by the NIA Board of Directors.

For membership information write to:

Joe J. Beres
1315 Old Mill Path
Broadview Hts., OH 44147

CROWN JEWELS OF THE WIRE

A monthly magazine devoted to all aspects of insulator collecting and related historical material concerning the telegraph and telephone industry.
For subscription information write to:

Crown Jewels of the Wire
Box 1003
St. Charles, IL 60174-1003
(708) 513-1544

ANTIQUE TELEPHONE COLLECTORS ASSOCIATION

The principal aims and purposes of the ATCA, chartered as a non-profit organization in the state of Kansas, are:

To promote the collecting of old telephones and related items.
To publicize the historical importance of telephony.
To establish and promote common courtesies and guidelines for use by association members when buying, selling, and trading old telephones and related items.
To provide a means of communication between association members.
To structure events and activities necessary for the accomplishment of the objectives stated above.

Members receive a monthly newsletter, a large part of which is devoted to members-only classified advertisements offering to buy, sell, or trade telephones or related items.
Membership is open to any person in sympathy with the objectives of the association. For full information on the ATCA write to:

Peg Chronister, Secretary
Antique Telephone Collectors Association
P.O. Box 94
Abilene, KS 67410
(913) 263-1757

Insulator Manufacturers in the United States (A Partial List)

Company Name	Years of Operation
Armstrong	1938–1969
Brookfield	1868–1922
Good, Robert	1895–1910
Hemingray	1871–1969
Kerr	1969–1975
Lynchburg	1923–1925
Maydwell	1935–1940
McLaughlin	1920–1935
Whitall Tatum	1920–1938

Hemingray, located at Muncie, Indiana, probably produced more than all the other makers combined, and this make is the one most commonly found by the new collector—that does not mean that some of the Hemingray insulators are not rare—they are! Good reference books on insulators include:

Insulators—A History and Guide to North American Pin Type Insulators (2 volumes), available from The McDougalds, P.O. Box 1003, St. Charles, IL 60174.

Milholland's Most About Glass Insulators, available from C. D. Walsh, P.O. Box 638, Freeland, Washington 98249.

Appendix 5

Telephone Manufacturers

1. Acme Telephone and Mfg. Co.
2. American Cushman Telephone Co.
3. American Electric Telephone Co.
4. American Speaking Telephone Co.
5. American Toll Telephone Co.
6. Automatic Electric Co.
7. Baird Mfg. Co.
8. Bell Telephone Co.
9. Bell Telephone Co., of Canada
10. B-R Electric & Telephone Mfg. Co.
11. Century Telephone Construction Co.
12. Chicago Telephone Supply Co.
13. Clark Automatic Telephone Switchboard Co.
14. Columbia Telephone Mfg. Co. (Chicago)
15. Columbia Telephone Mfg. Co. (New York)
16. Connecticut Telephone Co.
17. Cracraft-Leich Electric Co.
18. Davis and Watts
19. Dean Electric Co.
20. Electric Gas Lighting Co. (EGL Co.)
21. Electric Goods Mfg. Co. (EGM Co.)
22. Enochs Electric Co.
23. Ericsson, L. M., Telephone Mfg. Co.
24. Eureka Electric Co.
25. Farr Telephone & Construction Co.
26. Federal Telephone & Telegraph Co.
27. Fisk-Newhall Telephone Mfg. Co.
28. Garford Mfg. Co.
29. Gilliland Electric Mfg. Co.
30. Globe Automatic Telephone Co.
31. Gold and Stock Telegraph Co.
32. Green Telephone & Electric Mfg. Co.
33. Holcomb, J. R., & Co.
34. Illinois Electric Co.
35. Interstate Electric & Mfg. Co.
36. Julius Andrae & Sons
37. Kellogg Switchboard & Supply Co.
38. Keystone Telephone Co.
39. Kusal, D. A.
40. Leich Electric Co.
41. Lincoln Telephone & Telegraph Co.
42. Long Distance Telephone Mfg. Co.
43. Maryland Telephone Mfg. Co.
44. Monarch Telephone Mfg. Co.
45. Montgomery Ward & Co.
46. Munson Automatic Telephone Co.
47. Murdock & Taber
48. National Automatic Telephone Co.
49. North Electric Co.
50. Northern Electric & Mfg. Co.
51. Phoenix Electric Telephone Co.
52. Premier Electric Co.
53. Rawson Electric Co.
54. Rochester Telephone Co.
55. Screw Machine Products Co. (Select-O-Phone)
56. Sears Roebuck & Co.
57. Select-A-Phone Co. of America

58. Selectaphone Mfg. Co.
59. Shawk and Barton
60. Standard Electric & Supply Co.
61. Standard Electrical Works
62. Standard Telephone Mfg. Co.
63. Sterling Electric Co.
64. Stromberg-Carlson Mfg. Co.
65. Strowger Automatic Co.
66. Sumter Telephone Mfg. Co.
67. Sun Electric Mfg. Co.
68. Swedish American Telephone Co.
69. Taber & Mayer
70. Universal High Power Telephone Co. (Wonderphone)
71. Utica Fire Alarm Telegraph Co.
72. Viaduct Mfg. Co.
73. Vought-Berger Co.
74. Wesco Supply Co.
75. Western Electric Co.
76. Western Electrical Co. (Omaha)
77. Western Telephone Construction Co.
78. Western Telephone Mfg. Co.
79. Western Union Telegraph Co.
80. Wilhelm Telephone Mfg. Co.
81. Williams-Abbott Electric Co.
82. Williams Electric Co.
83. Williams Telephone & Supply Co.

Appendix 6

Some Communications Museums in the United States

Antique Wireless Association Museum
NY 5 & U.S. 20
Bloomfield, New York 14469

Cle Elum Telephone Museum
221 E. 1St
Cle Elum, Washington 98922

Edison National Historic Site
Main Street at Lakeside Ave.
West Orange, New Jersey 07052

French Cable Station Museum
Box 85, 41 Route 28
Orleans, Massachusetts 02653

GTE Telephone Museum
303 East Berry Street
Fort Wayne, Indiana

Henry Ford Museum
20900 Oakwood Avenue
Dearborn, Michigan

Historic Speedwell
333 Speedwell Ave.
Morristown, New Jersey 07960

Museum of Independent Telephony
412 S. Campbell
Abilene, Kansas 67410

The National Museum of Communications
6305 N. O'Connor
Irving, Texas 75081

Oliver P. Parks Telephone Museum
Illinois Bell
529 South 7th Street
Springfield, Illinois 62721

Telephone Pioneer Communication Museum
140 New Montgomery Street
San Francisco, California 94105

Telephone Pioneers
524 Armory Place
Basement East
Louisville, Kentucky

Telephone Pioneers
720 Frederica Street
Owensboro, Kentucky

Telephone Pioneers of America Museum
201 Third NW
Albuquerque, New Mexico 87102

U.S. Army Communications–Electronics Museum
Kaplan Hall, Bldg. 275
Fort Monmouth, New Jersey 07703

Appendix 7

Affidavits of Zenas Fisk Wilber*

WILBER'S FIRST AFFIDAVIT

October 21, 1885

I was in charge of electrical applications when an application was filed by Professor Alexander Graham Bell on Feb. 14th, 1876, which application became Letters Patent No. 174,465, dated March 7, 1876, and I made personal examination of said application, and personally made all the office actions made in said case, and personally "passed to issue," or granted said application; that is, certified that a patent should issue thereon, which patent was issued as noted above.

In the conduct of such application there was no fraud of any kind whatever, nor anything, any transaction, any communication, oral or written, which would support any such allegation in the least manner whatsoever, either on the part of Prof. Bell, his attorney, myself, or any other person whatsoever.

As elsewhere testified by me, I reached the said application for examination on the 19th of February, 1876, and found on that day that a caveat had been filed by one Elisha Gray on the 14th of February, 1876, for a new art of transmitting sounds telegraphically, which caveat, in my opinion, interfered with the first, fourth, and fifth claims of Bell's said application.

On said 19th of February, 1876, I notified Messrs. Pollok and Bailey, Bell's attorneys, that the first, fourth and fifth clauses of claim in said application—that is, in Bell's application—related to matters described in a pending caveat. This notification was an official communication in writing, and, as prepared by me for the official record, was as follows:

U.S. PATENT OFFICE
Washington, D.C., Feb'y 19, 1876

A. G. Bell,
Care Pollok & Bailey, Present
Telegraphy—Feb'y 14, 1876.

In this case it is found that the first, fourth and fifth clauses of claim relate to matters described in a pending caveat.

The caveator has been notified to complete, and this application is suspended as required by law.

(signed) Zenas F. Wilber, Exr.

*from the Washington Post, May 25, 1886.

198

This was copied on the proper official blank and transmitted to the attorneys for Prof. Bell. It contained all and every bit of information that I at any time gave to Prof. Bell or his attorneys. I never exhibited the said caveat of Gray's to Mr. Bell, his attorneys or any person whatever nor gave any information of its nature and contents except as disclosed in the said letter, as herein above copied.

As elsewhere testified to by me, it was customary in the Patent Office to give such information to applicants. Even the date of filing the caveat was sometimes given to applicants in such official notifications concerning suspension of an application to permit the interfering caveator to complete his invention. This may be ascertained by an examination of the files of the Patent Office.

As I have elsewhere testified, I afterward, on the 25th day of February, 1876, withdrew the suspension of Bell's application, in accordance with the instructions of the Commissioner of Patents. In the course of the proceedings leading to this action, I made the following indorsement in the case, as appears from a photographic copy of the indorsement in my handwriting, which I have before me:

Exr's Room 118, February 25, 1876.

The cash blotter in the chief clerk's room shows conclusively that the application was filed some time earlier on the 14th than the caveat.

The app'n was received also in 118 by noon of the 14th; the caveat not until the 15th.

(signed) Z. F. Wilber, Exr.

I have elsewhere testified in substance that the knowledge noted in this indorsement was all the proof I had upon which to base my conclusion that the application was filed prior to the caveat on the day of February 14th, 1876.

WILBER'S SECOND AFFIDAVIT

City of Washington
District of Columbia

Zenas Fisk Wilber being duly sworn deposes and says:

I am the same Zenas Fisk Wilber who was the principal examiner in the United States Patent Office in charge of a division embracing all applications for patents relating to electrical inventions, during the years 1875, 1876 and till May 1st 1877 about which latter date I was promoted to be Examiner of Interferences; that as such examiner the application of Alexander Graham Bell, upon which was granted to him Letters Patent of the United States No. 174,465, dated March 7th, 1876, for "Multiple Telegraphy," was referred to me and was by me *personally* examined and passed to issue.

And I am the same Zenas Fisk Wilber who has given affidavits in the telephone controversy, commonly called the "Bell controversy," in which a bill has been filed and suit brought in the Southern District of Ohio by the United States for the voidance of Letters Patents No. 174,465 issued March 7th, 1876, and No. 186,787 issued January 30th, 1877, both to Alexander Graham Bell, which affidavits so given by me were used at the hearing before the Commission in the Interior Department, consisting of Secretary Lamar, Assistant Secretaries Muldrow and Jenks and Commissioner of Patents Montgomery, which commission sat for the purpose of advising the Department of Justice as to the advisability and propriety of the General Government bringing the suit noted supra.

In none of such affidavits heretofore made by me and referred to in this affidavit, have the exact facts and the entire truth been told by me, in relation to the circumstances connected with the issuance of the said patent 174,465. Those affidavits were made by me under circumstances which I propose to relate herein, and obtained from me to save the ends and purpose of the parties who influenced me.

In order that justice may be vindicated and injustice rectified, I have concluded to tell the whole truth and nothing but the truth. It will be impossible for the Courts of the Country to meet [sic] out exact justice without a knowledge of the influences brought to bear upon me while examiner in the Patent Office in 1875, 1876 and 1877, which caused me to show Prof. Bell, Elisha Gray's caveat, then under my charge and control as by law provided, and which caused me to favor Bell in various ways in acting on several applications for patents by him made.

This conclusion has not come upon me suddenly, but after due and deliberate consideration, and after having carefully weighed the consequences which must result from this disclosure.

I am fully aware that it may place me in an awkward position with some of my friends and possibly before the public, that it may even alienate some of my friends from me, nevertheless I have concluded to do as above stated, regardless of consequences without the hope or promise of reward or favor on the one hand, and without fear of results on the other hand.

The affidavits hereinbefore referred to were executed July 30th and August 3rd, 1885 (these being duplicates), October 10th, 1885, Nov. 7th, 1885, and October 21st, 1885. One of these affidavits, the one of October 21st, 1885, given at request of Bell Co. by Mr. Swan of its counsel, was given when I was afflicted with and suffering from alcoholism and was obtained from me when I was so suffering, and after it had been so obtained from me, I was vilified and attacked before the Commission referred to. Under such conditions my faculties were not in their normal condition and I was in effect duped to sign it, not fully realizing then, as I do now, the statements therein contained. I had been drinking, was mentally depressed, nervous and not in a fit condition for so important a matter, as stated I did not realize (Could not in my then condition) the effect or scope of the affidavit, the data for which were supplied me by Mr. Swan, who paid me 100 dollars, therefor for the Bell Co.

In this instance and at this time I am entirely and absolutely free from any alcoholic taint whatever. I am perfectly sober and a conscious master of myself, mentally, and physically.

This affidavit is consequently the outcome of a changed mode of life and a desire on my part to aid in righting a great wrong done to an innocent man. I am convinced that by my action while examiner of patents, Elisha Gray was deprived of proper opportunity to establish his right to the invention of the telephone and I now propose to tell how it was done.

The attorneys for Prof. Bell in the matter of the application which became patent No. 174,465, were Messrs. Pollok and Bailey, then a leading firm of Patent Practitioners in Washington City (since dissolved and each in business for himself).

Major Bailey of that firm had the active management of the case and several times appeared before me during its pendency in relation thereto.

Major Bailey and I had then been acquainted for almost 13 years. We had for a time been officers in the same regiment and staff officers upon the staff of the same brigade commander. Upon my appointment in the Patent Office in 1870, our old acquaintance was renewed and for years we were exceedingly friendly and still are so, even to this day. I was poor when I became examiner and consequently was in constant and great straits for the lack of ready money. In such straits I had several times borrowed money from Major Bailey, not withstanding the fact that Commissioner Leggett had, in 1871 or 1872, issued an order prohibiting employees of the Patent Office from borrowing in any way or under any subterfuge from Attorneys practicing before the Office or from inventors, which order was then and is still in force.

I was consequently in debt to Major Bailey at the time the application of Bell was filed in the Office. In addition I was under obligation to him for a present to my wife, a very handsome and expensive gold hunting case ladies watch, which I understand he procured from Geo. P. Reed & Co. of Boston, Mass. I consequently felt under many and lasting obligations to him and necessarily felt like requiting him in some degree at least by favoring him in his practice whenever and however I could.

As I recollect I borrowed $100.00 dollars from him about the time the Bell application was filed. He was known as a liberal man and gave expensive presents and loaned money to others in the Office (for instance as I have been informed and believe, by Major Wm. H. Appleton, Prof. B. S. Hedrick, Dr. F. L. Freeman and others). Feeling thus in his power from the obligations noted, surrounded by such environments, I was called upon to act officially upon the applications of Alexander Graham Bell.

When I suspended Bell's application, because of the Gray Caveat, I did not in the Official letter to Bell, give the name of the caveator nor his date of filing. Major Bailey appearing before me in regard to such suspension, I allowed him to become acquainted with both facts, telling him, personally, the same, so that he immediately knew the exact facts upon which to base the protest he subsequently filed against such suspension, and which was referred by me to the commissioner in person for instructions. The Commissioner directed me to investigate and determine, if possible, which, the application of Bell or the Caveat of Gray was filed the earlier on February 14th, 1876, and to be governed by such finding of fact as to the maintenance or dissolution of such suspension.

From the circumstances hereinbefore detailed I was anxious to please Major Bailey, keep on the best and most friendly of terms with him, and hence was desirous of finding that the Bell application was the earlier filed and I did not make as thorough an examination as I should have done in justice to all concerned. So when I found in the "Cash Blotter," the entry of the receipt of Bell's fee ahead of the entry of the receipt of Gray's fee, I closed the examination and determined that Bell was the earlier, whereas I should have called for proofs from both Bell and Gray and have investigated in other directions, instead of being controlled by the entries alluded to and the statements of Major Bailey to me. The effect of this was to throw Gray out of court without his having had an opportunity to be heard or of having his rights protected, and the issuance of the patent hurriedly and in advance of its turn to Bell.

Immediately thereafter I again borrowed some money from Major Bailey, which has never been repaid. We have never had a settlement and for years I was constantly in debt to him and still am. He has as yet demanded no settlement or repayment from me.

After the suspension of Bell's application had been revoked, Prof. Bell called upon me in person at the Office and I showed him the original Drawing of Gray's caveat and fully explained Gray's method of transmitting and receiving. Prof. Bell was with me an hour, when I showed him the drawing and explained Gray's methods to him. This visit was either the next day or the 2d day after the revocation of the suspension.

There were several assistants and clerks in the room at the time who might have heard the conversation when I showed Prof. Bell the drawing and verbally explained to him the methods of Prof. Gray. Bell had been in the office before this on several occasions in relation to other cases, so we were then acquainted. On this visit he was alone and the visit occurred in the forenoon.

About 2 P.M. of the same day, he (Bell) returned to the Office for a short time. On his leaving I accompanied him into the hall and around the corner into a cross hall leading into the Court Yard, where Prof. Bell presented me with a $100.00 bill.

I am fully aware that this statement will be denied by Prof. Bell and that probably the statements I have made as to my relations with Major Bailey and his influence will be denied, but nevertheless they are *true*, and they are stated, subscribed and sworn to by me while my mind is clear and my conscience active and bent on rectifying as far as possible any wrong I may have done.

Gray's Caveat was a secret confidential document under the law, and I should not have been influenced to divulge the same, but I did so as hereinbefore related. Upon the following page I make a diagram of the room (No. 118), the hall and cross hall where Prof. Bell handed me the $100.00 bill.

[The original affidavit includes a floor plan of Room No. 118.]

The assistants and clerks had free access to the archives and records in the room. They could go in and out outside of regular office hours. The caveat was for some weeks in a file box on my desk and could have been taken therefrom and from the office and kept over night without my knowledge, either by a messenger, a watchman, a clerk or an assistant or by a clerk or assistant from other divisions. At that time Examiners rooms were not locked and the key kept at the desk of the Captain of the watch when the rooms were not occupied outside of hours as is now the case nor were passes then required for employees to enter the building outside of regular office hours.

The force then on duty in my division and room, was:

H. C. Townsend	1st Assistant Examiner
I. H. McDonald	2nd Assistant Examiner
Miss S. R. Noyes	3rd Assistant Examiner
W. S. Chase	Acting Examiner
Mrs. S. R. Andrews	Clerk

Prof. Bell in his testimony in the Dowd case admits having had a conversation with me in relation to the caveat, but says, as I remember it, that I declined to show him the caveat, which is *not true*, I did show him the original drawing as hereinbefore stated.

In corroboration of the fact stated herein that Major Bailey had an influence over me, I desire to refer to several other applications of Prof. Bell's which acted on and became patents in remarkably quick order, as will be shown by the records of the Patent Office.

The application for this patent 174,465 was filed February 14th, 1876, became a patent (after several actions thereon) March 7th, 1876. For No. 161,739 filed March 6th, patented April 6th, 1876. For No. 181,553 filed August 12th, patented August 29th, 1876. For No. 186,187 filed January 15th, patented January 30th, 1887. For No. 173,899 filed April 6th, 1876, suspended May 18th, 1876, on account of a possible interference with another pending application of Prof. Gray, was amended and protest against interference filed May 20th, suspension revoked, case passed to issue May 29th and patented June 6th, 1876.

Such rapid progress from applications to patents was exceptional, and few such instances, if any, can be found outside of Bell's case.

For the sake of justice, the easement of my own conscience and to place myself right in this matter, I have concluded to tell the whole truth thereabouts, in so far as I had any connection therewith in an official capacity, and this without regard to whom it may aid, help or hurt. And I have thus concluded after full frank consultation and conversation with my old college mate, comrade in arms and long time friend, Major Marion D. Van Horn and I shall entrust this document to him, hoping and trusting that I may yet be able to repair in some degree the wrongs done and I stand ready and shall always be ready and willing to verify this statement before any Court or proper tribunal in the land.

Zenas Fisk Wilber

Sworn to and subscribed before me this 8th day of April 1886.

(seal)   Thomas W. Soran, Notary Public

Appendix 8

Affidavit of Alexander Graham Bell in Reply to That of Zenas Fisk Wilber*

I, Alexander Graham Bell, being duly sworn on oath, depose and say: I reside in Washington, District of Columbia. I am the inventor to whom were issued letters patent of the United States No. 174,465, dated March 7, 1876.

I have read in *The Washington Post* of May 22, 1886, what purports to be an affidavit of Zenas Fisk Wilber, sworn to April 8, 1886.

I never presented, paid, gave or handed to Zenas Fisk Wilber a $100 bill or any other bill, or any money, or any valuable consideration or thing at the place he mentions or any other place for any purpose whatever. I never promised to, or understood to, or attempted to, or expressed any willingness to pay him any money, or any valuable consideration or thing whatever for any purpose.

I never knew or believed or heard that Mr. Bailey or Mr. Pollock or any one else, undertook to influence said Wilber, or made any attempts to do so, or employed or endeavored to employ any corrupt practices to obtain my said letters patent and do not believe so now.

So far as my personal acts or knowledge are concerned I know that all proceedings in the filing and prosecution of the application for my part and in the grant of it were free from fraud and trickery and honest in all respects; and I believe that all the acts of others concerned were also in all respects honest.

I make these statements in the fullest and broadest sense.

Mr. Wilber did not show me Gray's caveat or the drawings of it or any portion of either.

I have never seen the original papers of the caveat and I did not even see a copy of them until after the Dowd suit was brought, which was in the fall of 1878. When I saw Mr. Wilber about my application in 1876, he took up my original application papers and pointed out a paragraph which was in them when the application was originally filed, February 14, 1876, and has not been changed since, and which contained the following passage:

"The external resistance may also be varied. For instance, let mercury or some other liquid form part of a voltaic circuit, then the more deeply the conducting wire is immersed in the mercury or other liquid the less resistance does the liquid offer to the passage of the current. Hence the vibration of the conducting wire in

from the Washington Post, *May 25, 1886.*

204

mercury or other liquid included in the circuit occasions undulations in the current."

Mr. Wilber said that the caveat I have been put in interference with interfered with that. I did not have any other knowledge of the contents of Gray's caveat, specification or drawing, or either of them, until after Gray had published the caveat in 1878, in a letter which is in the records of proofs for my patent before the Secretary of the Interior. I testified to this in 1879.

Alexander Graham Bell

City of Washington
District of Columbia,

Subscribed and sworn to before me, a notary public in and for the city and district aforesaid, this 24th day of May, A.D. 1886.

Robert R. Shallabarger

Appendix 9

The Untold Story
of the Telephone*

On December 13, 1934, the newspapers noted the death of Thomas A. Watson, the man who, as the assistant of Alexander Graham Bell, was the first American to understand a sentence spoken over the telephone. With his demise went the last survivor of a small group of men who had a first-hand, uncensored knowledge of the circumstances surrounding the birth of the telephone. Much of the story of that great discovery they have given to the world. Other portions of it which they have left untold are perhaps of equal interest. Some of these untold portions are of record, though the records are widely scattered and there has been a surprising lack of competent endeavor to bring them together and integrate them with the more publicized parts of the story.

Some of the less well-known but more important portions are to be found in court and patent office records, in technical publications, in the proceedings of an investigating committee of the United States House of Representatives and in memoirs and personal correspondence of some of the principals. While it is unlikely that even the sum total of all these sources embodies the entire story of the telephone, it does bring out some points that place the publicized portions in a very different light than that in which they are commonly viewed.

The prevailing tendency to attribute great inventions exclusively to single individuals may be natural. It is certainly fostered by the way in which our patent laws are formulated and administered, but it creates a major problem for those who are interested in historical and scientific accuracy. In the sciences allowance is regularly made for the possibility of independent discoveries, whether simultaneous or not, and there are many important chapters of science in which that element is prominent. The impossibility of sharing credit within the framework of our patent law creates a prolific source of distortions of historical fact. The identification of Alexander Graham Bell with the birth of the telephone, to the exclusion of all others, is one example of this tendency. As in many other instances, the Bell tradition greatly oversimplifies the actual circumstances. It had its birth in a skillful combination of truth and silence out of which has grown the mighty myth that Bell was primarily responsible for the invention of the telephone.

by Lloyd W. Taylor, Department of Physics, Oberlin College, Oberlin, Ohio. Reprinted here by permission of the American Journal of Physics, *successor to the* American Physics Teacher. *This article originally appeared in the* American Physics Teacher, *December 1937.*

More than sixty years have passed since the momentous day in March, 1876, when Bell spoke the first sentence ever transmitted in this country by electricity. That exclamation, "Mr. Watson, come here, I want you!" is justly celebrated as the beginning of a new era in communication. The episode is fully authenticated; nor is there any good reason to suppose that it was antedated in this country by any other successful attempt of the same kind. The story has been told many times by the participants themselves. The most recent account is to be found in Watson's autobiography. He describes the event as follows:

It was during one of Bell's experiments on this kind of a telephone that the first sentence was transmitted and understood. I had made for Bell a new transmitter in which a wire, attached to a diaphragm, touched acidulated water contained in a metal cup, both included in a circuit through the battery and the receiving telephone. The depth of the wire in the acid and consequently the resistance of the circuit was varied as the voice made the diaphragm vibrate, which made the galvanic current undulate in speech form.

I carried the transmitter when finished to Exeter Place on the evening of March 10, 1876, intending to spend the night with Bell testing it. Neither of us had the least idea that we were about to try the best transmitter that had yet been devised. We filled the cup with diluted sulfuric acid, and connected it to the wire running between the two rooms. When all was ready I went into Bell's bedroom and stood by the bureau with my ear at the receiving telephone. Almost at once I was astonished to hear Bell's voice coming from it distinctly saying, "Mr. Watson, come here; I want you!" He had no receiving telephone at his end of the wire so I couldn't answer him, but as the tone of his voice indicated he needed help, I rushed down the hall into his room and found he upset the acid of a battery over his clothes. He forgot the incident in his joy over the success of the new transmitter when I told him how plainly I had heard his words; and his joy was increased when he went to the other end of the wire and heard how distinctly my voice came through.

There has never been any occasion for questioning the story as thus told by Watson. He and Bell have a clear priority to the claim of having conducted the first American telephone conversation. It is true that this story was not publicly told for several years after the event, but this was due, not to any suppression of it by opposing interest, but through the apparent intent of Bell himself. The most interesting feature of the episode is, however, the fact that Watson's account constitutes only a part of the story. There are some aspects of the story as a whole, now almost forgotten, which place it in an entirely different light than that in which it is customarily presented. For the entire story to have come to light would have been a catastrophe from Bell's point of view. Hence it may be that the delay in telling it arose from the necessity for waiting until the selection of certain portions of it and the discarding of others could be made with less danger of challenge.

Four of the most interesting elements in the setting of Watson's story which do not appear in that or any other of the official versions are the following:

First: That the transmitter into which Bell spoke on March 10, 1876, was a very different kind of instrument from that described and illustrated in his earlier patent.

Second: That the transmitter which he had constructed for the occasion had previously been described by a man named Elisha Gray in a confidential document about the contents of which Bell subsequently acknowledged having received information.

Third: That it was not until four years later that Bell made any claim to the type
of transmitter into which he spoke on that historic occasion.
Fourth: That Elisha Gray had made and publicly used several types of telephone receiver many months before Bell constructed his first one.

These theses may now be developed somewhat more fully. The first three deal
with the microphone type of transmitter, which is now universally used, and the
fourth with the metal diaphragm type of receiver, equally common. Both are commonplace today, but neither was a commonplace in 1876. The telephone controversy centers primarily in the transmitter.

The first point is, that *the transmitter into which Bell spoke on March 10, 1876,
was a very different kind of instrument from that described and illustrated in his
earlier patent.* Bell's exclamation to Watson had the great historical significance of
being the first words of any American experimenter to be spoken into a microphone
type of transmitter. Hence it is the first telephone conversation, if a one-way exclamation can be termed such, in which the prototype of the modern transmitter
played a part.

Now Bell had already invented a telephone transmitter, and several months
prior to his famous exploit of March 1876, had made attempts to operate it. A copy
of the original, made under the direction of Bell himself, is in existence today. . . .
During Bell's 1875 experiments, sounds had come through and been heard at the
distant receiver, but no words had ever been understood. Moreover, and this is the
significant point, the transmitter used in these earlier trials, and the transmitter
described and illustrated in his patent of early 1876, *was not* a microphone type of
transmitter, but was simply a receiver, of electromagnetic type, worked backward,
now a familiar device in the physics laboratory. The discovery that a receiver can
be so used orginated with Bell. He is clearly the inventor of the electromagnetic
type of transmitter. The point to be borne in mind is that his first successful
telephone conversation was conducted, not with that type of transmitter, but with
the so-called liquid transmitter, described by Watson, which can be recognized as
a microphone type, the precursor, however rudimentary of the modern transmitter.

That the transmitter which was described and illustrated in Bell's patent, the
application for which was filed on February 14 preceding his famous exploit of
March 10 in the same year, was not a microphone type, but an electromagnetic type,
the only drawing of a transmitter in Bell's patent constitutes an indication. The
descriptive material accompanying it treats quite explicitly its construction and
operation. It is also true, however, that Bell refers briefly in his patent to the
possibility of a liquid transmitter, a reference confined to eight lines out of a total
of about 190 printed lines. The legal status of this passing reference has never been
clarified. To the lay mind, and especially regarded as a scientific accomplishment,
it will be natural to feel that mere reference to a possible invention does not itself
constitute an invention. That is all that can be said for Bell's claim to the liquid
transmitter.

Even from the legal side, moreover, it is well to note that Bell's later victories
in litigation did not center in any claim that he may have made to the liquid transmitter. The main issue in all the suits in which this patent was involved was a different
paragraph ("claim") not connected in any way with the liquid transmitter. So far
from emphasizing the liquid transmitter, Bell explicitly stated his preference for the
receiver type of transmitter in his application. Indeed, he thought so little of the liquid transmitter that he made no reference to it in another version of his patent application, which he sent to England *after* he had written the American version, in
the hope of securing foreign telephone patent rights as well. So the transmitter into

which Bell spoke on March 10, 1876, was not only not the instrument described and illustrated in his earlier patent, but it was not even the instrument of Bell's preference up to and indeed long after, his experiment of March 10, 1876.

The second thesis is that *the transmitter used by Bell on this famous occasion had previously been described by Elisha Gray, a free-lance inventor in the telegraphic field, in a confidential document about which Bell subsequently acknowledged having received information.* On the same day that Bell filed his application in the Patent Office in Washington, February 14, 1876, his principal competitor in the inventive field, Elisha Gray, filed another document, describing a telephone. Though Gray's description was fully as explicit and complete as Bell's, it was not technically an application for a patent. It was what was known as a *caveat,* a type of document which no longer exists in patent law, which was in essence a formal notice of intention to perfect and file a patent application. It gave the claimant documentary evidence of priority of an idea in event of subsequent disputes. There was no reason why the papers of Bell and Gray should not have been of the same type, both of them applications for a patent, or both caveats; the two men were on the same footing, neither having reduced to practice the idea which he was describing. But their legal advisors apparently had each his different method of approach. As it proved, Gray was badly advised in submitting his idea in the form of a caveat. The legal technicalities involved in the two documents acted, in later court proceedings, to give Bell an enormous advantage which had no counterpart in any actual superiority or priority of his device. If both men had submitted the same type of document, whether caveat or application for a patent, the case could have been fought out on its merits instead of on the basis of a legal fiction. If Bell had submitted a caveat and Gray a patent application, thus reversing their positions before the law, we should, in all probability, have today the Gray Telephone Company in place of the Bell Telephone Company.

In addition to the difference in form, there was a difference in content of the two documents which was of even greater significance. Whereas Bell had made only parenthetical reference to the possibility of the liquid transmitter, devoting about one twenty-fifth of his application to it, Gray evidently considered the liquid transmitter to be of greatest importance. He described it in utmost detail, and illustrated it fully. Half of his entire document was devoted to it. Gray's description covers the principle and many of the structural details of the transmitter made by Watson for Bell less than a month later.

In pursuance of his official routine, the Patent Examiner notified Bell that his application came into conflict with a caveat which had been filed the same day. Since all such documents were confidential and the patent ethics of that time required that they remain so, the Examiner did not, of course, include in his notice to Bell any statements of the points at which the two claims interfered. Bell was acutely aware of the importance of his claims to invention of the telephone, doubtless feeling, and with the best of reason, as subsequent events have shown, that a fortune was at stake. Consequently he was deeply concerned at any possibility that this fortune might elude his grasp.

Apparently at the advice of his lawyer, he called on the Patent Examiner and asked to be informed about the nature of the interfering claims. Bell may have been entirely innocent in this move. Though he had had previous patent experience, he was not well versed in either the law or ethics of patent procedure, and may not have realized that he was asking for a breach of official confidence which would give him an unfair advantage over his competitor. He should, of course, have been instructed on this point by his lawyer. In any case, the only honorable course open

to the Patent Examiner was to refuse to divulge the requested information. For
some reason, however, he did not refuse. Pointing to the paragraph in Bell's application which mentioned the liquid transmitter, he told him that there was an interference at that point.

What led him to do this we shall probably never know. The fact that he did it
has been established by Bell's own repeated admissions in court. The Examiner
never appeared in court to deny it, nor did he ever make any denial outside of court.
The fact that Bell received this information is completely authenticated.

Statements have been made and evidence offered to the effect that the Examiner went much further than this, allowing Bell an extended examination of
Gray's caveat. The allegation seems not to have been adequately proven, though it
has certainly never been conclusively disproven. In any case, it is relatively unim-
portant. If the Examiner gave no more information than that which Bell admits having received from him, he violated the responsibility of his office. In doing so, he
gave Bell just the information that would spur him to the step he next took, construction and use of the device that his competitor had described, but never made.
There is no suggestion anywhere that up to this time Bell had ever made, or con-
templated making a liquid transmitter. Yet he immediately recalled his assistant,
Watson, whom he had previously laid off, and through activity on the part of the
two, succeeded in making and successfully using a liquid transmitter within less
than two weeks of the time that he received information about it through the Patent
Examiner. Thus not only had Bell's transmitter made by Watson and first used on
March 10, 1876, been previously described and the description come to Bell's
knowledge, but the subsequent occurrences indicate that he made good use of the
information, without which his first successful use of a telephone would at least have
been considerably delayed.

The third thesis is that *it was not until four years later that Bell made any claim
to the type of transmitter into which he spoke on that historic occasion.* The first successful transmission of speech in America by means of electricity was an historic
event. Bell might have been pardoned, indeed, he would have been fully justified,
in publishing it far and wide. Today it is universally considered the most dramatic
episode in the history of the telephone. It is somewhat of a shock, therefore, to
discover both that Bell did not at that time make any announcement of his accomplishment and that for several years he apparently made every attempt to conceal
it. Some of the principal occasions when, having an opportunity to tell of that now
famous episode, he nevertheless refrained from doing so, will be recounted presently.
In the meantime it may be observed that if he was to conceal the incident and yet
claim the distinction of having been the first to talk over a telephone of his own
make, he must reproduce the incident, using an instrument which he felt he could
claim. This he prepared immediately to do. He set about the task of so modifying
the receiver type of transmitter described in his patent that it would transmit
speech, and within three or four weeks he was successful, in a second episode which
deserves to rank with that of the preceding tenth of March.

Having so altered the telephone of his patent that it could be made to speak,
Bell was then in a position to make public announcement of accomplishment of the
electric transmission of speech and to demonstrate it without using a liquid transmitter.

This he did in two important public lectures in the late spring of the same year,
one before the American Academy of Arts and Sciences on May 10 and one before
the Society of Arts at a meeting held at the Massachusetts Institute of Technology
on May 25. Bell may have had his liquid transmitter with him on these occasions,

or even shown it to his audiences, though there is nothing in the printed record of his lectures to indicate that he did. Bell himself, when testifying a few years later, could not recall whether he had the liquid transmitter with him on those occasions. In any case, he did not demonstrate it in operation, though he did demonstrate his receiver-type instruments.

Bell must have felt very insecure about any claim which he could make to the liquid transmitter, for he continued for a long time this policy of secretiveness about his now famous experiment of March 10, 1876. An unprecedented opportunity for bringing his accomplishment to public notice presented itself in the Centennial Exhibition at Philadelphia in the same year. His demonstrations there, as in the case of his lectures were confined to his receiver-type instruments. Though he had a model of the liquid transmitter there, he did not use it. Moreover the judges make no mention of any liquid transmitter in their official reports of Bell's exhibits, though they describe his receiver-type instruments in detail.

In the trial of the Dowd case, the only occasion when the claims of Bell and Gray came directly into conflict in court, at no time, during entire nine days on the stand did Bell even mention his first transmission of speech on March 10, 1876, when a liquid transmitter was used.

In his patent of January 30, 1877, on *Improvement in Electric Telegraphy*, when, if ever, he would be expected to consolidate all improvements in the telephone to which he was entitled, Bell reiterates his preference for receiver-type transmitters but refers very guardedly to the possibility of other types, in these words: "I have heretofore described and exhibited such other means of transmitting sound, as will be seen by references to the proceedings of the American Academy of Arts and Sciences, Volume XII." It should be noted that he merely "described and exhibited" another type of transmitter. There is no claim to having invented it, either in the foregoing extract, nor in the article to which it refers.

It seems clear that, at least during the first four years of the telephone, Bell did not feel justified in claiming the liquid transmitter. Not until after the settlement of the Dowd case in 1879, by compromise between the contending parties, one of the terms of which was a division of all telephone royalties between them during the life of the patents in suit, did Bell begin to feel at all secure in his position with reference to the liquid transmitter. It was in 1880 that Bell made his first attempt to claim priority in conceiving it.

Bell's skill as a tactician reaped its full reward. During the crucial period of the struggle for supremacy, Gray and his advisers were completely misled. Gray was present at Bell's Centennial Exhibition but did not see any liquid transmitter. Had he seen it he would, of course, have instantly recognized it as his own and proceeded accordingly. Not knowing of its existence, he became convinced that he must concede priority to Bell because he supposed that the first successful performance of the telephone at Bell's hands had been with a transmitter quite different from his own. Gray summarized the case, in a letter written just before his death, in these words:

> It was not till eight or ten years — at least a long time after the telephone was in use — that I became convinced, chiefly through Bell's own testimony in the various suits, that I had shown him how to construct the telephone with which he obtained his first results.

With this brief summary of the evidence that Bell made no claim to the microphone type of transmitter until four years after the time of his first experiment with it, we turn from consideration of the part played by the transmitter in the telephone contest to the part played by the receiver. Gray's priority is perhaps even more pronounced here than with the transmitter, for, as will be adduced presently, he had unchallengeable patent priority on this point. Legal precedence is not the point at present under emphasis, however. It is rather the relative actual accomplishment of the two men, which is often quite distinct from mere legal advantage. The fact in connection with this part of the telephone contest is that *Elisha Gray had made and publicly used several types of telephone receivers many months before Bell constructed his first one.*

There are many ways in which the fluctuating electric currents that carry telephone messages from one place to another can be converted back into sounds resembling the sounds that created them. But of all the ways that are possible, the one that has almost universally prevailed in practice is to cause the fluctuating currents to act upon a diaphragm, especially a metal diaphragm, through the agency of an electromagnet. Through all its variations, the telephone receiver has embodied this principle almost exclusively. Any inquiry, therefore, into precedence in development of the telephone receiver, as between Bell and Gray, must center on the question of which of the two first developed and used the combination of an electromagnet and diaphragm, especially an electromagnet and metal diaphragm, to produce sound electrically.

Aside from Bell's use of one of his unmodified harmonic telegraph instruments as a makeshift receiver, his first attempt to construct an electromagnetic telephone receiver was in the summer of 1875, in an episode which is justly considered to be nearly as significant as his first experiment with the prototype of the modern transmitter in 1876. The diaphragm of this first receiver was of parchment however, not metal. . . . The first occasion upon which Bell publicly demonstrated a receiver possessing a metal diaphragm was the Centennial Exhibition in Philadelphia in June 1876, a year later.

But while it is impossible to attribute to Bell the development of the telephone receiver earlier than June 1875, Elisha Gray had constructed and publicly demonstrated, as early as 1874 and before February 1875, not less than four receivers which were prototypes of the modern telephone receiver. Each one of these consisted of a pair of electromagnets, near the end of which was placed a diaphragm of some form. The receivers differed from each other primarily in the variations in this diaphragm.

It is evident, from the documentation on the foregoing receivers, that, during the year preceding the earliest date that Bell can claim, Gray had made and exhibited to some hundreds of witnesses who were qualified to comprehend their principle and importance, four types of telephone receiver, all of which possessed thin metal diaphragms and hence anticipated the design of the modern telephone receiver much more closely than did the receiver which Bell first devised in 1875. But even these four were not his first successful ventures in this field. He had made, used, and published descriptions of at least three others prior to any of these four. But since the earlier models acted on a principle which could not have produced the modern receiver, they are not included here.

It should be understood that the tests and demonstrations made with these receivers during 1874 and 1875 involved only the production of musical tones from intermittent currents produced by tuned buzzers in the circuits. This was not because the receivers were incapable of reproducing speech, for three out of the four were capable of reproducing speech excellently, as later tests showed. That Gray had a strong suspicion that his receivers possessed this ability is made clear by his testimony before the Patent Commissioner, but it was not possible for him to test their ability to reproduce speech because at that time no method was known for getting speech *into* an electric system to be so reproduced. This had to await the invention of the transmitter.

For some reason, Gray's priority in the development of the telephone *receiver* has been allowed to escape general notice. That story has now been told. As for the *transmitter*, the story of how he was maneuvered by Bell and Bell's associates out of the maintenance of his proper claim to priority in design of the microphone type of telephone transmitter has also now been told. Gray's loss of credit for these two major contributions to the development of the telephone was quite possibly due in part to his own ineptitude as a tactician. As to the facts of his priority in both fields there is little room for controversy. The curious popular interpretation of those facts which gives exclusive credit to Bell for designs previously recorded and devices previously constructed by Gray is, alas, all too typical of common practice throughout the whole history of electrical communication.

Appendix 10

Alexander Graham Bell's
Original Telephone Patent Application, 1876

UNITED STATES PATENT OFFICE.

ALEXANDER GRAHAM BELL, OF SALEM, MASSACHUSETTS.

IMPROVEMENT IN TELEGRAPHY.

Specification forming part of Letters Patent No. **174,465**, dated March 7, 1876; application filed February 14, 1876.

To all whom it may concern:

Be it known that I, ALEXANDER GRAHAM BELL, of Salem, Massachusetts, have invented certain new and useful Improvements in Telegraphy, of which the following is a specification:

In Letters Patent granted to me April 6, 1875, No. 161,739, I have described a method of, and apparatus for, transmitting two or more telegraphic signals simultaneously along a single wire by the employment of transmitting-instruments, each of which occasions a succession of electrical impulses differing in rate from the others; and of receiving-instruments, each tuned to a pitch at which it will be put in vibration to produce its fundamental note by one only of the transmitting-instruments; and of vibratory circuit-breakers operating to convert the vibratory movement of the receiving-instrument into a permanent make or break (as the case may be) of a local circuit, in which is placed a Morse sounder, register, or other telegraphic apparatus. I have also therein described a form of autograph-telegraph based upon the action of the above-mentioned instruments.

In illustration of my method of multiple telegraphy I have shown in the patent aforesaid, as one form of transmitting-instrument, an electro-magnet having a steel-spring armature, which is kept in vibration by the action of a local battery. This armature in vibrating makes and breaks the main circuit, producing an intermittent current upon the line-wire. I have found, however, that upon this plan the limit to the number of signals that can be sent simultaneously over the same wire is very speedily reached; for, when a number of transmitting-instruments, having different rates of vibration, are simultaneously making and breaking the same circuit, the effect upon the main line is practically equivalent to one continuous current.

In a pending application for Letters Patent, filed in the United States Patent Office February 25, 1875, I have described two ways of producing the intermittent current—the one by actual make and break of contact, the other by alternately increasing and diminishing the intensity of the current without actually breaking the circuit. The current produced by the latter method I shall term, for distinction sake, a pulsatory current.

My present invention consists in the employment of a vibratory or undulatory current of electricity in contradistinction to a merely intermittent or pulsatory current, and of a method of, and apparatus for, producing electrical undulations upon the line-wire.

The distinction between an undulatory and a pulsatory current will be understood by considering that electrical pulsations are caused by sudden or instantaneous changes of intensity, and that electrical undulations result from gradual changes of intensity exactly analogous to the changes in the density of air occasioned by simple pendulous vibrations. The electrical movement, like the aerial motion, can be represented by a sinusoidal curve or by the resultant of several sinusoidal curves.

Intermittent or pulsatory and undulatory currents may be of two kinds, accordingly as the successive impulses have all the same polarity or are alternately positive and negative.

The advantages I claim to derive from the use of an undulatory current in place of a merely intermittent one are, first, that a very much larger number of signals can be transmitted simultaneously on the same circuit; second, that a closed circuit and single main battery may be used; third, that communication in both directions is established without the necessity of special induction-coils; fourth, that cable dispatches may be transmitted more rapidly than by means of an intermittent current or by the methods at present in use; for, as it is unnecessary to discharge the cable before a new signal can be made, the lagging of cable-signals is prevented; fifth, and that as the circuit is never broken a spark-arrester becomes unnecessary.

It has long been known that when a permanent magnet is caused to approach the pole of an electro-magnet a current of electricity is induced in the coils of the latter, and that when it is made to recede a current of opposite polarity to the first appears upon the wire. When, therefore, a permanent magnet is caused to vibrate in front of the pole of an electro-magnet an undulatory current of electricity is induced in the coils of the electro-magnet, the undulations of which correspond, in rapidity of succession, to the vibrations of the magnet, in polarity to the direction of its motion, and in intensity to the amplitude of its vibration.

That the difference between an undulatory and an intermittent current may be more clearly understood I shall describe the condition of the electrical current when the attempt is made to transmit two musical notes simultaneously—first upon the one plan and then upon the other. Let the interval between the two sounds be a major third; then their rates of vibration are in the ratio of 4 to 5. Now, when the intermittent current is used the circuit is made and broken four times by one transmitting-instrument in the same time that five makes and breaks are caused by the other. A and B, Figs. 1, 2, and 3, represent the intermittent currents produced, four impulses of B being made in the same time as five impulses of A. c c c, &c., show where and for how long time the circuit is made, and d d d, &c., indicate the duration of the breaks of the circuit. The line A and B shows the total effect upon the current when the transmitting-instruments for A and B are caused simultaneously to make and break the same circuit. The resultant effect depends very much upon the duration of the make relatively to the break. In Fig. 1 the ratio is as 1 to 4; in Fig. 2, as 1 to 2; and in Fig. 3 the makes and breaks are of equal duration. The combined effect, A and B, Fig. 3, is very nearly equivalent to a continuous current.

When many transmitting-instruments of different rates of vibration are simultaneously making and breaking the same circuit the current upon the main line becomes for all practical purposes continuous.

Next, consider the effect when an undulatory current is employed. Electrical undulations, induced by the vibration of a body capable of inductive action, can be represented graphically, without error, by the same sinusoidal curve which expresses the vibration of the inducing body itself, and the effect of its vibration upon the air; for, as above stated, the rate of oscillation in the electrical current corresponds to the rate of vibration of the inducing body—that is, to the pitch of the sound produced. The intensity of the current varies with the amplitude of the vibration—that is, with the loudness of the sound; and the polarity of the current corresponds to the direction of the vibrating body—that is, to the condensations and rarefactions of air produced by the vibration. Hence, the sinusoidal curve A or B, Fig. 4, represents, graphically, the electrical undulations induced in a circuit by the vibration of a body capable of inductive action.

The horizontal line a d e f, &c., represents the zero of current. The elevations b b b, &c., indicate impulses of positive electricity. The depressions c c c, &c., show impulses of negative electricity. The vertical distance b d or c f of any portion of the curve from the zero-line expresses the intensity of the positive or negative impulse at the part observed, and the horizontal distance a a indicates the duration of the electrical oscillation. The vibrations represented by the sinusoidal curves B and A, Fig. 4, are in the ratio aforesaid, of 4 to 5—that is, four oscillations of B are made in the same time as five oscillations of A.

The combined effect of A and B, when induced simultaneously on the same circuit, is expressed by the curve A+B, Fig. 4, which is the algebraical sum of the sinusoidal curves A and B. This curve A+B also indicates the actual motion of the air when the two musical notes considered are sounded simultaneously. Thus, when electrical undulations of different rates are simultaneously induced in the same circuit, an effect is produced exactly analogous to that occasioned in the air by the vibration of the inducing bodies. Hence, the coexistence upon a telegraphic circuit of electrical vibrations of different pitch is manifested, not by the obliteration of the vibratory character of the current, but by peculiarities in the shapes of the electrical undulations, or, in other words, by peculiarities in the shapes of the curves which represent those undulations.

There are many ways of producing undulatory currents of electricity, dependent for effect upon the vibrations or motions of bodies capable of inductive action. A few of the methods that may be employed I shall here specify. When a wire, through which a continuous current of electricity is passing, is caused to vibrate in the neighborhood of another wire, an undulatory current of electricity is induced in the latter. When a cylinder, upon which are arranged bar-magnets, is made to rotate in front of the pole of an electromagnet, an undulatory current of electricity is induced in the coils of the electro-magnet.

Undulations are caused in a continuous voltaic current by the vibration or motion of bodies capable of inductive action; or by the vibration of the conducting-wire itself in the neighborhood of such bodies. Electrical undulations may also be caused by alternately increasing and diminishing the resistance of the circuit, or by alternately increasing and diminishing the power of the battery. The internal resistance of a battery is diminished by bringing the voltaic elements nearer together, and increased by placing them farther apart. The reciprocal vibration of the elements of a battery, therefore, occasions an undulatory action in the voltaic current. The external resistance may also be varied. For instance, let mercury or some other liquid form part of a voltaic circuit, then the more deeply the conducting-wire is immersed in the mercury or other liquid, the less resistance does the liquid offer to the passage of the current. Hence, the vibration of the conducting-wire in mercury or other liquid included in the circuit occasions undulations in the current. The vertical vibrations of the elements of a battery in the liquid in which they are immersed produces an undulatory action in the current by alternately increasing and diminishing the power of the battery.

In illustration of the method of creating electrical undulations, I shall show and describe one form of apparatus for producing the effect. I prefer to employ for this purpose an electro-magnet, A, Fig. 5, having a coil upon only one of its legs b. A steel-spring armature, c, is firmly clamped by one extremity to the uncovered leg d of the magnet, and its free end is allowed to project above the pole of the covered leg. The armature c can be set in vibration in a variety of ways, one of which is by wind, and, in vibrating, it produces a musical note of a certain definite pitch.

When the instrument A is placed in a voltaic circuit, g b e f g, the armature c becomes magnetic, and the polarity of its free end is opposed to that of the magnet underneath. So long as the armature c remains at rest, no effect is produced upon the voltaic current, but the moment it is set in vibration to produce its musical note a powerful inductive action takes place, and electrical undulations traverse the circuit g b e f g. The vibratory current passing through the coil of the electromagnet f causes vibration in its armature h when the armatures c h of the two instruments A I are normally in unison with one another; but the armature h is unaffected by the passage of the undulatory current when the pitches of the two instruments are different.

A number of instruments may be placed upon a telegraphic circuit, as in Fig. 6. When the armature of any one of the instruments is set in vibration all the other instruments upon the circuit which are in unison with it respond, but those which have normally a different rate of vibration remain silent. Thus, if A, Fig. 6, is set in vibration, the armatures of A¹ and A² will vibrate also, but all the others on the circuit will remain still. So if B¹ is caused to emit its musical note the instruments B B² respond. They continue sounding so long as the mechanical vibration of B¹ is continued, but become silent with the cessation of its motion. The duration of the sound may be used to indicate the dot or dash of the Morse alphabet, and thus a telegraphic dispatch may be indicated by alternately interrupting and renewing the sound.

When two or more instruments of different pitch are simultaneously caused to vibrate, all the instruments of corresponding pitches upon the circuit are set in vibration, each responding to that one only of the transmitting instruments with which it is in unison. Thus the signals of A, Fig. 6, are repeated by A¹ and A², but by no other instrument upon the circuit; the signals of B¹ by B and B²; and the signals of C¹ by C and C²—whether A, B², and C are successively or simultaneously caused to vibrate. Hence by these instruments two or more telegraphic signals or messages may be sent simultaneously over the same circuit without interfering with one another.

I desire here to remark that there are many other uses to which these instruments may be put, such as the simultaneous transmission of musical notes, differing in loudness as well as in pitch, and the telegraphic transmission of noises or sounds of any kind.

When the armature e, Fig. 5, is set in vibration the armature h responds not only in pitch, but in loudness. Thus, when c vibrates with little amplitude, a very soft musical note proceeds from h; and when c vibrates forcibly the amplitude of the vibration of h is considerably increased, and the resulting sound becomes louder. So, if A and B, Fig. 6, are sounded simultaneously, (A loudly and B softly,) the instruments A¹ and A² repeat loudly the signals of A, and B¹ B² repeat softly those of B.

One of the ways in which the armature c, Fig. 5, may be set in vibration has been stated above to be by wind. Another mode is shown in Fig. 7, whereby motion can be imparted to the armature by the human voice or by means of a musical instrument.

The armature c, Fig. 7, is fastened loosely by one extremity to the uncovered leg d of the electro-magnet b, and its other extremity is attached to the center of a stretched membrane, a. A cone, A, is used to converge sound-vibrations upon the membrane. When a sound is uttered in the cone the membrane a is set in vibration, the armature c is forced to partake of the motion, and thus electrical undulations are created upon the circuit E b e f g. These undulations are similar in form to the air vibrations caused by the sound—that is, they are represented graphically by similar curves.

The undulatory current passing through the electro-magnet f influences its armature h to copy the motion of the armature c. A similar sound to that uttered into A is then heard to proceed from L.

In this specification the three words "oscillation," "vibration," and "undulation," are used synonymously, and in contradistinction to the terms "intermittent" and "pulsatory." By the terms "body capable of inductive action," I mean a body which, when in motion, produces dynamical electricity. I include in the category of bodies capable of inductive action—brass, copper, and other metals, as well as iron and steel.

Having described my invention, what I claim, and desire to secure by Letters Patent is as follows:

1. A system of telegraphy in which the receiver is set in vibration by the employment of undulatory currents of electricity, substantially as set forth.

2. The combination, substantially as set forth, of a permanent magnet or other body capable of inductive action, with a closed circuit, so that the vibration of the one shall occasion electrical undulations in the other, or in itself, and this I claim, whether the permanent magnet be set in vibration in the neighborhood of the conducting-wire form-

ing the circuit, or whether the conducting-wire be set in vibration in the neighborhood of the permanent magnet, or whether the conducting - wire and the permanent magnet both simultaneously be set in vibration in each other's neighborhood.

3. The method of producing nudulations in a continuous voltaic current by the vibration or motion of bodies capable of inductive action, or by the vibration or motion of the conducting-wire itself, in the neighborhood of such bodies, as set forth.

4. The method of producing undulations in a continuous voltaic circuit by gradually increasing and diminishing the resistance of the circuit, or by gradually increasing and diminishing the power of the battery, as set forth.

5. The method of, and apparatus for, transmitting vocal or other sounds telegraphically, as herein described, by causing electrical undulations, similar in form to the vibrations of the air accompanying the said vocal or other sound, substantially as set forth.

In testimony whereof I have hereunto signed my name this 20th day of January, A. D. 1876.

ALEX. GRAHAM BELL.

Witnesses:
THOMAS E. BARRY,
P. D. RICHARDS.

2 Sheets—Sheet 1.

A. G. BELL.
TELEGRAPHY.

No. 174,465.

Patented March 7, 1876.

Fig.1

Fig.2.

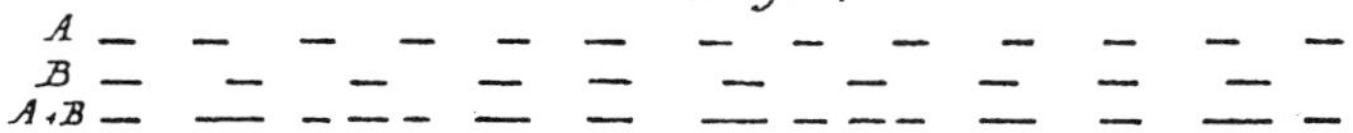

Fig.3.

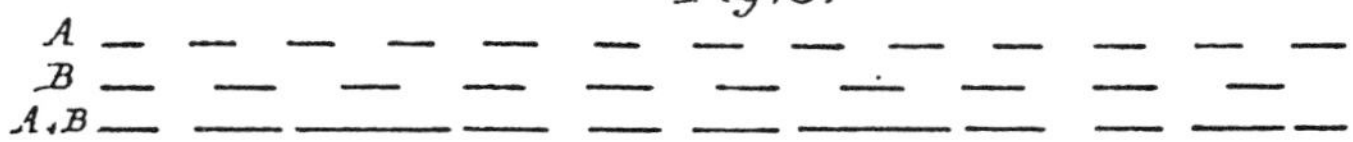

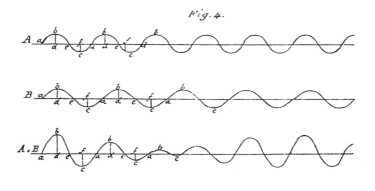

Fig.4.

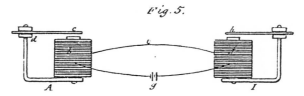

Fig.5.

Witnesses

Ewell Stock.
H. J. Hutchinson

Inventor:

A. Graham Bell
by attys Pollok & Baily

2 Sheets—Sheet 2.

A. G. BELL.

TELEGRAPHY.

No. 174,465. Patented March 7, 1876.

Fig 6.

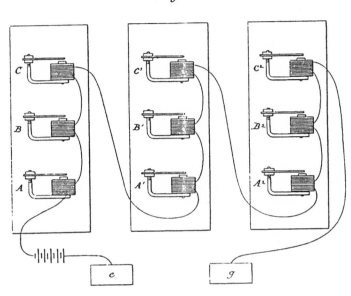

Fig. 7

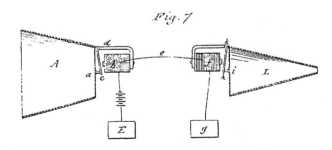

Witnesses

Inventor:

Appendix 11

Alexander Graham Bell's Patent Application, 1877

ALEXANDER GRAHAM BELL, OF BOSTON, MASSACHUSETTS.

IMPROVEMENT IN ELECTRIC TELEGRAPHY.

Specification forming part of Letters Patent No. 186,787, dated January 30, 1877; application filed January 15, 1877.

Il whom it may concern:

Be it known that I, ALEXANDER GRAHAM BELL, of Boston, Massachusetts, have invented certain new and useful Improvements in Electric Telephony, of which the following is a specification:

In Letters Patent granted to me on the 6th day of April, 1875, No. 161,739, and in an application for Letters Patent of the United States now pending, I have described a method of an apparatus for producing musical tones by the action of a rapidly-interrupted electrical current, whereby a number of telegraphic signals can be sent simultaneously along a single circuit.

In another application for Letters Patent now pending in the United States Patent Office I have described a method of, and apparatus for, inducing an intermittent current of electricity upon a line-wire, whereby musical tones can be produced, and a number of telegraphic signals be sent simultaneously over the same circuit, in either or in both directions; and in Letters Patent granted to me March 7, 1876, No. 174,465, I have shown and described a method of an apparatus for producing musical tones by the action of undulatory currents of electricity, whereby a number of telegraphic signals can be sent simultaneously over the same circuit, in either or in both directions, and a single battery be used for the whole circuit.

In the applications and patents above referred to, signals are transmitted simultaneously along a single wire by the employment of transmitting instruments, each of which occasions a succession of electrical impulses differing in rate from the others, and are received without confusion by means of receiving-instruments, each tuned to a pitch at which it will be put in vibration to produce its fundamental note by one only of the transmitting-instruments. A separate instrument is therefore employed for every pitch, each instrument being capable of transmitting or receiving but a single note, and thus as many separate instruments are required as there are messages or musical notes to be transmitted.

My invention has for its object, first, the transmission simultaneously of two or more musical notes or telegraphic signals along a single wire in either or both directions, and with a single battery for the whole circuit without the use of as many instruments as there are musical notes or telegraphic signals to be transmitted; second, the electrical transmission by the same means of articulate speech and sounds of every kind, whether musical or not; third, the electrical transmission of musical tones, articulate speech, or sounds of every kind without the necessity of using a voltaic battery.

In my Patent No. 174,465, dated March 7, 1876, I have shown as one form of transmitting-instrument a stretched membrane, to which the armature of an electro-magnet is attached, whereby motion can be imparted to the armature by the human voice, or by means of a musical instrument, or by sounds produced in any way.

In accordance with my present invention I substitute for the membrane and armature shown in the transmitting and receiving instruments alluded to above, a plate of iron or steel capable of being thrown into vibration by sounds made in its neighborhood.

The nature of my invention and the manner in which the same is or may be carried into effect will be understood by reference to the accompanying drawings, in which—

Figure 1 is a perspective view of one form of my electric telephone. Fig. 2 is a vertical section of the same, and Fig. 3 is a plan view of the apparatus. Fig. 4 is a diagram illustrating the arrangement upon circuit.

Similar letters in the drawings represent corresponding portions of the apparatus.

A, in said drawings, represents a plate of iron or steel, which is fastened at B and C to the cover or sounding box D. E represents a speaking-tube, by which sounds may be conveyed to or from the plate A. F is a bar of soft iron. G is a coil of insulated copper wire placed around the extremity of the end H of the bar F. I is an adjusting-screw, whereby the distance of the end H from the plate A may be regulated.

The electric telephones J, K, L, and M are placed at different stations upon a line, and are arranged upon circuit with a battery, N, as shown in diagram, Fig. 4.

I have shown the apparatus in one of its

simplest forms, it being well understood that the same may be varied in arrangement, combination, general construction, and form, as well as material of which the several parts are composed.

The operation and use of this instrument are as follows:

I would premise by saying that this instrument is and may be used both as a transmitter and as a receiver—that is to say, the sender of the message will use an instrument in every particular identical in construction and operation with that employed by the receiver, so that the same instrument can be used alternately as a receiver and a transmitter.

In order to transmit a telegraphic message by means of these instruments, it is only necessary for the operator at a telephone, (say J,) to make a musical sound, in any way, in the neighborhood of the plate A—for convenience of operation through the speaking-tube E—and to let the duration of the sound signify the dot or dash of the Morse alphabet, and for the operator, who receives his message, say at M, to listen to his telephone, preferably through the speaking-tube E. When two or more musical signals are being transmitted over the same circuit all the telephones reproduce the signals for all the messages; but as the signals for each message differ in pitch from those for the other messages it is easy for an operator to fix his attention upon one message and ignore the others.

When a large number of dispatches are being simultaneously transmitted it will be advisable for the operator to listen to his telephone through a resonator, which will re-enforce to his ear the signals which he desires to observe. In this way he is enabled to direct his attention to the signals for any given message without being distracted or disturbed by the signals for any other messages that may be passing over the line at the time.

The musical signals, if preferred, can be automatically received by means of a resonator, one end of which is closed by a membrane, which vibrates only when the note with which the resonator is in unison is emitted by the receiving-telephone. The vibrations of the membrane may be made to operate a circuit-breaker, which will actuate a Morse sounder or a telegraphic recording or registering apparatus.

One form of vibratory circuit-breaker which may be used for this purpose I have described in Letters Patent No. 178,399, June 6, 1876. Hence by this plan the simultaneous transmission of a number of telegraphic messages over a single circuit in the same or in both directions, with a single main battery for the whole circuit and a single telephone at each station, is rendered practicable. This is of great advantage in this, that, for the conveyance of several messages, or signals, or sounds over a single wire simultaneously, it is no longer necessary to have separate instruments correspondingly tuned for each given sound, which plan requires nice adjustment of the corresponding instruments, while the present improvement admits of a single instrument at each station; or, if for convenience several are employed, they all are alike in construction, and need not be adjusted or tuned to particular pitches.

Whatever sound is made in the neighborhood of any telephone, say at J, Fig. 4, is echoed in fac-simile by the telephones of all the other stations upon the circuit; hence, this plan is also adapted for the use of the transmitting intelligibly the exact sounds of articulate speech. To convey an articulate message it is only necessary for an operator to speak in the neighborhood of his telephone, preferably through the tube E, and for another operator at a distant station upon the same circuit to listen to the telephone at that station. If two persons speak simultaneously in the neighborhood of the same or different telephones, the utterances of the two speakers are reproduced simultaneously by all the other telephones on the same circuit; hence, by this plan a number of vocal messages may be transmitted simultaneously on the same circuit in either or both directions. All the effects noted above may be produced by the same instruments without a battery by rendering the central bar F H permanently magnetic. Another form of telephone for use without a battery is shown in Fig. 5, in which O is a compound permanent magnet, to the poles of which are affixed poll-pieces of soft iron P Q surrounded by helices of insulated wire R S.

Fig. 6 illustrates the arrangement upon circuits of similar instruments to that shown in Fig. 5.

In lieu of the plate A in above figures, iron or steel reeds of definite pitch may be placed in front of the electro-magnet O, and in connection with a series of such instruments of different pitches, an arrangement upon circuit may be employed similar to that shown in my Patent No. 174,465, and illustrated in Fig. 6 of Sheet 2 in said patent. The battery, of course, may be omitted.

This invention is not limited to the use of iron or steel, but includes within its scope any material capable of inductive action.

The essential feature of the invention consists in the armature of the receiving-instrument being vibrated by the varying attraction of the electro-magnet, so as to vibrate the air in the vicinity thereof in the same manner as the air is vibrated at the other end by the production of the sound. It is therefore by no means necessary or essential that the transmitting-instrument should be of the same construction as the receiving-instrument. Any instrument receiving and transmitting the impression of agitated air may be used as the transmitter, although for convenience, and for reciprocal communication, I prefer to use like instruments at either end of an electrical wire. I have heretofore described and exhibited such other means of transmitting sound, as will be seen by reference to the proceedings of the American Academy of Arts and Sciences, Volume XII.

For convenience, I prefer to apply to each instrument a call-bell. This may be arranged so as to ring, first, when the main circuit is opened; second, when the bar F comes into contact with the plate A. The first is done to call attention; the second indicates when it is necessary to readjust the magnet, for it is important that the distance of the magnet from the plate should be as little as possible, without, however, being in contact. I have also found that the electrical undulations produced upon the main line by the vibration of the plate A are intensified by placing the coil G at the end of the bar F nearest the plate A, and not extend it beyond the middle, or thereabout.

Having thus described my invention, what I claim, and desire to secure by Letters Patent, is—

1. The union upon, and by means of, an electric circuit of two or more instruments, constructed for operation substantially as herein shown and described, so that, if motion of any kind or form be produced in any way in the armature of any one of the said instruments, the armatures of all the other instruments upon the same circuit will be moved in like manner and form; and if such motion be produced in the former by sound, like sound will be produced by the motion of the latter.

2. In a system of electric telegraphy or telephony, consisting of transmitting and receiving instruments united upon an electric circuit, the production, in the armature of each receiving-instrument, of any given motion, by subjecting said armature to an attraction varying in intensity, however such variation may be produced in the magnet, and hence I claim the production of any given sound or sounds from the armature of the receiving-instrument,

by subjecting said armature to an attraction varying in intensity, in such manner as to throw the armature into that form of vibration that characterizes the given sound or sounds.

3. The combination, with an electro-magnet, of a plate of iron, or steel, or other material capable of inductive action, which can be thrown into vibration by the movement of surrounding air, or by the attraction of a magnet.

4. In combination with a plate and electro magnet, as before claimed, the means herein described, or their mechanical equivalents, of adjusting the relative position of the two, so that, without touching, they may be set as closely together as possible.

5. The formation, in an electric telephone, such as herein shown and described, of a magnet with a coil upon the end or ends of the magnet nearest the plate.

6. The combination, with an electric telephone, such as described, of a sounding-box, substantially as herein shown and set forth.

7. In combination with an electric telephone, as herein described, the employment of a speaking or hearing tube, for conveying sounds to or from the telephone, substantially as set forth.

8. In a system of electric telephony, the combination of a permanent magnet with a plate of iron or steel, or other material capable of inductive action, with coils upon the end or ends of said magnet nearest the plate, substantially as set forth.

In testimony whereof I have hereunto signed my name this 13th day of January, A. D. 1877.

A. GRAHAM BELL.

Witnesses:
HENRY R. ELLIOTT,
EWELL A. DICK.

2 Sheets—Sheet 1.

A. G. BELL.

ELECTRIC TELEGRAPHY.

No. 186,787.

Patented Jan. 30, 1877.

Fig. 1.

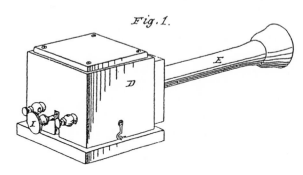

Fig. 2.

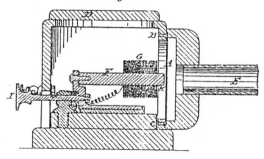

Fig. 3.

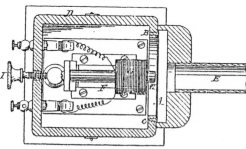

Attest

Inventor:

Alexander Graham Bell

Appendix 11

A. G. BELL.
ELECTRIC TELEGRAPHY.

No. 186,787.   Patented Jan. 30, 1877.

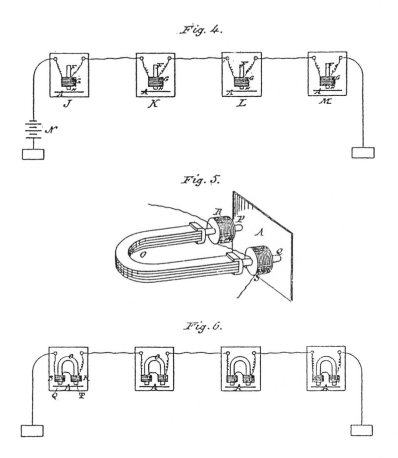

Fig. 4.

Fig. 5.

Fig. 6.

Attest:
P. Pollok
E. Wellasick

Inventor:
Alexander Graham Bell

Glossary of Telephone Terms

anti-sidetone	Circuitry to reduce volume of subscriber's voice in his own receiver.
battery	Direct current power from batteries or generators.
cable	Number of wires grouped together.
central office	Location of a switchboard for interconnecting subscribers.
common battery	Battery located in the central office.
cross talk	Voice currents heard in more than one line.
drop wire	Flexible wire from open pole line to subscriber's equipment.
generator	Small permanent magnet magneto used for ringing.
ground	Connection to the earth.
handset	Transmitter and receiver connected by a handle.
hook switch	Places telephone instrument in condition to receive incoming calls when receiver or handset is hung on it.
local battery	Provides talking power for subscriber's telephone.
distributing frame	Where incoming subscriber's lines are connected to the central office switchboard.
off hook	When subscriber's telephone is in talking condition.
on hook	When subscriber's telephone is in stand-by, ready to receive incoming calls.
open wire	Bare wire supported by insulators on poles.
outside plant	The portion of a telephone system outside the central office.
party line	A single telephone circuit serving two or more subscribers.
receiver	The earpiece which reproduces the distant voice.
repeater	Amplifying device to increase volume on toll lines.
ringer	The bell that signals an incoming call.
side tone	Subscriber's voice heard in his own receiver.
subscriber	Individual owner or user of a telephone.
switchboard	Provides a means of interconnecting subscribers.
toll line	Long-distance line between central offices.
transmitter	Changes voice sounds to electrical current.
transpose	To reverse position of parallel wires for reducing cross talk.
twisted pair	Flexible two-conductor insulated wire.

Bibliography

Aitken, William. *Who Invented the Telephone?* London and Glasgow: Blackie & Son, Ltd., 1939.

Appleyard, Rollo. *Pioneers of Electrical Communication.* Freeport, N.Y.: Books for Libraries, 1968.

Bell Laboratories. *A History of Engineering and Science in the Bell System: The Early Years (1875–1925).* New York, 1975.

Brooks, John. *Telephone: The First Hundred Years.* New York: Harper & Row, 1976.

Bruce, Robert V. *Bell: Alexander Graham Bell and the Conquest of Solitude.* Boston: Little, Brown & Co., 1973.

Clarke, Arthur C. *Voice Across the Sea.* New York: Harper & Row, 1974.

De Forest, Lee. *Father of Radio.* Chicago: Wilcox & Follett, 1950.

Garnet, Robert W. *The Telephone Enterprise: The Evolution of the Bell System's Horizontal Structure, 1876–1909.* Baltimore: Johns Hopkins University Press, 1985.

Harder, Warren, Jr. *Daniel Drawbaugh: The Edison of the Cumberland Valley.* Philadelphia: University of Pennsylvania Press, 1960.

Harlow, Alvin F. *Old Wires and New Waves.* New York: Appleton-Century, 1936.

Houston, Edwin J. *Electricity in Everyday Life.* New York: P. F. Collier, 1905.

Hylander, C. J. *American Inventors.* New York: Macmillan, 1934.

Mabon, Prescott C. *Mission Communications: The Story of Bell Laboratories.* Murray Hill, N.J.: Bell Telephone Laboratories, 1975.

McLuhan, Marshall. *The Global Village.* New York: Oxford University Press, 1989.

McMeen, Samuel G., and Kempster B. Miller. *Telephony.* Chicago: American Technical Society, 1923.

Miller, F. T. *Thomas A. Edison.* Philadelphia: Winston, 1931.

Report of the Chief Signal Officer. Washington, D.C.: Government Printing Office, 1919. Reprinted by Arno Press, 1974.

Rhodes, Frederick Leland. *Beginnings of Telephony.* New York: Harper & Brothers, 1929.

Sterling, Bruce. *The Hacker Crackdown: Law and Disorder on the Electronic Frontier.* New York: Bantam Books, 1992.

Thompson, Sylvanus P. *Philipp Reis, Inventor of the Telephone.* London: E. & F. N. Spon, 1883.

Wasserman, Neil. *From Invention to Innovation.* Baltimore: Johns Hopkins University Press, 1985.

Waterford, Van. *All About Telephones.* Summit, Penn.: TAB Books, 1983.

Wile, Frederick William. *Emile Berliner, Maker of the Microphone.* New York: Arno Press, 1926.

Index

Ader microphone 36
ALASCOM 155
Alaska Highway line 169, 170
Alaskan telephone system 114
Albert, E. 19
Albert, J. W. 19
Alexanderson, E. F. W. 145
Allen, Bob 136
amateurs' pioneer shortwaves 148
American Academy of Arts and Sciences 19
American Speaking Tel. Co. 79
Americas Cup Race 62
Annalen der Physik 18
anti-sidetone 174
Antique Telephone Collectors Assn. 122
ANZCAN cable 153, 154
Arlington radio transmitter 145
Armstrong, E. H. 64
Arnold, H. D. 45
AT&T 15, 135
Automatic Electric Co. 47, 111
automatic switching 53, 54, 55
Babcock, Clifford D. 63
Banholzer, Paul P. 44
Banker, Grace 89
Bardeen, John 46
Barnesville, Ohio 67
barrier button transmitter 124
Barton, E. M. 68
batteries 177
Behn, Hernand 56
Behn, Sothenes 56
Bell, Alexander Graham 1, 9, 10, 20, 21, 73
Bell Laboratories 46
Bell System divestiture 15, 79, 181
Beltz power posthole digger 66

Beresford, Major C. F. C. 97, 98
Berliner, Emile 31, 32, 33, 34, 35, 173
Blake, Francis 22, 76
blinker lamps 93
blue boxes 137, 138
Bocock, Paul 35
Bourseul, Charles 21, 23
Brandt, Nat 67
Brattain, Walter H. 46
Brewer, Mr. Justice 35
British Cable & Wireless 181
British Post Office 58
Brown, C. L. 182
Brown Telephone Co. 182
buzzer-phone 86
cable: coaxial L4 169; transatlantic 151
cable routes, hardened 169
call tracing 143
Campbell, George 58, 61
Canary Islanders 40
candlestick phone 97
Carterphone 15
Carty, Col. John J. 152
Casson, Herbert N. 73
Catalina Island 146
Centel 182
Channing, William F. 71
Chicopee, Massachusetts 8
Choctaw Indians 91
Churchill, Charles 67
Citizens Telephone Co. 50
coastal defense guns 72
common battery exchange 108
composite circuits 165
computer hackers 140
condenser 42
copper wire 157
Cornell, Ezra 75

crossbar switch 50
Cushman, S. D. 39, 40
Darr, William 25
De Forest, Lee 45, 62, 77, 145
Didaskalia 21
Dolbear, Amos E. 41, 42, 43
Dolbear Electric Tel. Co. 44
Dom Pedro, Emperor 1
Doolittle, Thomas 157
Dowd, Peter A. 43, 78
Dowd case 79
Drawbaugh, Daniel 25, 26, 27, 28, 29
dry cell batteries 106
Duell, Charles 46
du Moncel, M. 23
"dumpster divers" 139
earth telegraphy 156
Eastman Kodak 10
eavesdropping 146
Eberly's Mills 25
Edison, Thomas A. 3, 37, 76, 77, 173
Edison effect 63
Eiffel Tower 145
Ericson, Charles 50
Ericson, John 50
Fahlberg, Dr. Constantine 31
Faraday, Michael 38
Federal Telegraph Co. 64, 120, 121
Ferrar, Edward 39
Fessenden, Reginald 145
fiber-optics 154, 155, 171, 183
field telephone EE8 132
flash cutover 51
Fleming valve 63
Ford Model T 102
Fore River Ship & Engine Co. 12
Forest Service 132
Fort Sill, Oklahoma 85
Franklin, Benjamin 178
frequencies, low versus high 148
Fuller, A. C. 86
Fullerphone 86, 133, 134
gallows frame transmitter 9
Galva, Illinois 108
Garfield, President 51
Garnier's Institute 17, 18
General Electric Co. 45
Gifford, George 79
Goeken, Jack 181
Gold and Stock Telegraph Co. 43, 79
Gomera Island 41
Gray, Elisha 67; bathtub experiment 68; death of 74; early days at

Oberlin 67; files caveat 1, 13; joins Gray & Barton 68; sells tone telegraph to Postal Telegraph 69
Gray National Telautograph Co. 72
Graybar Electric Co. 169
Great Salt Lake 157
Greely, Gen. A. W. 85
ground panels 95
ground return circuits 156
GTE 49, 51
Hall, Charles Martin 67
Hammond organ 5
hand-cranked magneto generator 10
handsets 124
Harlan, Mr. Justice 35
Harlow, Alvin F. 13
harmonic telegraph 2
Harmonic Telegraph Co. 79
Harris, Joe 47
Harrison, W. H. 56
Hartford telephone system 8
Hayes, Hammond V. 78
Hayes, President 96
hearing aids 46
Heaviside, Oliver 22, 58, 59, 60, 179
heliograph 85
"hello" and "hoy" 78
Henry, Joseph 21, 38
Highland Park, Illinois 74
Hill, Lysander 26
hook switch 174
Hooke, Robert 41
Hoover, President 97
Horner, Capt. E. W. 91
House printing telegraph 75
Howe, Elias 13
Hubbard, Gardner 8
Hudson, John E. 35
Hughes, David E. 36
Hunnings, Henry 36
Hunnings transmitter 37
Hunter, Edward O. 45
Hush-a-Phone 45
Huxley, Professor 36
IBM 9
ID codes 139
independent telephone companies 53
induction balance 51
induction coil 173
insulators 158, 159, 160
International Tel. & Tel. Co. 56, 120
Japan 9
Johnston, Philip 91
Jones, C. E. & Bro. 14

KDKA 146
Keith, A. E. 50
Kellogg Switchboard & Supply Co. 3, 113
Kingsbury, Nathan C. 15, 80
Kingsbury Commitment 14
KR law 58
ladder line 93
Langmuir, Irving 45
La Porte, Indiana 48
La Porte County Historical Society 49
Legat, V. 22
Leich Electric Co. 108
lightning arrestor 176
Lincoln, President 96
Lincoln-Edison medal 9
linemen 160, 161, 163
liquid contact transmitter 2
loading coils 61
Lodge, Oliver 60
McDonough, James W. 40
McGowan, William G. 181, 182
McGraw, Max 182
Mackay, Clarence 80
Mackay Radio & Telegraph Co. 64
McKinley war room 96
McReynolds, James 80
magneto generator 174
magneto telephone 10
Marconi beam system 148
Maxwell, James Clerk 58
MCI 115, 180, 181
metallic circuit 156
Meucci, Antonio 29
Meyers, Sydney 63
microphone, carbon-pencil 36
microphonic contacts 21
microwave radio 170
microwave routes 185
Military Telegraph Corps 68
Mitchell, Billy 114
mobile subscriber equipment 99
Montgomery, Col. Benjamin F. 96
Montgomery Ward 41
Morgan, J. P. 80, 81
Morris, Illinois 51
Morse, Samuel F. B. 13, 73
Morse code 100
Mountain States Telephone Co. 157
National Electric Light Assn. 158, 159
National Inventors Hall of Fame 9
National Telephone Mfg. Co. 35
nationwide direct dialing 56
Navajo code talkers 91

Newark, New Jersey 54
Newtonville, Massachusetts 74
Northwest Indiana Tel. Co. 114
Oberlin, Ohio 67
Oberlin College 67
Oklahoma governor's speech 178
one-ring signal 138
open wire carrier 167
Orton, William 77
Pacific City, Oregon 155
Pacific Telephone Co. 146
Pack, R. F. 159
Page, Dr. Charles Grafton 21, 38
Panama-Pacific Exposition 66
party lines 104, 113
patent law 1, 7
PBX theft 140
Pentagon 100
People's Telephone Co. 26
phantom circuits 165
Philadelphia, Pennsylvania 8
Philadelphia Centennial 31
picture phone 183
pigeons, homing 94, 95
pin space 165
Poggendorff, Professor 18
polarized ringer 175
Polaroid 10
poles 165
Postal Telegraph 3, 75, 83
Power, Donald 56
power line carrier 149
Preece, William Henry 58, 59
Prescott, George B. 39
public address system 178
Pupin, Michael 58, 61
quadruplex 3
radio 185
Radio Act of 1912 185
railroad dispatching 125; *see also* telephones, railroad
RCA patent pool 64
red boxes 138
regeneration 63
Reis, Johann Philipp: becomes teacher at Garnier's 17; biography by Sylvanus Thompson 19; enters Garnier's Institute 16; invents "Telephon" 18; lecture before Physical Society 18; military service 17; paper rejected by Poggendorff 18; principal dates of Reis's life 23, 24; review of Reis telephone by Legat 22; ring off signal 175

Reis telephone in Scotland 21
Rocky Point antenna 147
Roosevelt, President Theodore 97
Roxbury, Kansas 106
rural mail delivery 102
Sanders, Thomas 12
Sarnoff, David 64
satellite communication 172
Schiavo, Giovanni E. 30
Sea Plow IV 152
security of ocean cables 152
selective ringing 113
Seward, Alaska 155
Shepard, Delia M. 69
Sherman Antitrust Act 80
Shields, W. C. 163
Shockley, William 46
"shop rights" 64
Shreeve, H. E. 61
Siberian telegraph line 75
Sibley, Hiram 75
Silliman, Professor 39
Smithsonian Institution 18, 84, 123
soap box transmitter 32
Spottiswoode, William 38
Sprint 180
Squier, Gen. George O. 149
Stager, Gen. Anson 68
Stanley steamer 157
static telephone 42
Statue of Liberty 31
Stein, Gertrude 102
Steinheil, Carl August 156
Stevenson, Robert Louis 8
Stockton, Lincoln C. 44
Storrow, James 35
Stromberg-Carlson 108
Strowger, Almon B. 47
Strowger Automatic Tel. Exch. 47
"stuffers" 137
Taft, President 97
taps on wires 141
TASI 151
Taylor, Dr. Lloyd W. 73
telautograph 71
telegraph key microphone 32
"teleloge" 40
telemarketing 142
telephone booth 12
telephone broadcast service 185
telephone companies, rural 103
telephone fraud 136, 137

telephone line: leakage 179; world's
  first 18
telephone manufacturers 119
telephone privacy 141, 142
telephone speech 176
telephone stamps 134
telephones: cellular 149; colored 134;
  cordless 149; field 86; French style
  123; railroad 125; tin can 41; without names 122; see also candlestick
  phone; magneto telephone
Theremin, Leon 65
Thompson, Sylvanus 19
Thompson, William 60
tone telegraphy 68
Touch Tone service 139
transcontinental line 65, 66
Tufts College 41
Twain, Mark 8
underground railroad 67
undulatory current 173
United Telephone 182
Vail, Theodore N. 80
Van der Weyd, Dr. P. H. 23
variable resistance 13
Vogel, Gen. Clayton B. 91
Walnut Street 8
water rheostat 69
Watson, Thomas A. 10, 12, 157, 173,
  174
Western Electric Co. 15, 50, 68
Western Union 5, 10, 37, 83
Western Union archives 84
Wheatstone, Sir Charles 17, 36, 41
White, A. C. 37
White, Samuel S. 70
White Alice network 114
White solid back transmitter 78
Whitefield, the Reverend Mr. 178
Wickersham, George W. 80
Wilber, Zenas 70
Williams, Charles 10, 12
Wilson, President 15, 97
wired wireless 149
women operators 89
wooden box phones 117
World War I 54, 85, 87
World's Fair 1893 72
Yale Light Artillery Battery 62
Yeates, S. M. 23
Yellow Breeches Creek 25